Glovebox Guide

Ohio State

"The writing style is very pers........as if I just had a conversation over a cup of coffee...what a vacation planner for the family!"

*-John Andreoni, Editor **-Ohio Out-of-Doors***

"More than just a visitors pilot, it's also a comfortable companion on a remarkable journey to Ohio's crown jewels."

*-Jeffrey L. Frischkorn **-The News-Herald***

"...destined to become the bible for campers and parks enthusiasts...well-done, comprehensive, accurate...and easy to use. But best of all...it provides just the sort of intriguing tidbits of lore that make you want to jump in the car and explore..."

*-Steve Pollick, Outdoor Editor **-The Blade, Toledo***

"Informative, well organized...vividly written...long over due...a must read."

*-Ellen Stein Burbach, Editor **-Ohio Magazine***

"...a treat...entertaining while providing tons of information. Must reading for visitors to Ohio's state parks!"

*Paul M. Liikala, Ohio Editor **-Outdoor Life***

"...this is the Atlas of Ohio state parks. Thoroughly researched, well organized and nicely written. A *must* for those who care about the outdoors in the Buckeye State."

*Tom Melody, Outdoor Editor **-Akron Beacon Journal***

Ohio State Park's Guidebook

by

Art Weber

Bill Bailey & Jim DuFresne

Glovebox Guidebooks takes you to
Ohio's great state parks!

A Glovebox Guidebook Original

Thanks to all the Ohio State Park's managers and their staff for the wonderful cooperation and unflagging support. A special thanks to Terri Carter and the entire Ohio Department of Natural Resources.

And thanks to all of our readers...remember, travel outdoors entails some unavoidable risks. Know your limitations, be prepared and alert, use good judgement, think safety, and enjoy Ohio's terrific outdoors! Be bold!

-Glovebox Guidebooks Publishing Company

Copyright © 1994 by Glovebox Guidebook Publishing Company
Reprinted/Revised in April 1994

Cover design by Dan Jacelone - Cover photo by Art Weber

Published by   **Glovebox Guidebook Publishing Company**
1112 Washburn Place East
Saginaw, Michigan 48602

Library of Congress - C.I.P.

Bailey, William L., 1952-
DuFresne, Jim, 1956-
Weber, Art,   1950-

Ohio State Park's Guidebook
(A Glovebox Guidebook)
ISBN 1-881139-04-2

Printed in the United States of America

10 9 8 7 6 5 4 3

Foreword

From the sandy shores of Lake Erie to the wooded banks of the Ohio River, from the rocky foothills of the Appalachian to the wind-swept plains of the cornbelt, Ohio's 72 state parks preserve and protect one of the most diverse and interesting state park systems in the world. To call Ohio's state park "world-class" is not just idly hyperbole. Ohio's 207,000 acres of parklands, streams and lakes offer the visitor an experience that is sometimes intimate and sometimes breathtaking; and always worth the trip. Entrance to Ohio's state parks remains free to all as a tribute to the quality of life these parks provide to all who pass this way.

There is an unheralded uniqueness to Ohio's parks which our visitors find surprisingly enjoyable. The four Lake Erie Island state parks attract vacationers because of their unique location in the Great Lakes and their cool combination of woods and rocky outcroppings. Their special topography provides a gentle counterpoint to the smooth blue water of Lake Erie for those who sit and relax upon the shore. As the visitor wanders through the parks, he or she "discovers" a world-renown exhibit of glacial grooves in the solid limestone surface of the islands. This "surprise" is a very pleasant result of "exploring the unknown" of our state parks. This delightful experience can be duplicated many times over throughout the entire system. I urge you all to go "exploring" in the Ohio State Park system.

Our almost 70 million visitors each year agree. Many come to enjoy the "best" boating or the "best" fishing or the "best" hiking or the "best" camping in the Midwest; among other superb experiences.

It is true that the largest lakes, the state and national record fish, the most scenic hiking trails and the most praised campground all lie within the Ohio State Parks. The draw of the "best" Ohio has to offer is not lost on native Ohioans as nearly half the population of our state comes to visit our state parks each year.

The quality of the visitor experience in Ohio State Parks is, in the end, a product of the experience he or she has through our state park employees. We are here to ensure that our customers have the very best outdoor recreational experience possible. If readers of this book find other than a quality experience in any state park I would greatly appreciate hearing from them personally at the address below. Although we cannot yet offer a guarantee on any park visit, we are striving daily to come as close as we possibly can.

Glen D. Alexander, Chief
Ohio Department of Natural Resources
Division of Parks and Recreation
1952 Belcher Drive, Building C-3
Columbus, Ohio 43224-1386

Introduction

Seventy-two parks, 72 different personalities.

Flatlands, wetlands, rolling hills, Appalachian foothills, deep hardwood forests, conifers, meadows, prairies, rivers, pristine streams, waterfalls, gorges, cliffs, caves, small ponds, big lakes, even a Great Lake -- it's all waiting for you in the state parks of Ohio.

Want to visit a working farm? Ohio's state parks has one. Want to see canal locks in operation? No problem. Wildlife? That's a cinch. Unbroken wilderness? Got that, too.

You can rough it in a primitive backpack camp, bring along a tent or RV and set up in a first-class campground, or pamper yourself in a resort lodge or cabin. Prepare your meals yourself over a campfire, in a deluxe cabin, or let someone else do it for you in a state park dining room.

If variety is the spice of life, Ohio's state parks offer a very tasty menu. Virtually anything you're looking for in the outdoors can be found in Ohio. In addition to the sheer scenic beauty are opportunities for enjoying dozens of outdoor pursuits including picnicking, walking, backpacking, bicycling, horseback riding, jogging, swimming, boating, canoeing, fishing, water skiing, hunting, sports, and nature photography,

Perhaps it is their diversity which explains why year in and year out Ohio is in the running for the highest state park attendance in the country.

Variety comes as no surprise in Ohio. Ohio is a diverse land of diverse peoples. The state is a melting pot of industry and agriculture, cultured cities and fertile rural life. It is a land of bounty and beauty, qualities reflected in its state parks.

Every area of the state is unique and together they provide a total outdoor experience. The Lake Plains, nearly level glaciated lands that were once at the bottom of Lake Erie's larger ancient predecessors, are concentrated in the western basin of Lake Erie and then eastward in a narrow band along the present lakeshore. Where natural areas remain they are largely wetlands and swamp forests, rich in wildlife and home to the largest concentrations of threatened and endangered plants in the state. Offshore from Port Clinton are the Lake Erie Islands, rocky outposts that still show the scars of the glaciers.

West and southwest Ohio are corn and soybean lands, lands of deep fertile soils pulverized in the passage of four major glaciers. These lands are known as the till plains, not as flat as the lake plains, but rivalling their value as agricultural lands.

The southeast is hill country, the Appalachian Highlands, a rugged region of hardwood forests that escaped the grinding, levelling action of the glaciers. Huge trees grow in the hollows and ravines, waterfalls tumble over ledges, and magnificent overlooks from the highest points of land reveal a contorted landscape that rolls as far as the eye can see. Northeast Ohio was very much like southeast Ohio before the glaciers made their way into Ohio, and today the region still shows considerable topography, the result of streams and rivers relentlessly cutting into the face of the landscape.

Each of these regions is represented among the 72 state parks which are more or less evenly distributed across the state. While each is unique, they have many points in common.

Hours: Almost all state parks are open from 6 a.m. until 11 p.m. but that doesn't apply across the boards. Facilities within state parks such as beach areas, hazardous trail areas, and concessions have shorter hours, while fishing access sites are open 24 hours a day.

Pets are allowed on leashes no longer than six feet in all state parks and campgrounds. In most campgrounds they are restricted to certain sites, in others they may be allowed throughout the camp. Pets are not permitted in buildings, on beaches, and certain other posted areas. The restrictions do not apply to seeing eye dogs.

Every state park has day-use facilities and nearly 60 of the 72 state parks offer **campgrounds**. All campgrounds are clean and well-kept but they vary in services and facilities. All have drinking water and restroom facilities, either flush or vault-type, along with fire rings and picnic tables. Some offer laundromats and heated showers and a few have commissaries stocked with groceries and camp supplies. Most offer some summer weekend nature programming.

Some of the campgrounds stretch over ridge-tops, others are small facilities tucked into ravines and hollows. Many are close to swimming beaches and also have nearby boat launches and tie-ups. Many have vehicle pads that can accommodate RVs up to 35 feet long but often offer beautifully situated tent-only sites as well.

No reservations are accepted for standard campground sites and generally there is a 14-day limit on your stay. Call a park in advance, though, to use group camps.

In between the choices of renting a lodge room or cabin and bringing your own equipment are the Rent-A-Camps available at 23 parks. Rent-a-camps consist of a 10x12 lodge-style tent and dining canopy. All basic equipment is provided including two cots, sleeping pads, cooler, propane stove, and lantern as well as the fire rings and picnic tables provided at regular campsites. Just bring your clothes and a sleeping bag. Call the appropriate park in advance to determine availability, but reservations must be made by mail.

Where **cabins** are offered, they are classified into three types:

Family Cabins are modern structures that accommodate six comfortably. They come with a fully equipped kitchen -- some have microwaves, a dining area, a master bedroom with double bed, a second bedroom with bunks, and a convertible sofa bed in the livingroom that invariably opens up to a screened porch, often with an overlook of a lake or ravine. Blankets, linens and towels are provided. These year-round cabins have central heat and a full bath, in a few parks they are also equipped with televisions and central air conditioning. In most parks these cabins are available only by the week between Memorial Day and Labor Day and on a daily basis the remainder of the year.

Standard Cabins are less common than family cabins. They lack central heat and, therefore, aren't open in late fall or winter. Their season is April 1 to October 31 of each year, except at Geneva State Park where the season in May 1 to September 30. Livingroom and kitchen areas are combined in these cabins and sleeping quarters are sometimes separated by a curtain divider. Both one bedroom and two bedroom cabins are available. Kitchens do have utensils and dishes for six people.

Sleeping Cabins are unique to Lake Hope State Park, these very popular rustic cabins are equipped with woodburning fireplaces which add a special atmosphere. They also come with central heat, full bath and a small kitchen. They are available in units ranging from one to four bedrooms.

The park system has recently implemented a $5 per day surcharge for six days before and six days after Memorial Day, the Fourth of July, Labor Day, and Thanksgiving.

Eight beautiful **resort lodges and conference centers** are open year-round in Burr Oak, Deer Creek, Hueston Woods, Maumee Bay, Mohican, Punderson, Salt Fork and Shawnee. Like the parks, each has its own personality yet they share the common quality of a luxury resort atmosphere in a natural setting. All offer dining rooms and lounges, swimming pools, outdoor and often indoor sports and games, exercise equipment, and, with the exception of Burr Oak, nearby golf courses. Nature trails are invariably located nearby as well as scenic views. The settings are perfect and the lodge atmosphere is a perfect getaway for recreation or business.

For current rates and **reservations** at the resort lodges and for all state park cabins call *1-800-ATA-PARK (1-800-282-7275)*. Information and reservations are also available directly through the appropriate park or lodge.

Generally, the reservation policy is to take reservations beginning the first of each month for the same month in the following year. For example, on December 1, 1993, the system will accept reservations for all dates in December, 1994.

Ohio's state parks have been working toward **handicapped accessibility** in its facilities and the system offers some wheelchair-accessible trails, picnic sites, restrooms, cabins, campsites, and lodge rooms.

Great **fishing** is available throughout the park system with largemouth bass, panfish, and catfish the most sought after species. A license is required for anglers sixteen years of age or older and all Ohio Division of Wildlife regulations apply. A booklet with current state-wide regulations should be obtained with the license.

Hunting is permitted in many state parks and in all state forest and wildlife areas. Familiarize yourself with state and local regulations in force and check with the park office for specific information before going into the field.

Ohio's state parks are invariably located near other visitor attractions, some of which are noted in this book. *For more information call 1-800-BUCKEYE, a toll-free nationwide number.*

Write to the Ohio State Parks' central office for an informational packet which includes current fee information and a calendar of events.

Ohio State Park Information Center
1952 Belcher Dr., Bldg. C-3
Columbus, Ohio 43224-1386

Resort Lodges

Tucked into Ohio's finest natural environs, the resort lodges of the state parks system range from elegant contemporary styling to Indian motif. All are open year-round, complete with modern meeting facilities, resort-like amenites that include golf, swimming pools, tennis, game rooms, courtesy docks, gift shops, fabulous food service, and much more for every group or family.

Reservations for each lodge can be made by calling *1-800-282-7275*.

Burr Oak: 60 rooms, five meeting rooms - *(614)767-2112*.

Deer Creek: 110 rooms, six meeting rooms - *(614)869-2020*.

Hueston Woods: 94 rooms, four meeting rooms - *(513)523-6381*.

Maumee Bay: 120 rooms, nine meeting rooms - (419)836-1466

Mohican: 96 rooms, three meeting rooms - *(800)472-6700*.

Punderson: 31 rooms, three meeting rooms - *(216)564-9144*.

Salt Fork: 148 rooms, six meeting rooms - *(614)439-2751*.

Shawnee: 50 rooms, four meeting rooms - *(614)858-6621*.

Cabins

Unique in the entire Midwest, cabins in the state park system range from rustic to modern, with many offering spectacular views, solitude, and all of the comforts of home. Cool screened porches for summer evenings and toasty warm woodburning fireplaces during the cold winter are featured in many of the 555 cabins scattered around the state.

Seventeen of the 72 Ohio State Parks offer cabins for rent. All but two of the parks operate the cabins year-round. Most of the cabins provide sleeping blankets, linens and towels, while family and standard cabins also offer kitchens equipped with cooking utensils and dishes, dining area and sleeping areas separated by curtains. Most cabins are booked well in advance, and many are rented only by the week during warm weather months. The following state parks operate cabins, *call ahead for details:*

Buck Creek	Burr Oak
Cowan Lake	Deer Creek
Dillon	Geneva
Hocking Hills	Hueston Woods
Lake Hope	Mohican
Maumee Bay	Pike Lake
Punderson	Pymatuning
Salt Fork	Shawnee

South Bass Island *(Cabents)*

Ohio State Parks

53 Oak Point
11 64 So. Bass Island
Catawba Island 35
26 Maumee Bay 47 19 Kellys Island 2 Cleveland 58
Harrison Lake 14 East Harbor Pymatuning
46 Toledo Crane Creek Cleveland Punderson 57 49
30 M. J. Thurston Lakefront 69 Mosquito
Independence Dam Tinkers Creek 52
70 W. Branch 71 41
Van Buren 20 Akron 56 Lake Milton
Findley Portage Lakes 59 Quail Hollow
25 Guilford Lake
45 5
Malabar Farms Beaver Creek
Lima 50 48
23 Mount Gilead Mohican
Grand Lake St. Marys 33
40 31 16 Jefferson Lake
Lake Loramie Indian Lake Delaware 61
36 2 Salt Fork
Kiser Lake Alum Creek
17 4
Columbus Dillon 51 Barkcamp
Muskingum River
7 8 6 72
Buck Creek Buckeye Lake Blue Rock Wolf Run
Dayton 34 44 3 Madison Lake A.W. Marion
67 John Byran 15 39
Sycamore Derr Creek Lake Logan
43 24 28 Hocking Hills
29 Little Miami Great Seal 68
Hueston Woods 10 Tar Hollow
Caesar Creek 9
13 Burr Oak
Cincinnati Cowan Lake Strouds Run
54 Scioto Trial 62 38 66
65 Paint Creek Lake Hope Forked Run
Stonelick 55 Pike Lake 37
18 60 42 Lake Alma
East Fork Rocky Fork Lake White
Adams Lake 1 32
Shawnee 63 Jackson Lake

W — S

14

Contents

Ohio State Parks

Ohio has some of the very best state parks in the Midwest.

Adams Lake

1 Adams Lake State Park

Land: 48 acres   Water: 47 acres

Adams Lake is bluegrass country. That's bluegrass as in geology and as in Kentucky. Those who want to impress their friends say Adams Lake is part of the interior low plateau.

Let's just say Adams Lake is in a very unique part of the state. It sits inside a small triangle of land that points up from the Ohio River and is almost totally restricted to Adams County, the only part of the state that's linked to the Bluegrass Region of Kentucky and the interior low plateau of the south-central states. Geologically, Adams Lake is a finger of unglaciated limestone between sandstone to the east and glaciated limestone to the west.

Adams Lake was almost in glaciated Ohio. In fact, those who sit in one of the picnic areas and look across the lake are looking at just about the furthest extent of the glaciers.

Botanically, what that means is that the plants of this part of Adams County are more in synch with Kentucky and points south than they are with the rest of Ohio. In fact, Adams County is second only to Lucas County and the Oak Openings Region in terms of numbers of state-listed endangered and threatened plants.

The soils here are generally light-colored and highly-erodible. Farmers found that out when they cleared the forest and tried to till the soil. Soon the farmland was abandoned for pastures, and finally abandoned altogether. That was too bad for the farmers, but one fascinating result of that turn of events was the xeric prairies that moved in on some of these abandoned lands.

Those who expect the huge horizon to horizon expanses of prairies once found out west will be disappointed to view the much smaller "pocket" prairies of Ohio. But the plants are none the less fascinating, both because of their beauty and because of their unique adaptations to be able to survive under extremely poor and harsh conditions.

When visiting Adams Lake, be sure to bring along some field guides about prairie wildflowers and grasses. Names like prairie dock, little bluestem, blazing star, prairie coneflower and agave or false aloe will have real meaning and add to your appreciation when you see the prairie blooming in all its glory.

Adams Lake itself was originally built as a drinking water supply for nearby West Union, but it is now strictly a recreation lake. In 1950, the lake and present parklands were purchased for operation as a state park. Because of the soils in the Adams Lake watershed, which became suspended in the lake after rainfalls, the water is rarely clear and not desirable as a swimming lake.

Information and Activities

Adams Lake State Park *
14633 SR41
West Union, Ohio 45693
(513) 544-3927

(* for quickest response, address correspondence and phone calls in care of nearby Shawnee State Park)

Directions: Located in Adams County, one mile north of West Union on SR41. State routes 41, 247, and 125 all intersect at West Union. Shawnee State Park is 20 miles west of West Union on SR125.

From Cincinnati or from US-23 take SR32 to SR41 and turn south.

Information: An information board is located just inside the park entrance at the maintenance building which serves as headquarters.

Campground: Camping is available at Shawnee State Park, 21 miles to the east.

Boating: A small launch is provided across the park road from park headquarters. The lake is restricted to electric motors.

Fishing: Fishing opportunities here are good, typical of small Ohio lakes with largemouth bass, bluegill, crappie, and channel catfish.

Hiking Trails: Two short walking trails are located in the adjacent Adams Lake State Nature Preserve. Both trails begin near the end of the main park road.

Post Oak Trail (0.5 mi. loop), is an easy walk through a dry oak forest dominated by white oak with an understory of flowering dogwood and redbud which are beautiful in spring.

Prairie Dock Trail (0.25 mi. loop) features a 300 foot boardwalk that rings a fine example of a xeric or dry prairie. An easy and fascinating walk that's best in the first or second week of August when the plants of the prairie are in bloom.

Day-use Areas: Excellent heavily shaded picnic areas that are nicely wooded to the lakeshore. A very nice open picnic shelter capable of holding up to 120 people is provided midway along the entrance road. Drinking water, vault toilets provided. An excellent timber-construction playground is located at the park entrance.

Swimming is not permitted in Adams Lake.

Nature Notes: The Division of Natural Areas and Preserves offers a number of unique programs in the Adams Lake Prairie on subjects varying from the prairie to geology to snakes. For further information contact the division at Bldg. F, Fountain Square, Columbus, 43224.

2 Alum Creek State Park

Land: 5213 acres   Water: 3387 acres

Quiet coves and shale cliffs await solitary fishermen in the park's northern reaches, while sunbathers and day-users convene by the thousands on Ohio's largest inland beach. Alum Creek, only minutes from capital city, Columbus, is nestled among the rich soils, beech-maple woodlots, shale deposits, and an array of other natural features.

Completed in 1974, the dam and park share operation of the area. An interesting history of Indian occupation, African Road and the Underground Railroad, fortresses, and modern day flood control efforts are everywhere. Over 40,000 slaves passed northward through Ohio and this area to freedom in the north.

The glacial deposits and rich soils offer thick natural vegetation of interest that supports a variety of wildlife. Spring wildflowers carpet the forest floor, while songbirds and many mammals are routinely seen by campers.

Information & Activities

Alum Creek State Park
3615 S. Old State Road
Delaware, Ohio 43015
(614)548-4631
(614)548-4039

Directions: Only minutes north of Columbus, between I-71 and US-23, reach the park headquarters by departing US 23 at Peachblow Road and travel east to the park office.

Information: The park headquarters is open 8 a.m. - 5 p.m. sometimes closed during the lunch hour, the campground office, which is located north of the park office on Cheshire Road (CR72), opens at 9 a.m. daily.

Campground: Alum Creek's campground, located on the west side of the lake just south of Cheshire Rd. off CR10, is one of the most private and shady in the state park system. Sites are separated by shrubbery, and many sites are under a canopy of leafy trees. With pop and ice machines near the park office, campers can also purchase wood for use at their camp site along one of the ten loops.

Sites G 25-27, 29, 31, 33, 35, are near the beach and very popular. Other camp sites located near the water include: B-34, 35, 37, 39; L-14-18; K-10, 15, 17, 19, 21, 22, 23; and M-8-13. B Loop is the most popular, but many regular campers seek L-15-17, and Loop E because of its canopy of mature trees. A short hiking trail is near G loop and along the shoreline and swimmer beach. A small boat ramp is near Loop L, pet sites are in zones J 1-18, and M 1-13. The campground also features a horseshoe court and playground equipment for the youngsters.

The campground beach is small, but busy on warm summer weekends. Five Rent-A-Camps are always full on weekends, but reservations can be made in March, or earlier, to insure a site for next summer.

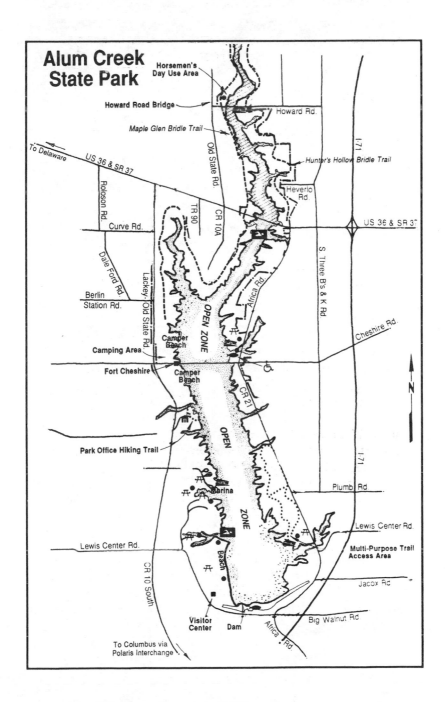

Alum Creek State Park

Horsemen's Day Use Area

Howard Road Bridge

Howard Rd.

Maple Glen Bridle Trail

To Delaware

US 36 & SR 37

Old State Rd.

Hunter's Hollow Bridle Trail

I-71

Heverlo Rd.

Roloson Rd.

TR 90

CR 10A

Curve Rd.

US 36 & SR 37

Dale Ford Rd.

Africa Rd.

S. Three B's & K Rd.

Berlin Station Rd.

Lackey-Old State Rd.

OPEN ZONE

Cheshire Rd.

Camper Beach

Camping Area

Fort Cheshire

Camper Beach

CR 21

OPEN ZONE

Park Office Hiking Trail

Marina

Plumb Rd.

I-71

Lewis Center Rd.

Lewis Center Rd.

Multi-Purpose Trail Access Area

CR 10 South

Beach

Jacox Rd.

Visitor Center

Dam

Africa Rd.

Big Walnut Rd.

To Columbus via Polaris Interchange

N

Only human or electric powered boats are allowed on the lake.

3   A. W. Marion State Park

Land: 216 acres   Water: 145 acres

Few people who drive the level, productive countryside of Pickaway County, past the fields along US-23 which in fall are dotted with the rich orange of pumpkins, through the county seat of Circleville, and on to the one part of Pickaway County where the terrain is hilly and the soil sandy and rocky, have the slightest idea why this beautiful, often over-looked, pocket of a state park is named after A.W. Marion.

There's a plaque prominently displayed in the large picnic area overlooking the blue, clear waters of Hargus Lake, but people seem content to walk by without learning that the park was named in 1962 after Pickaway County native A.W. Marion, the first director of the Ohio Department of Natural Resources.

A.W. Marion is on the edge of glaciated Ohio. Granite rocks scattered here and there in the park were deposited some 21,000 years ago by the fourth and most recent continental glacier to invade Ohio, the Wisconsin Glacier. The relatively rough terrain in and around A.W. Marion is the result of mounds of glacial till left by the glacier. Geologists call this particular band of rolling hills the Marcy Terminal Moraine, locals call it *"the devil's backbone."*

Information and Activities

A.W. Marion State Park
7317 Warner-Huffer Rd.
Circleville, Ohio   43113
(614) 474-3386

Directions: 23 miles south of Columbus, take US-23 to Circleville, east on US-22, left on Bolder-Pontius Rd. to main park entrance on Warner-Huffer Rd. For campground follow US-23, then US-22 past Bolder-Pontius Rd., to East Ringgold-Southern Rd. north to Township Rd. 77, follow it west to the campground.

Information: The park office is located on Warner-Huffer Road, turning right takes you to the office, left to the main picnic area.

Campground: If you like wooded campgrounds and don't mind the absence of electrical hook-ups, showerhouses, and flush toilets, you'll love A.W. Marion. A very nice camp with 60 sites located above and 200 yards east of lake, pop and ice machine in campground near site #1, VIP Camper-Host at Site #16, vault-type restrooms, small amphitheater and horseshoe pits. Although it can fill-up for Memorial Day and Fourth of July, the campground fills much later than nearby Deer Creek State Park. Other than holidays, you'll likely find a spot. Pets are welcome throughout camp. Basic supplies are available at the boat concession across the lake from camp, others in Circleville five miles away.

Campers desiring full hook-ups will find them at nearby Airy Acres, 300 sites with full hook-ups located next to the park's boat launch.

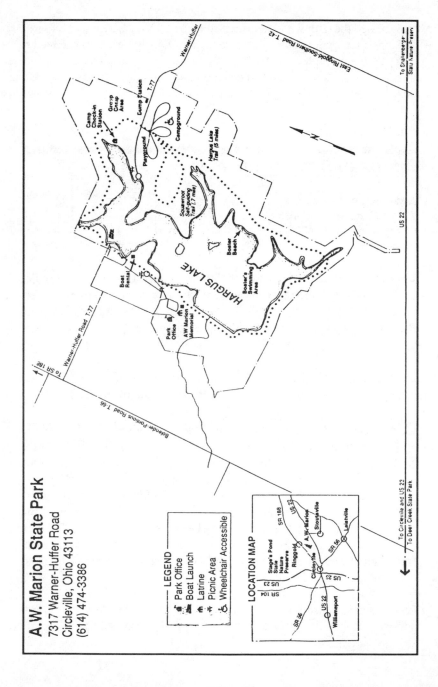

A.W. Marion State Park
7317 Warner-Huffer Road
Circleville, Ohio 43113
(614) 474-3386

LEGEND
- Park Office
- Boat Launch
- Latrine
- Picnic Area
- Wheelchair Accessible

LOCATION MAP

28

Day-use Facilities: Even though it lacks a swimming beach, A.W. Marion is a heavy day-use park with a large beautiful picnic area overlooking Hargus Lake, a small picnic area below the camp used primarily by fishermen (look to the north into the cove to see beaver activity), and a unique picnic site on a small island accessible only by boat.

Hiking Trails: Only two trails are available. The Squawroot Self-Guiding Trail (0.7 mi.) which loops out of the picnic area on an easy course down to and through the lowlands along the lake. Before taking the trail, check in the park office for a booklet describing features along the trail. The Hargus Lake Trail (5 mi.), as the name implies, loops around the lake. It is a somewhat challenging trail, a favorite for locals whose doctors have ordered exercise. The trail crosses four feeder streams, one of which isn't bridged.

Boating: Hargus Lake is held behind an earthen dam originally constructed in 1948 to dam Hargus Creek. It was drained in 1956 to rework the dam, and again in 1986 when structure was added and rough fish removed. Hargus Lake is a deep lake with the rich blue waters you'd expect in the North Woods -- in fact, one day while I was there a common loon floated lazily offshore in the deep waters. The lake is 55 feet deep in the main channel with many weed beds on the shelf along the shore and at the islands.

Only electric motors are allowed on the lake. A boat launch and concession are located just north of the picnic area. The concession is open April thru September and offers rowboats, some with electric motors, canoes and paddleboats as well as basic camp supplies, sandwiches and snacks.

An area is buoyed off in the southeast part of the lake as an offshore swimming area for boaters. No lifeguards, no beach.

Hargus Lake, unfortunately, is one of the first two Ohio inland lakes known to be invaded by the zebra mussel, a difficult to control European species that has flourished in Lake Erie and can be transferred from one body of water to another by boaters unless proper precautions are taken. Boaters should familiarize themselves with the mussel and learn the precautions to do their part in stemming the spread of zebra mussels.

Fishing: The lake is known as a bluegill lake, although most people fish it from shore for catfish and a monthly catfish tournament is held here. When I was there a six-pound plus largemouth bass and 44" muskie had just been taken. Kids love the lake, dropping a wax worm, red worm or nightcrawler from a cane pole on shore and always catching something.

Nature Notes: In spite of its small size and seemingly suburban location, A.W. Marion sports a variety of wildlife with excellent rabbit and squirrel populations, pheasant and deer. Hunting is allowed after October 14, away from buildings, camps, trails and other public use areas. Waterfowl hunting is also popular here.

In the summer, movies are shown in the campground amphitheater as visitors enjoy the relaxed setting.

Special Notes: Nearby Circleville is home of "the greatest free show on earth," the Circleville Pumpkin Festival held over a four-day October weekend. Entertainment, parades, pumpkin carving, pie eating, and more draw more than 400,000 visitors.

One of the last Mail Pouch barn signs by painter Harry Warwick, Jr.

4 Barkcamp State Park

Land: 1,232 acres   Water: 117 acres

Barkcamp was once just that, the site of a logging operation nestled in the heart of Belmont County where logs were stripped of their bark in preparation for delivery to a mill. But that was a long time ago and the second-growth oak-hickory woods are back crowding the creeks and covering the rolling park terrain. Today, Barkcamp is one of the nicest small parks in the system, a gem that's little known outside Belmont County.

The region was first inhabited by moundbuilders, and later was a vast hunting area for Wyandots, Chippewas and Potawatomis. Wildlife, including the large predators -- wolf, bear, and mountain lion -- was abundant. Although frontiersmen made this rugged wilderness along the upper Ohio River their home in the early 18th century, it was 1800 before the Barkcamp area was settled. The Society of Friends (Quakers) brought the first church to the area and later was active in the Abolitionist movement

31

and the 120 miles of Underground Railroad which funneled runaway slaves to safe havens in Canada. Freed slaves began to settle the county in the 1820s, Irish and Scotch-Irish Immigrants settled here in the mid-1800s.

Agriculture became the basis of the local economy, although today Belmont County is the state's leader in coal production. Barkcamp sits between those two worlds -- crops and cattle dominate the rolling hills along SR 149 approaching the park, but on the other side of the park, to the north and west, is strip mining.

Once inside the park, though, surrounding land uses are the furthest thing from your mind as you drive through the tunnel of dogwoods that bloom in late April on the way to the beach.

Information and Activities

Barkcamp State Park
65330 Barkcamp Road
Belmont, Ohio 43718
(614)484-4064

Directions: East of Cambridge and the I-70/I-71 interchange. Depart at exit 208 off I-70 and proceed two miles south on SR 149 to Barkcamp Park Rd.

Information: The park office is located on Barkcamp Road at the campground entrance not far from the main park entry.

Campground: Barkcamp is a heavy day-use park with a large campground that rarely, if ever, fills up. Although it lacks amenities such as electric hook-ups, flush toilets, and laundry facilities, it does have a wheelchair accessible showerhouse and very nice selection of shaded and open campsites on a series of ridgetops. Among its 150 sites are 14 for tents only (sites 136-149) located on an open knoll surrounded by woods on three sides. Pets are permitted on sites 42-67.

Special features include five very popular Rent-A-Camp sites and two sites

BARKCAMP STATE PARK

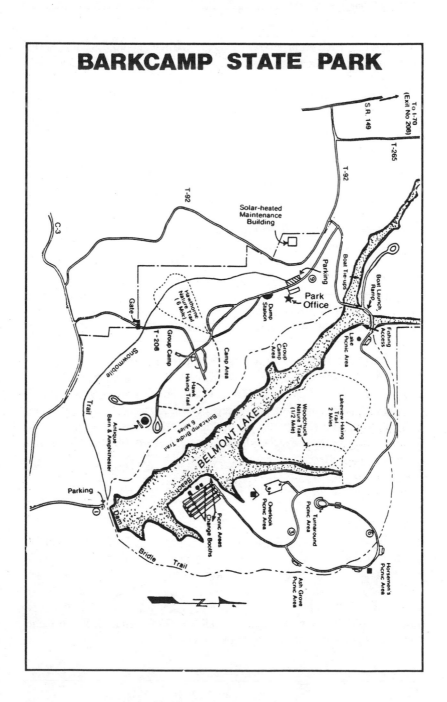

equipped with a paved-around fire ring and extra wide pull-up pads for the convenience of those in wheelchairs.

Day-use Facilities:
Seven picnic areas are provided including two large well-used areas at the 700 foot-long beach located across the lake from the campground. Above the beach, roads follow a ridge to three higher picnic areas, one a Horsemen's Picnic Area that is open to everyone but has tie-ups and easy access to the park's nine-mile Bridle Trail. In between is the large Overlook Picnic Area and shelter. One of the nicest areas, though, is the smaller Lake Picnic Area snuggled in on the upper end of the lake.

Boating:
Only electric motors are permitted on Belmont Lake, a relatively shallow lake that averages 10 to 12 feet in depth, up to 40 feet at the earthen dam. A boat rental and snack concession has been available at the beach, but it's closed until another concessionaire can be found. A small launch ramp is located at the Lake Picnic Area and tie-ups are available through the park office. Three fingers of Barkcamp Creek converge here so there's plenty of coves and shallow bays to explore.

Fishing:
Electroshock studies have shown that there are a lot of big bass here, but fishermen haven't found the formula for catching them. There's a slot limit in effect on Belmont Lake, fishermen must return bass in the 12 inch to 15 inch range but may keep others. Locals like to fish with nightcrawlers and roostertails. For the several thousand rainbow and golden trout which are stocked here each year, the popular formula is as simple as pasteurized cheese on a spinning rod.

Of special note is the wheelchair-accessible fishing dock and restrooms at the Lake Picnic Area.

Hiking/Bridle Trails:
Joggers and walkers love Barkcamp's miles of trails. Two trails, the Lakeview Hiking Trail (2.0 mi.) and Woodchuck Nature Trail (0.5 mi.) loop from a trailhead near the Overlook Picnic Area. The Lakeview Trail parallels the lakeshore over half its distance, is an excellent woodland birding trail with great lake views, but no real vistas. Lakeview is flatter than the shorter Woodchuck Trail which scales a hill and follows a course through an oak/hickory woods.

Two trails begin at the campground, the Hawthorne Nature Trail (0.6 mi.) a slightly rolling, relatively easy woodland loop, and the Hawk Hiking Trail (0.5 mi.) which connects to the barn/amphitheater area where nature programs are held regularly.

Nature Notes: In summer, programs are held regularly at the amphitheater.

Barkcamp is the only state-owned public hunting area in Belmont County with its healthy population of whitetail deer, ruffed grouse and squirrel. No trapping is permitted, however. Many non-game species are found here as well as beaver, osprey, barn owls, towhees, orioles and more.

Special Features: The old barn at the end of the campground loop is an unusual feature in itself, but be sure to check out the Mail Pouch advertisement on the barn's exterior which like most Mail Pouch signs in the eastern U.S. was painted by Harry Warwick, Jr., Belmont resident and the last of the Mail Pouch painters. The barn with its antique farm equipment and historic information is the main stop on the paved Pioneer Trail for the Handicapped which features everything from nature interpretation, a stop at an old outhouse complete with the half moon, and a plaque commemorating the accomplishments of the colorful and famous local Indian fighter Lewis Wetzel who supposedly killed four Indians there.

Historic Village at Beaver Creek State Park.

5 *Beaver Creek State Park*

Land: 3038 acres Water: River

The first Ohio river to be designated Wild and Scenic is Little Beaver Creek and in Beaver Creek State Park it lives up to its grand title. Within the Columbiana County park, the river flows seven miles past the rugged foothills of the Appalachian Mountains, through forested glens and beneath towering cliffs.

It also flows past the remnants of one of the most interesting chapters in the state's history; the canal era. After the Ohio and Erie Canal was constructed in 1825 to connect Portsmouth on the Ohio River to Cleveland on Lake Erie, several feeder canals were added to access the larger markets. One of them was the Sandy and Beaver Canal.

A most unusual project because it was privately financed through the sale of stock, the Sandy and Beaver Canal connected the Ohio-Erie Canal at Bolivar with the Ohio River at Glasgow. Although construction began in

1828, financial problems delayed its completion until 1848. By then railroads were already putting an end to the canal era. Still the Sandy and Beaver Canal operated successfully for four years until a reservoir project outside of New Lisbon caused extensive property damage and ruined a large section of the canal. The canal company went broke trying to settle the resulting lawsuits.

Today, remains of the area's colorful past can be seen throughout the park. Near the headquarters there is Pioneer Village with Gaston's Mill, blacksmith's shop, log cabin and a covered bridge. In the southeast corner is Sprucevale, a "ghost town" from the canal era and the site of Hambleton's stone grist mill which according to legends was haunted for more than a century by a Quaker preacher.

Most of all you'll find locks, eight of them stretched along the river where it's possible to stop and reflect on the amazing workmanship that keeps them standing more than a century later. Beaver Creek, one of Ohio's finest state parks, offers more than just a history lesson however. A wide range of activities are possible including hiking, horseback riding, camping, fishing and canoeing.

Information & Activities

Beaver Creek State Park
12021 Echo Dell Road
East Liverpool, Ohio 43920
(216) 385-3091

Directions: Beaver Creek is located 8 miles northwest of East Liverpool off of SR7. Continue on the state route after it departs from US-30/SR11 and then head east on Bell School Road to Echo Dell Road. Head north on Echo Dell to reach the park office, Pioneer Village and three of the four picnic areas along Little Beaver Creek.

Information: The office is on Echo Dell Road near the Pioneer Village. Hours are 8 a.m. to 5 p.m.

Campgrounds: Beaver Creek has three camping areas. A family campground is reached from the park office by crossing the river to continue north along Echo Dell Road and then west a short ways on Leslie

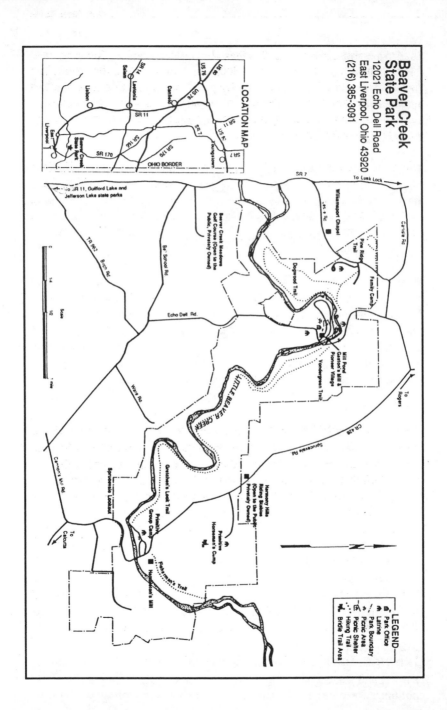

Beaver Creek
State Park
12021 Echo Dell Road
East Liverpool, Ohio 43920
(216) 385-3091

Road. The rustic 55-site facility has vault toilets, tables, fire rings and gravel spurs along two loops. Both loops are well wooded, the second in a pine plantation, and laid out on a ridge top. A few sites have a view of the rugged valley below while the best overlook is just a short walk from site number 23. There is a dump station near the entrance. The campground rarely fills up, even on holiday weekends.

At the southeast end of the park, reached from Sprucevale Road (CR428) is a primitive Horseman's Camp in a large grassy clearing with water, vault toilets and fire rings. Within the old Sprucevale townsite is a rustic group campground where grassy sites overlook Little Beaver Creek. The group camp, which has vault toilets but no water, can be reserved by contacting the park office 14 days in advance.

Day-use Areas: The park has four picnic areas, all of them overlooking the river. Near Pioneer Village are two picnic areas with tables, grills, vault toilets and play equipment in a grove of red pine. Cross the Echo Dell Bridge, a historic iron bridge constructed in 1910, and you'll reach a third picnic area with more tables, grills and play equipment in a stand of hardwoods along the river. The trailhead for the Dogwood Trail is posted at the back of this loop. A fourth picnic area is located in the Sprucevale area near Hambleton's Lock and the remains of the old lock tender's home.

Locks and Mills: The heart of Pioneer Village near the park office is Gaston's Mill and the mill pond it overlooks. Built in 1830 by Samuel Conkle, the mill originally powered by water then steam and finally gas engines before it discontinued operations in the late 1920s. Nearby are Theo Appley Blacksmith Shop, the Paul Dailey Schoolhouse, a barn, Floyd Lower's log cabin and Thomas Malone Bridge. The covered bridge was built in 1870 along SR154 between Lisbon and Elkton, but eventually was moved and converted into a storage shed. It was "re-discovered" and renovated in 1971.

Most of the buildings in the village are furnished and open Saturday and Sunday 1-5 p.m. At the same time volunteers operate the mill for visitors. The other mill in the park is Hambleton's stone grist mill at Sprucevale.

The park has eight locks, all of them part of the Sandy Beaver Canal, the

73.5-mile man-route that featured a total of 90 locks and 30 dams. Three locks are accessible from the road. The most impressive by far is Lusk Lock in a separate area of the park that is reached by heading north on SR7 to Middle Beaver Road (CR419) and then heading west. Here you'll find a parking lot and stairs that lead into one of the largest canal locks in the world. Built in 1836, Lusk still displays the exceptional masonry work needed in canal lock construction. Near Pioneer Village is recently restored Lock 36 while in the Sprucevale picnic area is Hambleton's Lock, also referred to as Lock No. 42. The other five locks are seen along the Sandy Beaver Trail that spans from the Echo Dell Bridge to Sprucevale. Grey's Lock is a mile from the bridge, the extremely well preserved Vondergreen's Lock along with Lock No. 39 and Lock No. 40 are two miles and Gretchen's Lock is 2.8 miles or less than a mile from Sprucevale.

Fishing: Beaver Creek has 7 miles of river bank open to anglers and most of it is accessible from the park's trail system. Anglers cast for a variety of fish including smallmouth bass, bluegill, rock bass and catfish.

Hiking: Beaver Creek has more than 16 miles of hiking trails. Near the family campground is Pine Ridge Trail, a 0.5-mile loop up the ridge. Dogwood Trail is a 2.2 mile loop from the picnic area on the north side of the river at Echo Dell Bridge while departing in the opposite direction from the iron bridge is Vondergreen Trail, a five mile loop to the lock of the same name.

The Vondergreen Trail is actually part of Sandy Beaver Trail, a 21-mile backpacking route that follows the original Sandy and Beaver Canal from Elkton to the Ohio River at East Liverpool. Built and maintained by the Boy Scouts, the most scenic section of this long distance trail is the 3.5-mile stretch through the state park, beginning at the Echo Dell Bridge and ending at Sprucevale. Along the way you view five locks, old stone foundations and the cliffs along the river.

Canoeing: The park is the put-in site for a 12-mile paddle down Little Beaver Creek. The scenery is delightful through the park and includes remnants of locks and high cliffs. But hazards include rocks, downed trees and low water during the middle of the summer. The river can also be fast in spots, including a stretch of Class III rapids at the Fredericktown Bridge outside the park.

Bridle Trails: Beaver Creek has excellent facilities for trail riders and is a favorite for equestrians. There are 25 miles of bridle trails and the main trailhead is in the Horseman's Campground. The trail range from the mile-long Leisure Loop and Whispering Pines Trail, a 7-mile loop to Hoof Beat Loop, the longest ride. Hoof Beat is a 16-mile trail that winds up Little Beaver Creek Valley and across the river four times as well as over ridgetops and through other rugged terrain. This ride is stunning during fall colors.

Ohio's first Wild and Scenic river.

Remote Blue Rock State Park is a favorite camping destination.

6   Blue Rock State Park

Land: 335 acres   Water: 15 acres

There really is blue rock in Blue Rock State Park. It's there, but it's not easy to find. It's said there's some to be seen in the spillway below Cutler Lake. Blue Rock, and the surrounding 4,573 acre Blue Rock State Forest of which it was a part of until 1949, got their names from the outcrops of shale along the nearby Muskingum River which actually appear blue, particularly when wet.

The park and state forest were once marginally productive farmland originally acquired by the federal government in the 1930s under the Depression-era Resettlement Administration, then transferred to the state under the Federal Land Utilization Program. The land has since been reforested, transforming it into one of Ohio's most beautiful forests.

Cutler Lake, the focal point of Blue Rock State Park, was laboriously dug in the mid-1930s by WPA workers using teams of horses and drags. Before becoming a lake the area was known as Oil City complete with a number of shallow Berea wells. In 1949, the lake and adjoining lands were turned over to state parks.

Blue Rock is out-of-the-way. Getting there is off the beaten path, leaving SR60 and climbing away from the Muskingum River along a narrow, winding, mostly residential street, past a vacation farm, through a portion of the heavily wooded Blue Rock State Forest and, finally, into the beautiful, quiet, secluded family-oriented park.

Information and Activities

Blue Rock State Park
7924 Cutler Lake Rd.
Blue Rock, Ohio 43720
(614) 674-4794

Directions: Depart I-70 at Zanesville's SR60 south exit, follow it 13 miles to Duncan Falls, turn left on Cutler Lake Rd. and take it 6.5 miles to Blue Rock.

Information: The park office is located off Park Road 3, opposite the beach, the first left turn after entering the park.

Campground: Blue Rock is a quiet, low-pressure park, and the campground is no different. The 101 sites fill up only on the Memorial Day and Fourth of July holidays, otherwise there's a nice spot somewhere here for you. Registration is thru the ranger or camp attendant who will visit your site. Paved drive-ups, drinking water, vault toilets, picnic table and fire ring are provided at each site. A coin-operated shower is available at the beach. There are no electric hook-ups.

The campground is separated into two distinct loops, both on the west side of the lake. Although almost all sites are nice the upper, and older, loop is preferred. A very nice little stream cuts thru the upper loop -- actually it's the outlet stream from the lake -- a favorite for kids who splash around in it for crawdads, salamanders, and the like. For best sites in the upper loop check 54-56, 76, 86, and 89 for their relative seclusion and shaded to open character. Three Rent-A-Camps are available in the summer months in the upper loop. Contact the park office for Rent-A-Camp information.

The lower loop is newer and up on a oak-wooded ridge. Pets are allowed on this loop only. Check sites 12, 24, 35, and 41 before you settle on a spot, but virtually all sites provide shade.

A primitive tents-only walk-in camp area is located at the opposite end of the lake, a one-half mile hike off Cutler Lake Road to the top of a hill in a big, open field surrounded by woods. Only latrines and trash containers are provided. Camping is free in this little-used area, but sites still must be registered with the ranger.

No camping is available in the adjacent Blue Rock State Forest.

Boating: Cutler Lake is restricted to electric motors only, and is ideal for a quiet excursion in a rowboat or canoe. A small launch ramp is off Cutler Lake Road beyond the beach bathhouse.

Fishing: Cutler is a shallow lake, only 20 feet deep at the dam and much shallower elsewhere, especially in the eastern end of the lake which is now a cattail marsh and near a cove to the north which is choked with American lotus.

Water quality is usually very good. Good structure in the lake and stocking of bluegill, channel catfish and largemouth bass offers anglers good to fair fishing. In the summer months, fishermen work on the bass with artificial lures.

Hiking/Bridle Trails: Three miles of hiking trails are available in Blue Rock, with some ten miles of bridle trails that double very nicely as hiking trails located in the nearby state forest. Unfortunately for horseback enthusiasts there is no livery in the area.

Day-use Areas: Four picnic areas and three shelterhouses can be used

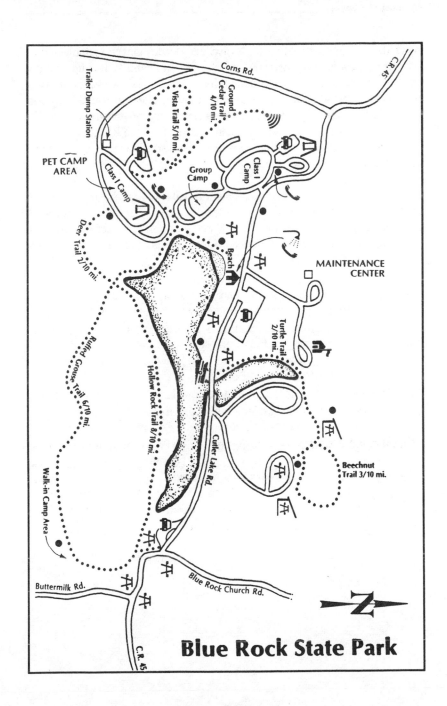

Blue Rock State Park

45

by visitors. The beach picnic area is nice, very traditional and popular. Two other areas, each with large shelters, are alongside and above the shallow cove of the lake that crosses under Cutler Lake Road. The lower shelter is a more open woodland setting than the upper shelter. A fourth area and shelter is maintained by the park at the old fire tower in the state forest. To reach it travel 1 1/4 miles north on Cutler Lake Road to Ridgeview Road, then the same distance on Ridgeview to the tower. The tower steps can be climbed, but at your own risk.

A 200 foot beach is just north of the dam. Lifeguards are present during peak hours, otherwise swim at your own risk. Only daylight swimming is permitted. The showerhouse with its change booths, lockers, restrooms, and coin-operated warm showers is open, while the beach snack bar concession offers lots of goodies.

Nature Notes: Blue Rock shares a seasonal naturalist with nearby Dillon State Park, but still offers a variety of programs on Wednesday, Thursday and Saturday, culminating with movies in the campground amphitheater on Saturday night. The three-session Naturalist Aid Program for young people is offered there as are "owl prowls" and discovery walks.

Hunting: Hunting is not permitted in Blue Rock State Park but is permitted in season in the surrounding state forest.

Winter Activities: Camping and hiking can be enjoyed year-round in Blue Rock. Although far enough south to escape heavy snows and most of the harsh winter, there are days when ice fishing, ice skating and sledding can be enjoyed.

Cabins, camping, quality fishing, and a beach await you at Buck Creek.

7 Buck Creek State Park

Land: 1910 acres   Water: 2120 acres

The C.J. Brown Reservoir is located at Buck Creek State Park, 2 miles northeast of Springfield. The large reservoir has 2,120 surface acres and 10.5 miles of shoreline that is designed to help with flood control and water supply. It impounds Buck Creek and drains an area of 82 square miles. The U.S. Army Corp of Engineers finished construction of the dam in 1973.

The earthern dam is 6,600 feet long and 72 feet high, and the maximum depth is 50 feet at the dam. The northern end of the reservoir is shallow and many standing trees continue to support excellent fish habitat.

The state park is one of the most modern, with the campground completed in 1987. With 1.2 million visitors annually, Buck Creek and the Corp's visitor center near the dam makes this one of the busiest parks in the Ohio system. Well known as a good fishing lake, all types of boaters, skiiers, and even scuba divers use the facility.

Information & Activities

Buck Creek State Park
1901 Buck Creek Lane
Springfield, Ohio 45502
(513) 322-5284

Directions: On the northeast corner of Springfield, in Clark Country, Buck Creek is about seven miles above its confluence with the Mad River, a tributary of the Miami River. Depart I-70 at exit 62 and go west 3 miles, turn right on Bird Rd, which becomes Buck Creek Ln.

LOCATION MAP

Information: The park headquarters is located at the end of Buck Creek Lane, which is off Old Columbus Road, is open Monday - Friday, 8 a.m. - 5 p.m. The beach, boat launching, and picnic area is nearby.

Campground: 89 of the 101 camp sites at Buck Creek have electricity (non-electric sites are 21-26 & 29-34), the pet sites are numbers 1-5 and 45-49. The first loop, sites 1-40 have virtually no shade, frankly, they are pretty sterile. Sites number 21-28 are carved into a field for tent campers. Sites 80-85 have a lake view but the shade is light. Sites 41-74 have light shade and are open. Because of the parks relative newness, many of the shade trees and other landscaping in the campground are still growing.

The campground is not heavily used and there are usually sites available even on summer holiday weekends. Showers, flush toilets, and a dump station are located conveniently. The campground is located north of the park office on a peninsula near the cabins. Buck Creek's cabins are among the shadiest and most private in the park system. Cabin number 14, 16, 17 and 18 have a great lake view. All of the cabins are pleasant and private and booked well in advance, call early, 513-322-5284.

Buck Creek State Park

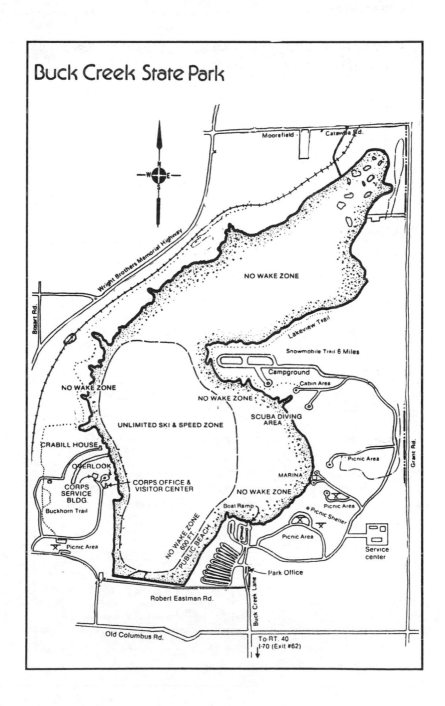

Boating: The Buck Creek State Park Marina, 2250 Buck Creek Road (phone: 513-322-5992) offers full service for the boater. Snack bar, marine accessories, bait/tackle, ski equipment, fishing license, fuel and boat rentals also.

You can rent a humble canoe or skip from wave-top to wave-top on a snorting and revving jet ski. Pedal boats, fishing boats, and pontoons are also in the rental slips. The lake is designed for unlimited horsepower boats but there is a no wake zone along most of the shoreline including a large no wake zone at the northern end of the lake.

Fishing: Walleyes, catfish and crappies have been stocked in the lake. Largemouth bass, black crappies, bluegills, suckers, carp, bullhead catfish, and other sunfish have entered the lake from Buck Creek.

The Ohio Division of Wildlife conducts stocking programs, monitors the adult fish population, installation of fish habitat structures, and conducts studies to determine spawning success, survival, and growth of important game species.

Springtime walleye can be caught along riprap shorelines such as the dam using jigs tipped with minnows or twister tails. Summer walleyes can be taken by trolling or drifting deep diving crankbaits or spinners tipped with

	Jan.	Feb.	Mar.	Apr.	May	Jun.	Jul.	Aug.	Sep.	Oct.	Nov.	Dec.
Largemouth bass				●	●	●	●	●	●	●		
Crappies				●	●	●				●		
Bluegill						●	●	●				
Channel catfish					●	●	●	●	●			
Walleye			●	●	●	●		●				

Peak Action Fishing Calendar

nightcrawlers. Some walleyes can be taken in the tailwater pool below the dam.

Springtime crappies are found throughout the lake and can be taken in brushy areas, around fish habitat structure additions, and along riprap shorelines by still fishing with minnows, small flies, jigs tipped with waxworms, etc. Drifting or trolling over old roadbed or other structure with minnows or waxworms can be producive. Hungry bluegills hit redworms and waxworms during the warmer season around any type of shoreline or natural cover.

Largemouth bass can be taken from spring until fall by casting artifical lures and live bait at the drop-offs, roadbeds, and old stream channels. Night fishing for all species can be productive, many anglers night fish around the marina with fair to good results. Channel catfish can be taken in the spring in the creek mouth and upper end of the lake by fishing shrimp, chicken liver, or cut bait.

Hiking: Although Buck Creek has only 5.5 miles of hiking trails, walkers
will find the trails easily, interesting, and near the water. The Buck Horn Trail begins at the southeast corner of the lake near the U.S. Army Corps of Engineers Visitor Center off Croft Road. The leisurely trail wanders along the lakeshore to Catawba Road, a total of three miles of walking through fields and forest. The trail parallels an active railroad track.

The Lakeview Trail is located on the east side of the lake begins at the cabins and runs northward along the shoreline. Bring your panfishing rod along on this easy hike.

Day-use Areas: Because the lake is a very good to excellent fishing
reservoir shoreline anglers ply their craft along the miles of flat shoreline. The picnic and shoreline fishing area near the Corps Visitor Center is the most popular area for day-use. Visitors can also enjoy scuba diving in the designated area, picnic tables and grills are also located throughout.

With the huge dam tower in the distance, swimmers will enjoy one of the longest beaches in the entire state park system. The 2400-foot beach is sandy and complete with bathhouse and buzzing water skiiers racing nearby. There is a handicapped accessible fishing area.

Nature Notes: Once again, the Corps of Engineers, the builders of the dam and managers of the flood control project, offer an excellent visitor center that interprets the natural history and water dynamics of the area.

The overlook and Visitor Center is located off Croft Road at the southeast end of the lake and offers detailed educational displays that explain flood controls and natural history. Staff conducts a variety of educational programming in cooperation with the state park. The naturalist staff reports regular sighting of mute swans, loons, hummingbirds, and a variety of wildlife. They also conduct nature hikes, and are managing a prairie re-development project next to the visitor center.

Nearby is the Crabill House, a living history museum that is operated by the Clark County Historical Society, call (513)324-0657 for exact times and dates of operation. The late Federal-style house, built in the early 1820's, has two wings; a kitchen wing and the main house.

A visitor to the historic house and the visitor center is an excellent half-day family outing only minutes from the campground, beach, and fishing areas.

Aside from the above managed areas, the Ohio Division of Natural Areas and Preserves in cooperation with the Corps of Engineers administers the Prairie Road Fen State Nature Preserve, the largest and finest prairie fen in Ohio. *You must have a permit to enter the fen, issued by the Corps Office.*

Fens are alkaline wetlands found in the glaciated region of North America. They occur where groundwater moving through calcareous gravel reaches a lower area and forms a spring. During the subterranean journey, the water becomes cold, oxygen deficient and hard.

The harsh conditions of a fen are unique, with specialized plants evolving and thriving. In the coldest and most alkaline areas Kalm's lobelia, false asphodel, grass-of-Parnassis and seaside arrow-grass grow. Away from the fen, where water temperatures moderate and fallen organic matter offers some protection from the marl, a sedge-meadow forms. Here are found stubby cinquefoil, Canadian burnet, small fringed gentian, and Ohio goldenrod.

Boat launch at Buckeye State Park

8 *Buckeye Lake State Park*

Land: 175 acres   Water: 3,382 acres

There are about twenty acres of water to every acre of land in Buckeye Lake State Park. It doesn't take a rocket scientist to figure out that just about everything there happens on, in, or next to the lake.

Buckeye Lake is a park with strong roots in the past, and an island in the middle of the lake that's not rooted to anything at all.

When the last of the glaciers retreated from Ohio some 18,000 years ago it left in its wake innumerable lakes, kettles and wetlands. One such lake was at present-day Buckeye Lake, only that prehistoric lake was actually much larger than the present lake. By the 1700s when the first European settlers were entering the region, Buckeye Lake had largely silted in and became a bog dominated by sphagnum moss and other northern plants.

These plants that are today more typical of Canada were holdovers from the glacial days when the area's climate really was much more like Canada. One early explorer dubbed the area, which more properly should have been called the Great Bog, the "Great Swamp."

The return of Buckeye Lake was not a natural but a man-made occurrence. In the 1820s, Ohio caught canal fever and towns across the state fought to have a canal connecting them to important markets in the east and south. The result was a network of canals that didn't work unless there was water in them and sometimes feeder lakes were required to supply it. A dike was built around the west end of the swamp and the Great Swamp became the Licking-Summit Reservoir.

Those who have worked with sphagnum moss in their gardens know of its amazing capacity for absorbing and holding water. As though in an act of defiance, 50 acres of the most buoyant section of the sphagnum moss absorbed and stretched and expanded until it broke through to the surface and created what is known today as Cranberry Bog which appears as an island just east of Picnic Point. Cranberry Bog is unique to the lake -- the other islands here are simply lands above lake levels. It's not unusual to have a floating bog mat, not unusual at all, it occurs frequently in Canada, for example. But bog mats typically surround the lake, at Buckeye Lake the lake surrounds the mat.

The coming of the railroads doomed the canals -- after all, they could operate year-round and make better time -- and in 1894 the state abandoned the Licking-Summit Reservoir for canal purposes, changed its name to Buckeye Lake, and made it a recreation lake. Within a few years Buckeye Lake became a popular resort area, and much of the area today has the feel of a long-established lake retreat.

Out in the lake, Cranberry Bog is fading in spite of its status as a state nature preserve and national natural landmark. It started as fifty acres, dwindled to 23 acres by 1955, and is well under 19 acres today. Its sphagnum moss meadow interior is still rich in bog plants such as cranberry and northern pitcher plant, but for how long isn't known. Studies say there's nothing to be done to stabilize the bog except protect it as much as possible from the wake of passing boats. No one is permitted on Cranberry Bog without written permission from the chief of the Ohio Division of Natural Areas and

Preserves, Fountain Square, Bldg. F, Columbus, 43324. The Division schedules a day each year when the public can visit the island and walk the boardwalk trail.

Information and Activities

Buckeye Lake State Park
Box 488
Millersport, Ohio 43046
(614)467-2690

Directions: Buckeye Lake is a large lake with several park activity areas.

Park headquarters just outside Millersport is located on Liebs Island about 22 miles east of the I-270/I-70 interchange on the west side of Columbus. Take I-70 east out of Columbus 17 miles to SR37, proceed south three miles on SR37 to SR204, turn east on SR204 and follow to Millersport, where SR204 seems to deadend (but doesn't) is Millersport Road, turn north (left) one mile to Liebs Island Road, turn east (right) and follow the road to park headquarters.

Three miles further east off I-70 is the Village of Buckeye Lake with the North Shore Ramp picnicking and launch facilities. Follow I-70 to SR79, turn south on SR79, the park facility is one mile away on SR79.

Information: Park headquarters is located on the right hand side of Lieb's Island Road just past the boat launches. Office hours are Monday through Friday from 8 a.m. until noon and 1 p.m. to 5 p.m.

Boating: Buckeye Lake is an unlimited horsepower lake where virtually every size, type, or style of boat can be seen. It's estimated there are over 3,000 private boats on the lake. But the lake is over seven miles long and an average of one-half mile wide, so there's plenty of room for everyone.

Weekdays during the boating season are great days for a leisurely family boat trip or a lazy day of fishing. Weekends are generally quiet in the mornings but the mood changes in the afternoon when the power boats and jet skis strut their stuff.

Sailboating is very popular. It's claimed the Buckeye Lake Yacht Club, which is primarily a sailing club, is the largest club on an inland lake in the United States.

No wake zones are in effect 300 feet from any land mass and in the central zone of the lake between Picnic Point and Harbor Hills. That zone protects Cranberry Bog. There are also no wake zones between the southwest shore of the lake and the series of islands offshore, and at either end of the lake. A 10 mph speed limit is in effect from sunset to sunrise.

A selection of four launch locations is available including a pair of two-lane iaunches at Liebs Island, a modern two lane ramp at North Shore in Buckeye Lake, and older ramps suitable for smaller boats at Fairfield Beach at the mid-point of the southern shore and Brooks Park near Millersport. The Fairfield Beach ramp has limited parking, the other sites have plenty.

Two boat swim areas are buoyed off at each end of the lake, one is east of Lieb's Island and the second is off the south shore opposite Avondale Park.

Fishing: Like boaters, fishing enthusiasts find a lot to like here. Big fish, little fish, perch, bluegill, crappie, muskellunge, largemouth bass, channel catfish and bullheads are all favorite quarry here. In spite of its shallow depth -- the lake averages only 4 1/2 feet of water -- it's one of the better musky lakes in the state. And the other species aren't shabby either. The word is there are some monster fish in Buckeye Lake. The word must be spreading because the lake hosts a fishing tournament virtually every weekend from March through July, including as many as four pro tournaments each year.

The season starts in March as soon as the ice is off the lake when bass and crappie are hitting back in the coves and along wooded banks. The best tip is to be aware of temperature gradients in this lake. It's shallow and warms up quickly, by August it can be bathtub warm.

Best fishing is from a boat, and the least pressure is along the south shore.

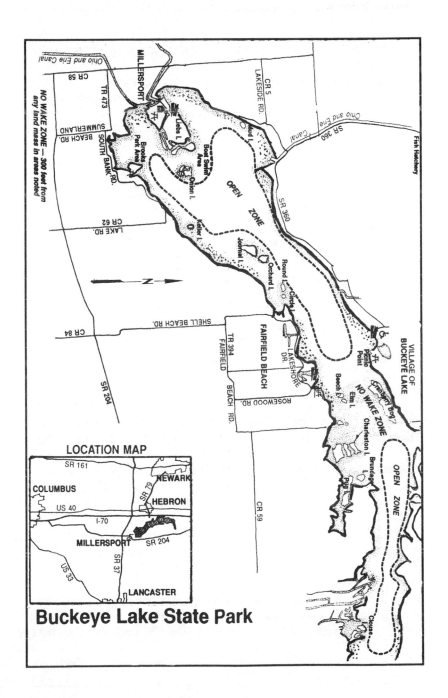

Buckeye Lake State Park

It's along some of the points on the south shore that the musky are caught.

Shore fishing is popular at Lieb's Island where crappie and catfish are caught along the wall next to the launch, and at North Shore Ramp. At North Shore there is a recently built jetty that stretches into the lake affording a very nice walkway into the lake and also some excellent fishing for catfish. Green Lake, a protected bay off the lake at North Shore, has a special 10 foot square fishing pier that's wheelchair accessible. Virtually all facilities at North Shore at handicapped accessible including the flush restrooms and the jetty.

About every third year the ice is thick enough on Buckeye Lake for ice fishing, ice boating, and snowmobiling. The favored ice fishing spots are on the east end of the lake north of Clouse Island where the perch hit. Lieb's Island is the best staging area for snowmobiles.

Day-use Areas: Buckeye Lake is actually five small parks scattered around the lake. There are no facilities at present at Edgewater Beach, and Brooks Park Area has been greatly expanded in recent years by depositing dredge materials. There's a large parking area there now along with the boat launch and picnicking facilities. Future plans for the site include a nice beach.

Lieb's Island has a small but nice picnic area shaded by big cottonwoods. Fishermen like the spot, too, so tables are often right at the water's edge.

The North Shore Ramp property now includes the old site of the Buckeye Lake Amusement Park which was the place to be in the 30s and 40s but petered out by the mid-70s. All that's left of the park where Tommy Dorsey and all the other big names of the era used to play is a fountain that will, hopefully, be restored to working condition. The nicest picnic sites here are out on Picnic Point, a grassed area with plenty of shade right on the lake. The flush toilets are unheated so are closed in winter.

Fairfield Beach is the prettiest area in the park with its old-style picnic shelter, nicely shaded scattered picnic sites and grills, an open play area, and 100 foot beach that's lightly used during the week and even many weekends through the summer.

Hunting: Buckeye Lake is strictly for waterfowlers. Even though the lake is off the flyways there are enough puddle ducks that a good hunter can get the limit. Hunting blinds are assigned through the state but hunters can also use boats. Depending upon the year, Buckeye Lake has been considered both in the North and South Zones for hunting season. Be sure to contact Buckeye Lake or the Ohio Division of Wildlife for information.

Fog hangs over hollows and ravines where ruggedly-rolling terrain stretches to the horizon.

9 Burr Oak State Park

Land: 3,265 acres   Water: 640 acres

Take to the high ground at Burr Oak State Park. Do it in the morning or evening when the low slanting rays of the sun are shooting light and shadow across the ruggedly-rolling countryside, when more often than not a fog is dramatically hanging in the hollows and ravines, when you can look out for miles and miles and see a great forest seemingly unbroken by the hand of man. It's a view that's certainly not much different than the earliest settlers might have seen.

It's appropriate that this park is named for a tree, because the deep oak-hickory forest is everywhere. Unfortunately, though, the only burr oaks to be found in the park now are in the R.J. Miller Memorial Grove near the cabins, planted in 1968.

The park actually takes its name from the town of Burr Oak which once thrived along Sunday Creek near today's dam and park entrance off SR13. Before they were timbered, great burr oaks -- some of them giants with trunks that stretched 100 feet to the first branches -- crowded the hillsides surrounding the village. Only a few homes remain of the original town. Beneath Burr Oak Lake are seven covered bridges left in place when the lake was created in 1950. Burr Oak State Park was created in 1952 and has proven to be one of the most beautiful and popular in the state.

To find out why, venture north on SR78, the "rim of the world" highway, and feast on the splendor of the exaggerated hills and deep forest of the region. SR78 is a winding rolling highway, a fun ride in itself, but if you want to step up the adventure a notch try SR555 between Ringgold and Portersville.

Burr Oak State Park is the heart of the region but there are other public lands as well. A portion of the Wayne National Forest borders the park at the dam and Sunday Creek Wildlife Area is also adjacent. Trimble Wildlife Area is on SR78 east of Glouster and Wolf Creek Wildlife Area is also on SR78, five miles northeast of the lodge entrance.

Information and Activities

Burr Oak State Park
Route 2, Box 286
Glouster, Ohio 45732
(614) 767-7570

Burr Oak Lodge
Route 2, Box 128
Glouster, Ohio 45732
(614) 767-2112   Reservations: (800) 282-7275

Directions: Take SR13 south off I-70, approximately 40 miles to main camping, beach and park office area. For lodge and cabins follow SR13 to SR78 at Glouster, follow 78 east and north, through Bishopville then two miles to entrance.

Information: Park office is located one mile off SR13 on CR63.

The campground check-in station located at the main campground entrance just past the office is attended Memorial Day through Labor Day. On the other side of the park, off SR78, try the Park Patrol Office/nature center located at the first stop sign on that road. The desk in the Burr Oak Lodge is open 24 hours daily.

Campground: The main campground off SR13 features 93 camp-sites, 60 with trailer access for up to 25 foot RVs, 30 tent sites, and three Rent-A-Camps. The campground is largely open pine and hardwood located high above Burr Oak Lake. Showerhouses, flush toilets, a laundromat, and play equipment are conveniently located here. Showerhouses remain open through the deer season and then reopen in mid-April. No electric hook-ups are available. Trailer sites 23-27 are located furthest on the point overlooking the lake and provide the best view. Sites 4-22 have glimpses of the water below while 43-49 are located right on the main camp road. Pets are allowed on sites 58-66.

The tent area overlooks a deep ravine and has some beautiful sites. Parking is available at all sites, but there is a short downhill carry. Site 76 is isolated at the head of the ravine, 79-83 overlook the steep hillside which drops to the beach parking, and 88-90 are set off by themselves as the camp drive approaches the entry road.

Additional but more primitive camping is available at boat docks 2 and 3, both on the east side of Burr Oak Lake. Drinking water and vault toilets are available at both areas. Dock 2 has 15 sites located just up off a small cove while Dock 3 has eight sites on the water, sites 4-8 have boat tie-ups right at the site. Both camps are located on the Burr Oak Backpack Trail, but are used primarily by fishermen who love the on-the-water location of the sites.

The main camp is particularly popular on Memorial Day and Fourth of July, be sure to arrive several days in advance of those holidays. Otherwise, you can usually find a good site there.

Nineteen family camping sites are also available through the Wayne National Forest at Burr Oak Cove located off CR63 before reaching the state park office.

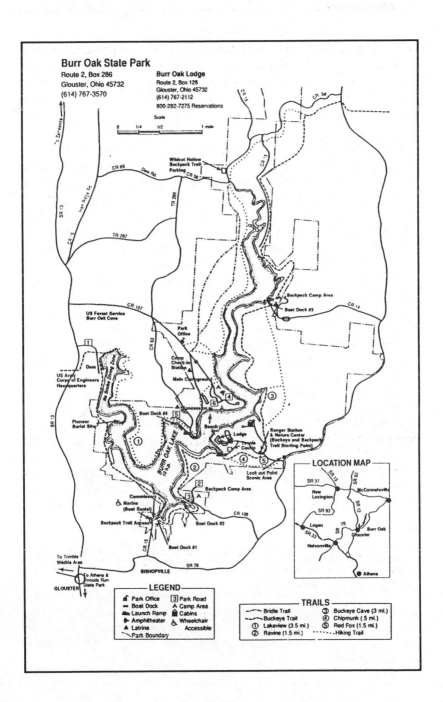

Supplies can be found at the bait store in Corning just north on SR13 or at grocery stores in Glouster and Bishopville. Basic needs such as fuel and firewood can be purchased at the nearby beach concession.

Resort Lodge: The 60-room Burr Oak Lodge is one of the older state park lodges, but its modern glass and beam construction retains its rugged charm and good looks. The lodge's cathedral-ceilinged sitting area is one of the most inviting anywhere, the kind of place you can picture yourself when the autumn leaves are ablaze or a fire is crackling in the giant stone fireplace while snow drifts outside. The view is beautiful to the woods and lake below, whether you're inside, on the balconies, or on the steep walkway down to the lake and swimming beach reserved for lodge/cabin guests. Among the many amenities here are the Cardinal Dining Room with its wonderful views and country atmosphere, the Wren Lounge, five meeting rooms, a game room, an indoor/outdoor pool, tennis courts, a gift shop and more. Nearby are a launch ramp and courtesy docks for guests. The restaurant is a popular eating place for local residents as well as travellers. Recreation facilities are open to both lodge and cabin guests. The only disappointment here is that the rooms don't feature balconies as they do in newer lodges, but the setting more than makes up for that small oversight.

Cabins: Thirty family cabins located near the lodge in a dense woodland above the lake are booked a year in advance with the period from Memorial Day through the deer season in great demand. The cabins are operated through the lodge. Cabins 1-22 are located on a Y-shaped spur reached by turning right at the park patrol office. For those concerned about access, cabins 20 and 21 are located up a series of 14 steps and #22 is across the road and up from the available parking. Cabins 23-30 are on a loop near the lodge, within walking distance of the resort amenities. Many have glimpses of the lake through summer foliage. Cabin 29 sits on the inside of the loop without the benefit of forest, its porch overlooks the road.

Boating: Burr Oak Lake was created for flood control and local water supply when the Tom Jenkins Dam was constructed in 1950 across Sunday Creek. The dam, named for the senator who was instrumental in building the project, is operated by the Corps of Engineers, and is an integral unit in flood control for the Ohio River.

In addition to the launch ramp and courtesy docks at the lodge, the park offers four launch/docks facilities conveniently located around the lake. Concrete ramps are available at dock #1 and 4, with dirt ramps at #2 and 3. Among the areas are 173 floating docks and 396 tie-ups available for rental by the season. Dock #1 at Bishopville has the largest marina along with a rental facility for canoes, johnboats, and pontoon boats. There's also a commissary with basics from fuel to soft drinks, candy, and chips. There's a boat rental at dock #4 near the beach which offers everything except pontoon boats.

The lake has a 10 hp limit so the lake has a very nice, quiet, wild feel. It's an excellent lake to explore due to its long narrow configuration and the many coves and backwaters.

Fishing:

Most fishing on Burr Oak Lake is from a boat to take full advantage of access to the many weed beds and the excellent structure in the lake. Water quality and fishing is excellent through the entire lake which averages 18-20 feet but is deepest at the dam where you'll find walleye, saugeye and big catfish in the 35 foot deep water. The lake is now stocked annually with saugeye instead of walleye, but young walleye are still being caught, an indication they're naturally reproducing. The bulk of the lake is great for crappie and saugeye, with dock #3 area furthest from the dam known for catfish. Fishing is especially good in spring when largemouth bass are caught mostly on crankbaits and crappie on live minnows. Locals claim the lake is one of the best in the state for largemouth, several eight pounders are taken every year.

Hiking/Bridle Trails:

Burr Oak is a hiker's paradise. The great unbroken woods with very few man-made intrusions, a long trail that can be easily broken into short jaunts, the lake vistas, and a connection to the Buckeye Trail which traverses the state contribute to its popularity.

Burr Oak Backpack Trail. This 29-mile trail has its official start above the dock 4 marina with designated trail access points also at the dock 1 area and at the dam where the Buckeye Trail is also accessible. The backpack trail which makes a loop around the lake through oak-hickory forest is designed to be done in two to three days. Camping is permitted only in the designated campgrounds. Most of the trail is fairly easy walking with many small but somewhat steep inclines. However, there are some very steep slopes on the east section of the trail which require caution. Although there is no fee for using the trail or primitive camps, hikers are required to self-register at the trailhead.

The shorter trails, excepting the Chipmunk Trail, are actually sections of the 29-mile Burr Oak Backpack Trail.

Chipmunk Trail (0.3 mile loop) An easy walk through an upland woods accessed either at the lodge or patrol office.

Buckeye Cave Trail (1.0 mi. one-way) A moderate trail, also beginning at the patrol office, to Buckeye Cave, which is actually an overhanging ledge.

Lakeview Trail (3.5 mi. one-way) One of the prettiest trails you'll find, especially in October. This moderate trail connects dock 4 with the dam.

Ravine Trail (1.5 mi., one-way) Follows the lakeshore from the lodge to dock 2 including a stretch on a narrow peninsula into the lake.

Red Fox Trail (1.5 mi. one-way) A longer and rougher version of the Chipmunk Trail that connects the lodge dock area with the patrol office, occasionally steep and strenuous.

Day-use Areas: Beaches, boating, trails, and picnicking are all favored here by day-users.

A 1,000 foot public beach is available near the main camp and dock 4, complete with lifeguards, a showerhouse and flush toilets. A large shaded picnic area is located above the beach and a smaller picnic area is nearby at dock 4.

Horseback riding is available on private bridle trails from a private concession near dock 2.

Nature Notes: Burr Oak's relatively unspoiled hill country setting is

rich in flora and fauna. Its hillsides, hollows and ravines provide wonderful habitat for turkey, ruffed grouse and deer, and there have been some hints that bobcat may be roaming the area. The spring showing of wildflowers includes orchids, trilliums, jack-in-the-pulpits, and violets -- a display that rivals the spectacular fall colors of the region.

Calling attention to the natural riches of the area is a full summer schedule of naturalist-led programs including weekend movies in the campground amphitheater and a number of day and evening programs in both the main camp and at the nature center.

Hunting: Hunting opportunities are excellent in the park and on adjacent and nearby wildlife areas.

Special Notes: The Paul Bunyon Show, a very unique festival full of lumberjack events, is held the first weekend of October, Friday through Sunday, at Hocking Technical College in nearby Nelsonville. No rides, no neon lights, just good food, good music, and old-fashioned competition.

Also of note are the Parade of the Hills in Nelsonville with its Old Time Fiddler's Convention the third week of August, and the Old Settlers' Reunion in nearby Jacksonville with its fiddler's contest and carnival atmosphere.

Caesar Creek State Park is one of the most modern parks in Ohio.

10 Caesar Creek State Park

Land: 7941   Water: 2830

Caesar Creek State Park is a diverse area with meadows and scattered woodland in the south and heavily wooded, steep revines in the north. Unlike many flood control projects, Caesar Creek also boasts a large land base. Naturally diverse, the oak-hickory and beech-maple woodland cloak the ridges and hillsides.

One of the newer state parks, Caesar Creek dam construction started in 1971 and was operational in 1978. The huge flood control project provides water storage and water quality control while also offering excellent fish and wildlife recreation.

Although not heavily used, Caesar Creek has some of the best facilities and amenities in the park system. Facilities include the regional U.S. Army Corps Visitor Center, Youth Hostel house, nearby Caesar Creek Gorge State Natural Preserve, Corps trail system, Pioneer Village, a full service nature center, fossil observation areas, environmental education programs and much more.

Information & Activities

Caesar Creek State Park
8570 E. Street Rt. 73
Waynesville, Ohio 45068
(513)897-3055

Directions: From I-71 depart on SR73 north to park office. About ten miles south of Xenia and Dayton.

Information: The park headquarters is open weekdays, 8 a.m. - 5 p.m. They have complete brochures of the area, camping information and so on. The campground is 11 miles from the park office.

Campground: There is no beach at the 287 site campground. The newly built camping area is lightly used and has little shade due to very young trees that have recently been planted. The campground is too new to draw big crowds. Nevertheless, the amenities are very clean and modern. Loops A and C are very open, loops E and F are pretty good sites near the water. Maybe the best sites are number #79 and #56.

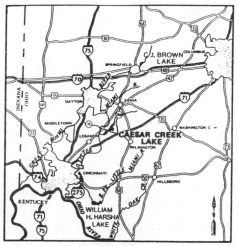

VICINITY MAP

There are four Rent-A-Camps, modern shower houses and restrooms that dot the campground. The sparsely shaded campground has lots of picnic tables, grills, and open spaces. Play equipment and bike-riding children love the openness. A small boat launch ramp is at the west end of the campground and a AYH house is on Center Road before the campground entrance.

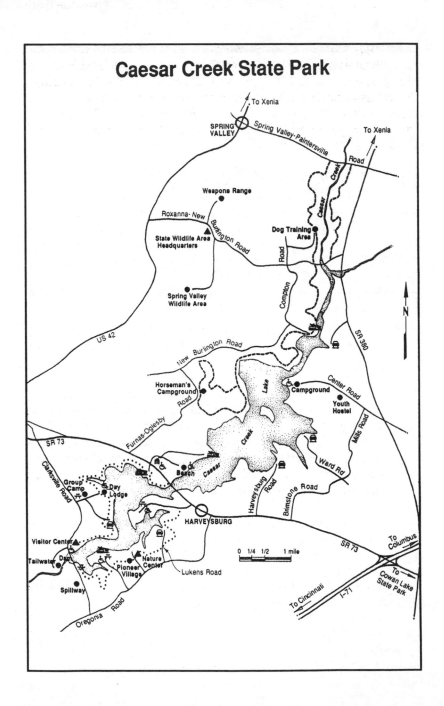

Caesar Creek State Park

To Xenia

SPRING VALLEY

Spring Valley-Paintersville

To Xenia

Caesar Creek Road

Weapons Range

Roxanna- New

Burlington Road

State Wildlife Area Headquarters

Dog Training Area

Compton Road

Spring Valley Wildlife Area

N

SR 380

US 42

New Burlington Road

Horseman's Campground

Lake

Campground

Center Road

Youth Hostel

Mills Road

Furnas-Oglesby Road

SR 73

Caesar Creek

Beach

Clarksville Road

Group Camp

Day Lodge

Harveysburg Road

Ward Rd

Brimstone Road

Visitor Center

HARVEYSBURG

0 1/4 1/2   1 mile

SR 73

To Columbus

Tailwater Dam

Nature Center

Pioneer Village

Lukens Road

To Cincinnati

I-71

To Cowan Lake State Park

Spillway

Oregonia Road

70

Boating: Caesar Creek Lake is designed for unlimited horsepower but there are no wake zones. The large body of water is active with skiiers, powerboat enthusiasts, and high-powered bass boats. Five launch ramps are well signed and located around the entire perimeter of the lake. The two larger ramps are near the park office off SR73 just south of Corwin. The remaining ramps are on the south side of the lake, with one serving the campground. Boating activity is heavy on weekends.

Fishing: The diverse habitat and large size of the lake offers anglers coves and bays, inlets and underwater structure that hold a variety of species. White bass have exploded on the scene through feeder rivers, possibily threatening walleye populations. Both walleye and saugeye are stocked annually, biologists are researching ways to increase the survival rates of planted fry. Crappie fishing is poor to fair, and despite heavy fishing pressures, largemouth and smallmouth bass are taken in good numbers. Weekdays are the most enjoyable time to fish on Caesar Creek Lake.

Hiking: Some excellent hiking trails, including the nearby Buckeye Trail, are maintained by the Army Corps Visitor Station. The Little Miami Trail is also accessed near Corwin, north of the park.

A total of 32 miles of hiking trails are in the park offering easy to rugged hiking experiences. Near the Dam's Visitor Center, 4020 North Clarksville Rd., a large, high quality regional interpretive center, is a number of short trails including a handicapped trail that begins at the dam overlook. A self-guided, half-mile long trail also starts in front of the Visitor Center. Also in the immediate area is a 3/4-mile long Bluebird Trail that begins at the small pond and travels through the field areas of Caesar Creek.

The one-mile long Gorge Trail is a hugged hike that begins at the parking lot near the Tailwater area. The Caesar Creek Gorge, which is not technically part of the state park, is a large 484 acre scenic natural area that was dedicated in 1975. Formed by glacial meltwater that cut down to the exposed Ordovician limestone and shale over 180 feet deep, the creek flows through the gorge for more than two miles to the Little Miami River.

For easier hiking try the Flat Fork Ridge to Wellman Meadows trail. Nearly three miles long, this trail is moderately difficult and leads to the ridge top overlooks, the trail also crosses a swinging bridge.

The Wellman Meadows to Furnas Shores trail is four-miles long and moderate in difficulty. To Pioneer Village crosses a waterfall, be sure to pick up a map at the Corps of Engineers Visitor Station near the dam.

For a rugged hike through forested lands, near Saddle Dam, along this northern route you'll pass through some bottomlands, and near the lakeshore. This is the Furnas to Visitor Center hike of six miles.

Day-use Areas: Picnic areas with tables and grills, scattered shelters, and shoreline fishing are well marked and located around the entire large park. A Day Lodge, complete with kitchen and indoor area is available as a rental for groups. Four very nice picnic shelters are located near the Pioneer Village and right on the shoreline just off SR73.

Aside from many shoreline fishing areas, trails, natural areas, a newly developed nature center near the Pioneer Village, off Clarksville Road on the south side of the lake, is the Corps Visitor Center. The regional center is impressive complete with hands-on displays, and Ohio River diorama, history displays, flood control diagrams, aquariums, videos, observation platform, and knowledge staff. An excellent interpretive facility open daily, call (513)897-1050.

The popular Pioneer Village, on the south side of the lake off Oregonia Road near Clarksville Road, features living history and special events conducted in an authenic village of dozens of log houses, restored shops, and tools and equipment of the 18th and 19th century (tel. 513-897-1120). Open daily, volunteers great and educate visitors on the weekends.

The beach, about 1300 feet long, and a small concession and changing rooms offer swimmers a chance to escape the heat. The beach is located near the park office, off SR73 south of Furnas-Oglesby Road.

Nature Notes: The staff of the Visitor Center often issue day-use fossil collecting permits, and does an excellent job of developing and presenting all types of environmental education programs for groups. The nature center and seasonal naturalist present regular programs. The Visitor Center also offers a wide variety of environmental education programs.

Bridle Trial: 25 miles long, Horsemans's camp area and staging area.

Fishing access is great, and so is the action at Catawba Island State Park.

11 Catawba Island State Park

Land: 18 acres Water: Lake Erie

Grouped together are three parks, Catawba Island, South Bass Island and Kelleys Island; that are referred to as the Lake Erie Islands State Parks. But Catawba Island is not only the smallest, it isn't even a true island. The 18-acre unit is located on the northwest corner of Catawba Island Peninsula, land that was once Ottawa and Wyandot Indian territory and in 1786 served as the northwest boundary of the Connecticut Western Reserve.

The peninsula is now rich with vineyards and is the center for much of Ohio's winemaking industry while the state park draws more than 650,000 visitors a year, the vast majority of anglers are eager to hook into a Lake Erie walleye.

Information & Activities

**Catawba Island State Park
4049 E. Moores Dock Road
Port Clinton, Ohio 43452
(419) 797-4530**

Directions: The park is just east of Port Clinton. Follow SR163 towards Marblehead and then turn north on SR53. Immediately swing west onto West Catawba Road and follow it 5 miles to Moores Dock Road where the park is posted. Turn left on Moores Dock and the entrance is reached in half mile.

Information: An office is located in the park and can provide information, ferry schedules and maps for all three Lake Erie island state parks. Hours are 8 a.m. to noon and 1-5 p.m. Monday through Friday.

Day-use Area: There is a lightly shaded picnic area overlooking the lake and boat ramp with tables, grills and a large shelter.

Fishing: The main attraction at Catawba Island is its boating facilities which provide quick access for anglers interested in Western Lake Erie walleye fishery. The park maintains a four-ramp boat launch with loading docks and parking for 200 vehicles and trailers. The fishery is so popular that the parking area is usually filled early on the weekends.

Many say the Western Basin of Lake Erie offers some of the finest walleye fishing in the country. May and June are the prime months as the fish are through spawning and are forming large schools. At this time anglers often turn to weight-forward spinners tipped with nightcrawlers and search for walleyes in relatively shallow areas such as the reefs offshore of Locust Point and in the Bass Islands area. Later in the summer, the walleye typically form suspended schools over deep, muddy bottoms known as "that flats", extending from West Sister to Middle Sister Islands and eastward towards Rattlesnake and Green Islands. To reach these walleye, anglers often troll with downriggers or planer boards with leadcore line that can get crankbaits down to depths of 40 feet or more.

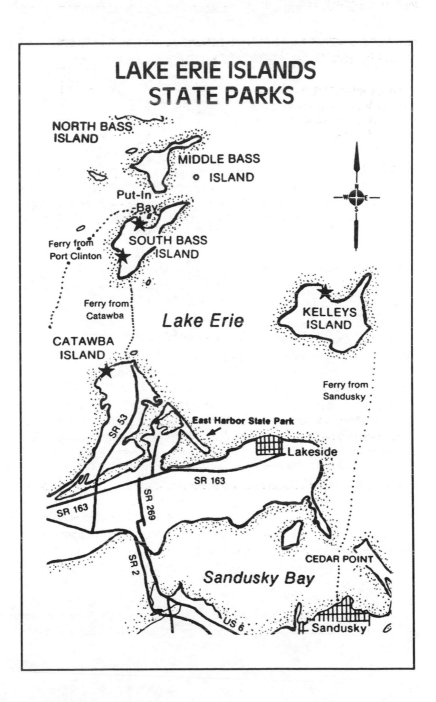

LAKE ERIE ISLANDS
STATE PARKS

NORTH BASS
ISLAND

MIDDLE BASS
ISLAND

Put-In
Bay

SOUTH BASS
ISLAND

Ferry from
Port Clinton

Ferry from
Catawba

Lake Erie

KELLEYS
ISLAND

CATAWBA
ISLAND

Ferry from
Sandusky

SR 53

East Harbor State Park

Lakeside

SR 163

SR 163

SR 269

CEDAR POINT

SR 2

Sandusky Bay

US 6

Sandusky

75

Catawaba Island State Park

The park also has a large fishing pier with lights and benches for shore anglers. The most sought after species from the pier is yellow perch which can be found close to shore April and May and then again from late August through the end of autumn. Anglers also catch smallmouth bass from the pier, catfish and even walleye in the late fall.

Winter Activities: When there is safe ice of three inches or more on Lake Erie, Catawba Island draws a large number of ice fishermen during the winter who jig for walleye and perch.

12　Cleveland Lakefront State Park

476: Acres　　Lake: Erie

The busiest unit in the Ohio State Park system and one of the top three state parks in the country is Cleveland Lakefront. The day-use park along Lake Erie in Cuyahoga County draws between eight and 10 million visitors a year, the vast majority from the surrounding metropolitan area.

Composed of six separate areas, Cleveland Lakefront is also one of the most spread out units in the state park system. It stretches 14 miles from Edgewater Park, west of downtown Cleveland, to Wildwood Park in Euclid. Several of the parcels are historical parks developed by the City of Cleveland in the 19th century. When the municipality was unable to provide the funds for park restoration in 1977 it leased four lakefront strips to the state which created Cleveland Lakefront State Park the following year. In 1982, historical Edgewater Beach was added and the newest area, Villa Angela Park, in 1992.

Presently the focal point of Cleveland Lakefront is Edgewater Park, the largest section at 131 acres. But that could change after the park opens up the Villa Angela in 1995. This 41-acre parcel will connect Euclid Beach with Wildwood Park, creating a 191-acre lakefront strip that will feature one of the longest public beaches in the Cleveland area. All park units are handicapped accessible and open from 6 a.m. to 11 p.m. year round.

Information & Activities

Cleveland Lakefront State Park
8701 Lakeshore Blvd. NE
Cleveland, Ohio 44108
(216) 881-8141

Directions: The park is six units, each with a separate entrance that lies east and west of Cleveland. Edgewater is west of the downtown area and reached by departing US2 at the Edgewater Park exit and following signs right into the park. East 55th Street Marina and Gordon Park are just east of downtown Cleveland and reached from I-90 from the East 55th Street exit or the East 72nd Street exit.

Euclid Beach, Villa Angela and Wildwood are near the town of Euclid. From Cleveland head east on I-90 and depart north at SR283 exit. The entrances are reached in 4 miles along Lakeshore Boulevard.

Information: The Cleveland Lakefront office is located in Gordon Park on Lakeshore Boulevard NE west of the village of Bratenahl. Hours are 8 a.m. to 5 p.m. Monday through Friday.

Edgewater Park: Purchased from J.B. Perkins, the son of a wealthy railroad tycoon, Edgewater became a public park in 1894 and part of the state park in 1978. The 131-acre unit is divided into Lower Edgewater and Upper Edgewater and connected by a paved bicycle path. Lower Edgewater features a large grassy picnic area and a 900-foot long and very wide beach

Cleveland Lakefront State Park

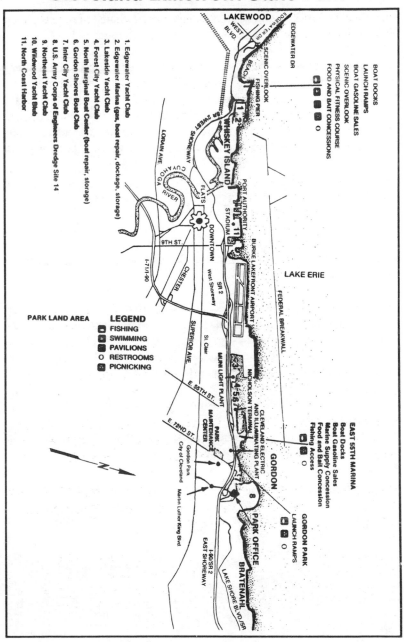

1. Edgewater Yacht Club
2. Edgewater Marina (gas, boat repair, dockage, storage)
3. Lakeside Yacht Club
4. Forest City Yacht Club
5. North Marginal Boat Center (boat repair, storage)
6. Gordon Shores Boat Club
7. Inter City Yacht Club
8. U.S. Army Corps of Engineers Dredge Site 14
9. Northeast Yacht Club
10. Wildwood Yacht Club
11. North Coast Harbor

LEGEND
- ▣ FISHING
- ▣ SWIMMING
- ▣ PAVILIONS
- O RESTROOMS
- ▣ PICNICKING

PARK LAND AREA

LAKE ERIE

with a marked off swimming area and a large bathhouse. There is also a beach concession here and a 1.6-mile long fitness trail.

Fishing facilities in Lower Edgewater include rock breakwalls, fishing platforms and a handicapped accessible, T-shaped pier that extends 90 feet into the lake. From the pier and the shoreline anglers catch perch, panfish, white bass, rock bass and sheepshead. Bait is available from a concessionaire nearby. There is also a 10-ramp boat launch separated from the rest of the park by the Edgewater Yacht Club that has boat fuel as well as loading docks and parking for vehicles and trailers.

Further to the west is Upper Edgewater, a lightly shaded picnic area that is situated on a high bluff above the lake. Facilities include tables, grills, a restored pavilion and play equipment. Near the pavilion is a statue of Conrad Mizar, father of concerts in the park and the oldest monument in Cleveland. The view of the downtown skyline and Lake Erie is excellent from the edge of the bluff here.

East 55th Street Marina: The marina was constructed from a landfill area in 1969 and serves both boaters and the anglers. The marina has 335 docks with water and electrical hook-ups for rent on a seasonal basis as well as concessionaires for gasoline, marine supplies, bait and food. During the month of August boaters can register at the park office for a slip lottery held the third Saturday in September. There is also a breakwall here that has been developed into a 1,200-feet long fishing platform for shore anglers.

Gordon Park: The 105-acre Gordon Park was first developed as a park in 1893 after William J. Gordon bequeathed his estate to the city of Cleveland. The park features six launch ramps with a parking area for vehicles and trailers, a picnic area and the park headquarters. Anglers are attracted to onshore fishing platforms while next to the park the Cleveland Electric and Illuminating Co. hot discharge offers winter catches of steelhead and salmon.

Euclid Beach: Euclid Beach Amusement Park existed from 1895 to 1969 and during its peak in the 1920s was world renown. It was added to the state park in 1982 and has a 650-foot long beach with picnic area, pavilion, a scenic observation pier and food concession. Pets are not allowed in this park.

Wildwood: Wildwood was also a resort that featured cabins and a dancehall, where in the 1920s couples could check their coats for three cents and dance all night for the same price. The dancehall is gone but the 19th century farmhouse of the land's original owner still stands in the park. Wildwood offers boat rentals, food and bait concessions, a six-ramp boat launch and a picnic area. Along with access to the summer walleye fishery in the Central Basin of Lake Erie, Wildwood has lengthy rock breakwalls to accommodate shore anglers. The park also provides access to Euclid Creek that attracts anglers in the spring for coho salmon.

One of the 27 deluxe two-bedroom cabins at Cowan Lake.

13 Cowan Lake State Park

Land: 1076 acres   Water: 700 acres

Gently rolling, the land was shaped by the regions last glacier that receded about 10,000 years ago. Once a shallow sea, shale deposits are vast, interesting, and filled with fossils of the era. Both Liberty Shale and Waynesville Shale can be seen at the spillways area near the Cowan Lake Dam. Fossil hunters comb the bedrock areas around Cowan Creek looking for signs of prehistoric lifeforms. Cowan Lake has an interesting prehistory that park naturalists interpret during regular programs each summer.

The park was dedicated in 1968. Shortly after World War II the property was purchased by the state and development soon began. By 1950 the dam was completed impounding a 700-acre body of water that continues to offer quality recreational opportunities.

The coves and bays, shallows and shorelines makes Cowan Lake one of the most scenic and user friendly parks in southwestern Ohio.

Information & Activities

Cowan Lake State Park
729 Beechwood Road
Wilmington, Ohio 45177
(513) 289-2105

Directions: Only seven miles southwest of Wilmington, and within a one hour drive from Cincinnati. From US68 (which runs north and south through Wilmington) depart at SR350 and go west to Beechwood Road and follow signs to the park office.

Information: The park headquarters is located at the end of Beechwood Road on the southeastern edge of Cowan Lake. Hours are 8 a.m. - 5 p.m., Monday - Friday. Watercraft liscense can be purchased at the office.

Campground: Cowan Lake has 237 campsites on four loops located on the north side of the lake, with the entrance off Osborn Road. Each campsite is paved to accommodate up to 35 foot RV's with 50 amp electrical service. There are two handicapped accessible sites with paved patios and grills and picnic tables designed for handicapped use.

A private beach, boat launch ramp, and docking facilities are available for camping and cabin guests. Campers with pets are permitted to use sites 211-237 only. About 50% of all campsites are shady, the nicest group of sites are #110-130. The campsites along the perimeter are the best. There are nine restrooms and two large showerhouses, dump station, and park store located halfway to the beach.

Cowan Lake is one of the finest campgrounds in the region, often filled by mid-week from Memorial Day to Labor Day.

Open year-round, Cowan Lake's 27 family cabins accept reservations up to one year in advance. They are very nice, and very popular, well worth taking the time to plan and make reservations. Cabins are heated and sleep up to six, complete with showers, kitchen, dining area, screen porch, and full bath. All cabins are furnished with blankets, linens, towels, cooking

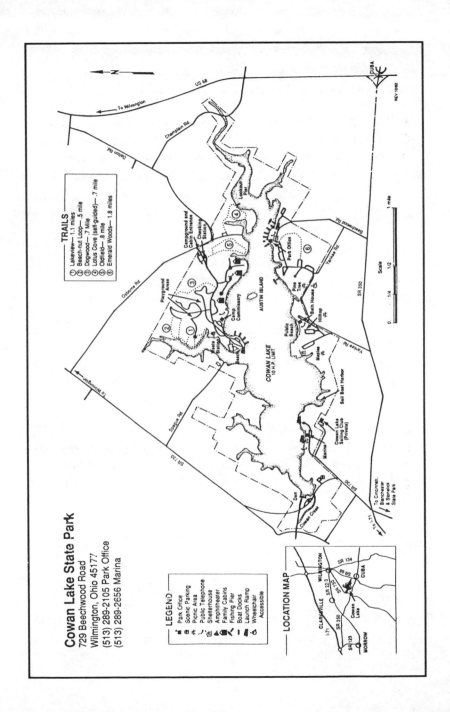

Cowan Lake State Park
729 Beechwood Road
Wilmington, Ohio 45177
(513) 289-2105 Park Office
(513) 289-2656 Marina

LEGEND

Park Office
Scenic Parking
Picnic Area
Public Telephone
Shelterhouse
Amphitheater
Family Cabins
Fishing Pier
Boat Docks
Launch Ramp
Wheelchair
Accessible

LOCATION MAP

TRAILS

① Lakeview— 1.1 miles
② Beech-nut Loop— .5 mile
③ Dogwood— .7 mile
④ Lotus Cove (self-guided)— .7 mile
⑤ Oldfield— .8 mile
⑥ Emerald Woods— 1.8 miles

84

utensils and tableware. All of the two bedroom cabins are shady, and most have a water view. Cabins 8 and 9, and 17-25 have the best water view and location. The one-mile long Oldfield Trail is nearby.

Boating: Boats are restricted to using ten horsepower or smaller motors on Cowan Lake. Boats can be rented and stored at the state park also. Open seven days, 7 a.m.- 8 p.m. in the summer, the South Shore Marina (tel. 513-289-2656) offers fuel, bait, food concession, docking, and fishing tackle, licenses and information.

The private Cowan Lake Sailing Club (tel. 513-289-7207) occupies a small cove near the boat concession. One of the two public ramps is also in this area at the end of SR730. The large ramp, located at the end of Beechwood Road near the park office has eight ramps, nearby docks, parking, picnic tables, and shoreline fishing areas.

Fishing: Cowan Lake is heavily fished, but good populations of largemouth bass, crappies, and bluegill keep anglers happy. Channel catfish and muskies are also tempting species many fisherman pursue. Bass under 15 inches in length must be released unharmed. It is possible to catch 20-30 bass daily, but most will not be keepers. Cowan Lake and Rocky Fork are both known for fair to good muskie fishing.

Cowan Lake unofficial fishing records includes: muskie - 23 lbs., 43.5 inches; largemouth bass - 6 lbs; smallmouth bass - 4 lbs., 14 inches; crappie - 2 lbs; and shovelhead catfish a whopping 50 pounds and 40 inches in length. Anglers should check with the South Shore Marina for fishing tips, updates and "secrets." A lake map showing depth/structure is available.

Hiking: Cowan Lake has 4.5 miles of hiking trails ranging in length from one-half to one mile in length. Each trail is marked with a color coded hiking symbol and direction arrows. Emerald Trail (one mile), Beechnut Trail (0.5 mile) and Lakeview Trail (0.5 mile) are considered easy hikes. Old- field (3/4-mile), Dog Wood Trail (3/4-mile) and Lotus Cove (one mile) are moderate. The Lotus Cove Trail features a lovely boardwalk that overlooks a lilly pond. The trail system offers linkages between park amenities. The Lakeview Trail, just north of the campground is delightful with gentle lake breezes.

Day-use Areas: Six picnic areas, two docks, and five playgrounds offer excellent places for family outings and day visits.

The public beach, located on the south side of the lake at the end of Yankee Road is along a small cove complete with lifeguard, parking and lots of picnicking sites. The campground beach is small, but clean and busy.

With lots of hilly open spaces, the day-use areas are often busy with shoreline anglers, walkers, and picnickers. The Hilltop Picnic area, near the public beach is large enough for group outings and family reunions. The 151 boat slips and sailing club are interesting places for a slow walk.

Nature Notes: The park presents a variety of naturalist programs during the summer season that are designed to sharpen your outdoor knowledge. Programs are usually in the evening, mid-June through Labor Day. A youth program is offered for children 7-14 years old. A special canoe excursion lead by park naturalists is available by pre-registration at the campground office. A weekly list of activities is posted.

Fossil hunting along the Cowan Creek bedrock is popular year-round with hunters often finding imprints of prehistoric plants and animals which have been preserved in sediments for over 400 million years. Please limit collecting.

The cool waters and sandy beaches of Lake Erie are popular with kids.

14   Crane Creek State Park

Land: 79 acres on Lake Erie

Crane Creek State Park takes its name from the stream that flows into the lake on the park's western boundary. There are no cranes in Crane Creek, but there are large numbers of great blue herons and great egrets, two species that people often mistakenly call cranes.

Especially in early summer, the herons and egrets can be easily seen ferrying back and forth between the nearby marshes where they catch their food, and their rookery or nesting sites on West Sister Island. West Sister Island, which can be seen on the horizon almost due north from Crane Creek, is Ohio's only federally designated wilderness area and is home to the largest heron rookery in the entire Great Lakes basin. The island is strictly off limits to human visitors.

Though herons are common, it was ducks that saved the Lake Erie marshes that remain. These marshes became famous for offering some of the finest duck hunting anywhere and their reputation attracted such luminaries as President Eisenhower who talked fondly of his duck hunting experiences in the marshes of Lake Erie's western basin. Their value as hunting preserves led to their protection under the ownership of private hunting clubs. What is now Crane Creek and the adjoining Magee Marsh were purchased in 1951 from private clubs.

Driving into Crane Creek is an experience in itself. Between the park office and the beach is Magee Marsh, 1,821 acres of wetlands operated by the Ohio Division of Wildlife through the Crane Creek Wildlife Experiment Station. Seen from the park entrance drive it is obvious that the marsh is divided by dikes into units. Water levels in each unit are carefully managed to provide a variety of habitats to benefit a wide range of species. Research done at the station has pioneered new techniques in wetland management and, for example, played a large role in the amazing comeback of the Canada goose.

Magee Marsh and the similar philosophy of management practiced next door at the 6,000 acre Ottawa National Wildlife Refuge make this area one of the most productive wetlands in the Midwest. Bald eagles nest in the area and are often seen along public trails in both of these marshes. These marshes are important stopovers for migrating birds and waterfowl on both the Mississippi and Atlantic Flyways. Twenty-nine species of ducks, four of geese, and tundra swans are present, some species numbering into the thousands. In the winter months, when driving this stretch be observant for short-eared owls, prairie natives that are often common from December through March.

But in summer it is the park's beach that capture visitor's attention. It's a three-quarter mile long sandy beach, three hundred feet wide, and dotted with shady oases of cottonwoods. It's a great place to catch some rays, play a little beach volleyball, get some swimming in, and relax while reading a book. Not a bad way to spend a day.

Information and Activities

Crane Creek State Park
13531 W. State Route 2
Oak Harbor, Ohio 43449
(419) 898-2495

Crane Creek Wildlife Experiment Station
Ohio Division of Wildlife
13229 West State Route 2
Oak Harbor, Ohio 43449-9988
(419) 898-0960

Directions: Located midway between Toledo and Port Clinton, 17 miles east of I-280 on SR2. I-280 is at Gate 5 of the Ohio Turnpike.

Information: The park office is located just inside the park entrance off SR2, Monday through Friday, 6 a.m. to dusk through the summer season. There is no staff on duty so if the office is vacant the duty ranger will be on patrol at the beach.

For wildlife information and the offices for the Crane Creek Wildlife Experiment Station go to the Sportsmen's Migratory Bird Center which is located on the park road past the park office. The Center is open May 1 to September 1, weekdays 8 a.m. to 5 p.m., Saturdays, 8 a.m. to 5 p.m. and Sundays from noon until 6 p.m. It is open the rest of the year Monday through Friday 8 a.m. to 5 p.m. and Sundays from noon to 5 p.m.

Campground: The nearest state park campground facilities are at Maumee Bay State Park, 15 miles to the west on SR2 and five miles north on North Curtice Road.

Boating: Offshore powerboating, sailboating, and fishing are popular in Lake Erie. The nearest public launch is a modern ramp at Metzger Marsh State Wildlife Area, seven miles west off SR2 at Bono. Jet skis, catamarans, and boats up to fourteen feet can be hand-carried across the beach and put in at the east end of the park's beach. All craft are prohibited from venturing inside the buoyed swimming area.

There is a small ramp at Turtle Creek Fishing Access which is east of the Magee Marsh with a separate access of SR2. Small boats only should use this ramp due to the shallow water in Turtle Creek which has access to Lake Erie.

Fishing: The western basin of Lake Erie offers some of the finest walleye and yellow perch fishing anywhere, with excellent opportunities to fish for white bass and smallmouth bass as well. Even though perch is the most sought after sport fish in Lake Erie, walleye is king in the western basin. So fine is the walleye fishery that the western basin has been dubbed *"the walleye capital of the world."*

Lake Erie walleye start hitting in April and continue through the summer. The Ohio Division of Wildlife recommends pursuing walleye by drifting and casting with weight-forward spinners baited with worms, and trolling with deep diving lures. Perch can be caught year-round from the shoreline, piers and boats. The nearby pier at Metzger Marsh is an extremely popular fishing access, especially August through October. Try using emerald shiner minnows for bait on spreaders. Maps, information, bait and lures are available at numerous bait stores along SR2

Fishing in Lake Erie is permitted from the stone breakwall on the east end of the beach and along the lakeshore dike in Magee Marsh. Crappie and smallmouth bass are sought in spring and perch from late July through October.

Crane Creek is a staging area for ice fishing on Lake Erie. A ramp is provided at the parking area for unloading and loading snowmobiles which can be driven on a designated trail directly onto the lake.

Walking Trails

Magee Marsh Bird Trail (1.0 mi., one-way) Though short, this boardwalk trail south of the beach parking area is considered one of the best birding hot spots in the Midwest. Though commonly thought to be part of the state park, the trail is actually in the Magee Marsh Wildlife Area managed by the

Ohio Division of Wildlife. All walkers are asked to stay on the boardwalk and not stray off the trail.

The trail, which is wheelchair accessible, traverses a swamp beach ridge and skirts several ponds and marsh meadows. The habitat is extremely important as a gathering area for migrating birds preparing to cross Lake Erie in spring, and as landing areas for the southern migration in fall. It is possible to observe more than 100 species of birds in a single day. Timing a visit to see the migration depends upon which species are being sought. Mother's Day weekend is generally an excellent time to plan to walk the bird trail.

Walkers are also welcome along the Magee Marsh Wildlife Area beach, a mile-long continuation of the Crane Creek beach where swimming and picnicking are not permitted but hiking and birding are. That beach is open from dawn to dusk.

Day-use Areas: Although surrounded by thousands of acres of wetlands managed for wildlife by the Ohio Division of Wildlife and the United States Fish and Wildlife Service, the reason for Crane Creek's existence is not wildlife, but the beach. Tens of thousands of swimmers find their way to Crane Creek each year making it one of the hot -- uh, cool spots on Lake Erie each season.

Because the park is centered on the beach hours are from sunrise to sunset only. Lifeguard stations are staffed throughout the summer season. Unless the waves are large, the beach is safe for children. The lake bottom at Crane Creek slopes very gradually into deep water. Floatation devices, pets, and alcohol are all prohibited.

The zebra mussel, a small exotic species that has invaded Lake Erie by hitching a ride on cargo ships from Europe, is readily apparent on the beaches. Visitors in recent years have found the shell remains strewn all along the beach, a situation which was corrected in 1992 with the use of a beach sanitizer which will remove them and other unwanted debris.

Picnic tables and grills are scattered all along the beach back in the stands of cottonwoods. A picnic area and shelter are located on the east end of the

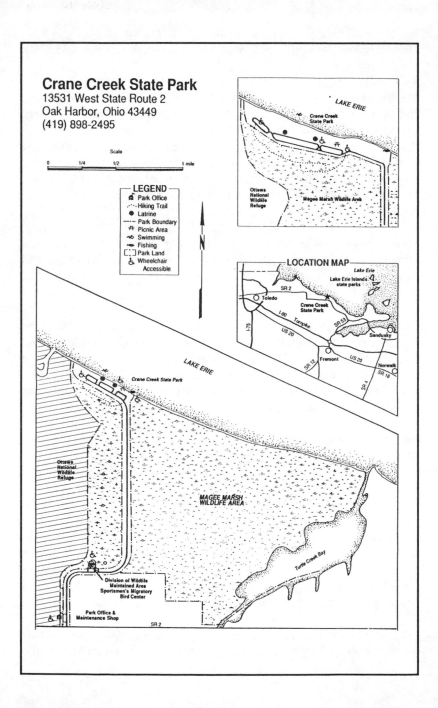

Crane Creek State Park
13531 West State Route 2
Oak Harbor, Ohio 43449
(419) 898-2495

Scale

0   1/4   1/2   1 mile

LEGEND
- 🏠 Park Office
- ⋯ Hiking Trail
- ● Latrine
- — Park Boundary
- ⚲ Picnic Area
- ⤳ Swimming
- ⬳ Fishing
- ⌐⌐ Park Land
- ♿ Wheelchair
       Accessible

N

LAKE ERIE

Crane Creek State Park

Ottawa
National
Wildlife
Refuge

MAGEE MARSH
WILDLIFE AREA

Turtle Creek Bay

Division of Wildlife
Maintained Area
Sportsmen's Migratory
Bird Center

Park Office &
Maintenance Shop

SR 2

LAKE ERIE

Crane Creek
State Park

Ottawa
National
Wildlife
Refuge

Magee Marsh Wildlife Area

LOCATION MAP

Lake Erie

Lake Erie Islands
state parks

SR 2

Toledo

Crane Creek
State Park

I-80 Turnpike

I-75

US 20

SR 53

Sandusky

SR 12

Fremont

US 20

Norwalk

SR 18

SR 4

beach behind a lakeshore dike.

A special picnic pad to accommodate wheelchairs is also provided at the east end of the beach. It is equipped with two picnic tables, a grill and nearby accessible vault-type restroom. Concrete sidewalks are also provided so wheelchairs can have access to the beach.

Nature Notes: Although the park does not offer nature programs, the Sportsmen's Migratory Bird Center has displays of interest to those wanting to know more about waterfowl and other marshland wildlife. The Center can accommodate wheelchairs. A wildlife observation tower provides an excellent vantage point for observing marsh life, migrating hawks, etc. Public programs and workshops are held in the center, call for information.

On the last Sunday of each September the Lake Erie Wildfowlers sponsor a waterfowler's festival which features bird dog trials, skeet shooting, decoy carving and competition, numerous displays of outdoor gear in a trading post, and displays by local wildlife woodcarvers and artists.

Hunting: Goose and duck hunting is available in season, by lottery in Magee Marsh. Contact Crane Creek Wildlife Experiment Station for information.

Uncrowded and relaxing, by the pool, or near the lake.

15   Deer Creek State Park

Land: 3,107 acres   Water: 1,277 acres

Rural agriculture dominates the scene approaching Deer Creek State Park. Flat to slightly rolling land -- the trademarks of the till plains of glaciated Ohio -- covered with crops of corn, beans and wheat that seem to stretch to the horizon. Thin green lines of second-growth trees meander through the fields filling the lower creases in the land.

Long before the farmer, nearly 4,000 years ago, nomads roamed here. They were hunters and gatherers who lived off the animals and plants of an area until they were exhausted, then moved on. From artifacts it is known that for some time they inhabited a camp on Tick Ridge where today's modern cabins stand. Those people knew this area as a mixed oak forest that occasionally opened up into grass-dominated wet prairie communities.

The farmer cleared the land to bring agriculture to the good soils of this area. The impact of farming in what is now Deer Creek is obvious. The park is dominated by old field plant communities, that is, old farm fields that nature is gradually reclaiming, first as meadows, then with woody plants. Taller, older trees exist only as isolated individuals or in small woodlots.

Be sure to check these large trees as you walk or drive through the park. They are favorite roosts for the hawks, owls and turkey vultures who search the surrounding fields for prey. On one recent five-minute drive to the lodge on a late July evening I observed a great horned owl and red-tailed hawk in the woodlot near the campground, and five vultures gathering at dusk in an old snag. The drive was topped off with five deer along the roadside and more woodchucks than I can recall. July also proved an excellent time to observe meadow wildflowers, including butterfly weed, black-eyed susans and the old field invaders like Queen Anne's lace and goldenrod.

Deer Creek is a destination park, the kind of park people come from long distances to enjoy its wide variety of facilities. In this park, though, all roads lead to the lake. The 93 foot high, nearly 4,000 foot long earthen dam that created the lake was completed in 1968. It's worth the visit just to walk out on the dam.

Information and Activities

Deer Creek State Park
20635 Waterloo Rd.
Mt. Sterling, Ohio 43143

Park office: (614)869-3124
Campground: (614)869-3508
Golf Course: (614)869-3088
Lake Conditions:(614)869-3728

Deer Creek Resort and Conference Center
P.O. Box 127
Mt. Sterling, Ohio 43143
(614) 869-2020 Reservations: (800)282-7275

Directions: From Columbus take I-71 to SR56, follow SR56 southeast to Mt. Sterling, then south SR207, east on Dawson-Yankeetown Rd.

From Cincinnati take I-71 to SR38. Follow SR38 southeast to Bloomingburg to SR62-3, northeast on 62-3 to Yankeetown Pike.

Information: The park office is located on the main park entrance road off Dawson-Yankeetown Rd.

Campground: An excellent campground located off the main park entrance drive has 232 sites, all equipped with electric hook-ups. Sites can handle RVs up to 35 feet in length. Four washhouses with showers and flush toilets are provided along with two playgrounds and six vault toilets. The washhouse near sites 217-224 is handicapped accessible. There's a very nice selection of sites with something for every taste, about one-third are heavily wooded, one-third open with shade, and one-third open. The general observation here is older campers prefer the open sites, while the younger congregate in the wooded sites. Some to check include sites 1-48, 90-93, 112-114 and 134-139 in the heavy woods; 49-79 and 94-111 are higher open sites that slope back to foliage; 115-133 are mostly open sites as are virtually all sites in the pet area, 140-224.

Four VIPs are strategically located throughout the campground helping with minor problems, keeping the camp area clean, answering questions and handling the campground's five Rent-A-Camps.

The campground is busy from mid-May through mid-August so summer campers should plan to arrive as much ahead of the weekend as possible. Also available are three horsemen's camps near the main camp equipped with vault toilets. Water is available at the nearby campground. Also a similarly equipped group camp that can accommodate up to 60 people in one or more groups.

Camping supplies are available at the Deer Creek Marina and in stores along SR207.

Lodge: Deer Creek Lodge is the second largest, second newest resort and conference center (built 1982) in the state parks. It's an interesting blend

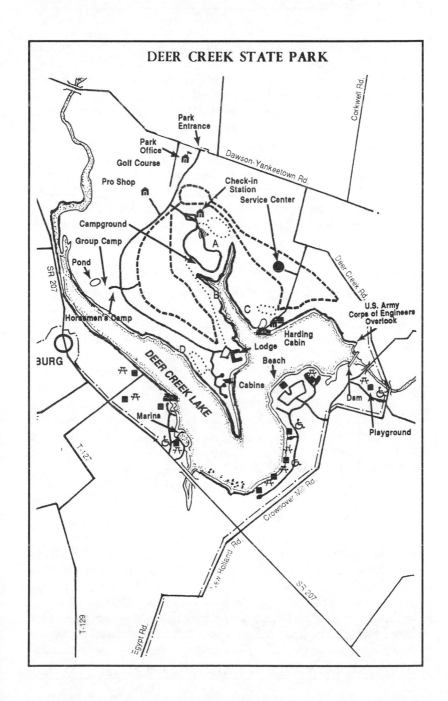

DEER CREEK STATE PARK

Corkwell Rd.

Park Entrance

Park Office

Golf Course

Dawson-Yankeetown Rd.

Pro Shop

Check-in Station

Service Center

Campground

A

Group Camp

Pond

B

C

SR 207

Deer Creek Rd.

U.S. Army Corps of Engineers Overlook

Horsemen's Camp

D

Lodge

Harding Cabin

BURG

DEER CREEK LAKE

Beach

Cabins

Dam

Marina

Playground

T-127

Crownover Mill Rd.

T-129

Egypt Rd.

New Holland Rd.

SR 207

of modern architecture and thinking -- heating is supplemented by solar collectors -- and traditional stone and timber construction that blends nicely with its setting on the shore of Deer Creek Lake. It's an inviting atmosphere from the spacious sitting area equipped, of course, with a huge fireplace, to the TV lounge to the restaurant overlooking the lake. Also indoors are a game room, indoor pool and whirlpool, sauna, exercise room, and gift shop. Cradled by the main section of the lodge is a very attractive outdoor recreation area that includes an outdoor pool equipped with dozens of lounge chairs, shuffleboard, children's play area, putting green and basketball. Nearby are tennis and volleyball courts, and courtesy docks. Accommodations are roomy -- ask for loft rooms if you need more space -- well equipped and include a balcony. Your choice whether you want to overlook the action around the pool or quieter park and lake scenes.

Cabins: Twenty-five modern family cabins are spread on three loops near the Lodge on Tick Ridge. Tick Ridge extends into the lake and some cabins have nice lake views when foliage is off. Try cabins 3, 4, 10-12, 17, 18, or 23. Like most state park cabins, they are available only by the week from Memorial Day to Labor Day.

For something really different try the Harding Cabin, a rustic one and one-half story cabin built in 1918 overlooking the valley that is now the lake. It was built by William Daugherty, attorney general in the Harding administration, and President Warren G. Harding used the cabin as sort of a poor man's Camp David. It's in a great isolated setting away from other facilities and with more amenities than the family cabins. Not surprisingly, it's so popular in spite of the understandably higher rental rates a lottery system is used for reservations. The cabin sleeps up to nine in three bedrooms upstairs and on a sleeper sofa. Included is a screened porch, private dock, and dishwasher.

Golf Course: It lacks the topography of the golf course at Salt Fork or the uniqueness of the links-style course at Maumee Bay, but the ten ponds and 52 sand traps on the well-manicured 350 acre, 6,574 yard Deer Creek golf course present a challenge nevertheless. The par 72 course opened in 1983 so the landscaping has matured somewhat and promises to get even better with age. Tee times are recommended on weekdays, required on weekends and holidays until 3 p.m. Lodge and cabin guests can call in advance for times. Rental clubs and carts available as is a snack bar.

Boating: Deer Creek Lake is an unlimited horsepower lake popular for water skiing, pleasure boating and fishing. Two improved launch ramps are available, the most popular is at the Deer Creek marina off SR207 and another near the Harding Cabin which is reached via Yankeetown Rd. and Twp 197. A wide variety of boats ranging from pedalboats to 25 hp runabouts to pontoon ski boats are also available for rent by the hour, day or week at the marina.

Remember Deer Creek is a flood control lake and it begins to take on a very different look in mid-September when the Corps of Engineers drops the water levels by 15 feet. Most boats are off the lake by the end of the month.

Fishing: Deer Creek Lake is a good fishing lake. Water depth averages only 12 to 15 feet but is as much as 60 feet at the dam. The tailwater pond below the dam is always popular with anglers, but especially in late winter and early spring for saugeye. Deer Creek, upstream from Yankeetown Rd. is productive for white bass in mid to late spring, and for smallmouth and rock bass. In low water, old SR207 below Pancoastburg is good for fishing smallmouth bass with crankbaits. Crappie fishing has been good from spring well into summer with most caught on yellow and hot pink jigs with brightly colored plastic worms. Crappie fishing has been best along the brushy shorelines in the creek channel above the lake. Channel catfish are caught mostly in the upper lake and in the stream channel. Bluegill fishing is very good along the deeper shorelines in the lower half of the lake, especially in June and July. No matter the species, when using artificial bait the brighter colors such as chartreuse and yellow generally work best in the dark waters of Deer Creek Lake.

Hiking/Bridle Trails: Deer Creek has several trails of interest for visitors:

Rolling Hills Trail (3.2 mi. one-way). A new walking trail that starts from near site 224 in the campground and connects to the lodge. The longest walking trail in the park, it's a very pleasant rolling trail with some lake views and a few large oaks along the way.

Hawkview Meadow Trail (1.0 mi. loop). This self-guiding trail begins just past the campground check-in station and is perhaps the best to experience the natural assets of the area. Along the trail's route there are twenty information stops to point out the various features. The trail passes through an oak woodlot that opens into a gently rolling meadow bordered by Clark Run Creek. A two-acre portion of the meadow is managed by the park crew to keep woody plants from taking over. Watch for beaver cuttings and a beaver dam.

Ridge Trail (1.0 mi. loop). Begins from the lodge/cabin area through some smaller second-growth woods, providing some open lake views. About one-third mile in on the right trail fork is a wildlife observation blind where walkers can watch park wildlife attracted to the area by salt blocks, feeders, habitat boxes, etc. The trail crosses some gullies but is not strenuous.

Marsh Walk Trail (1.0 mi. loop). Begins from the Harding Cabin area along the lake, crossing two creeks, through a mixed hardwood forest.

Snowmobile and Bridle Trail (14 mi. in two loops). The staging area is at the trail's midpoint off the parking area at the campground check-in station. To the west is the lodge/cabin area loop, east goes toward the dam and Harding Cabin. Bikes and APVs are prohibited on the trail. Walkers are welcome to use the trail but the surface conditions are often marginal due to horse traffic. Snowfall in this area is generally insufficient to provide enough base for snowmobiles.

Day-use Areas: Deer Creek features an excellent 1,600 foot sand beach with lifeguards on the 300' mid-section in season. A beach concession with snack bar is available.

Picnicking is on scattered sites throughout the park, at the marina, the beach, off small parking areas along the shore up the road from the beach, and below the dam. Most are nicely wooded sites.

Nature Notes: Throughout the summer, there's a variety of naturalist-led walks and programs from night hikes, to the naturalist aide sessions, to inside looks at the Deer Creek Dam. Most programs focus on the nature center and nearby amphitheater located near the campground check-in station. The nature center is open briefly before evening programs.

Hunting: Hunting, in season, is open in some park areas after Labor

Day, others after October 15. Check at the park office for details. Deer, pheasant, rabbit, and some squirrel hunting is popular here and in the surrounding 3,710 acre Deer Creek Wildlife Area. A shotgun, pistol, and archery range located just off SR207 on Yankeetown Road is available year-round.

Fishing at Deer Creek Lake is considered very good.

Delaware is only minutes north of Columbus.

16   Delaware State Park
Land: 1815 acres   Water: 1330 acres

Setting on 350 million year old bedrock, which was quarried and used to build the nearby state capital, Delaware State Park has ancient roots---and modern use that began in 1951. Once clothed in majestic hardwoods, then heavily tilled for lush crops, old farm fields around the park area are returning to mature woodlands that support native wildlife and recreation.

The land east of the lake is preserved as Delaware Wildlife Area where a series of more than 50 farm ponds further enhances the habitat's diversity. Delaware State Park and adjoining properties are excellent places for birding and wildlife observation.

The entire park is replanted with trees, including many southern species like bald cypress and sweetgum.

Information & Activities

Delaware State Park
5202 US 23 North
Delaware,Ohio 43015
(614)369-2761
(614)363-1617

Directions: About 20 miles north of downtown Columbus on US-23. Five miles north of Deleware, entrance is on US-23.

Information: The park office is located just off US-23, and is open 8 a.m. - 5 p.m.

Campground: Delaware State Park's campground is located along the west side of the lake on Camp Road, the camp office is open daily during warm weather months. Four sections compose the campground and section A (sites 1-50) has no elecricity. There are 214 campsites at Delaware. Loop B is open year-round. Pet sites are available in each section.

Although there are no waterside sites, there are many sites near the water that boaters and fisherman often request because they can tie their small boats at the adjacent shoreline and walk back and forth.

Loop A has many shady sites that are private and non-electric, the best are sites numbered 9, 10, 12, 13, 31.

Loop B, which offers nearby boat mooring, has good sites that include 62, 66, 74, and 75.

Loop C also has boat tie-ups located at the end of a tiny gravel roadway that leads to the lake. The best sites for those that want access to their boat are numbers 114-119. Sites C 148 and 155 are also popular.

Loop D is the most shady of the sections, but about 1.5 mile from the camp office. Boat tie-up sites are 195-200. Weekend campground activities include wagon rides, seasonal naturalist programs, and movies.

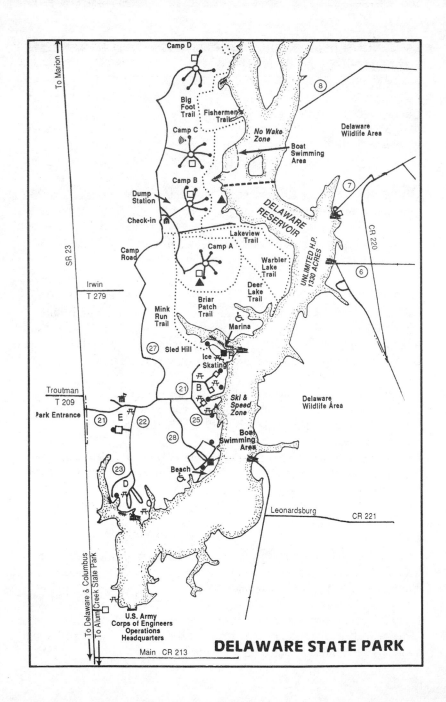

DELAWARE STATE PARK

Boating: The boat tie-up area near the campground are a convenient way to enjoy the lake and the campground. The northern third of the lake is reserved for no wake boating activites, but the southern portion is open to all horsepower boats pulling skiers or pleasure cruising. The state park has two boat launching ramps, one at the southeastern end that has two ramps, additional parking, restrooms, and the nearby Hickory Grove Picnic Area; and the marina launch that has two ramps, docks, concession, live bait, and boat rental.

Fishing: Bass fishing in Delaware Reservior is very good to excellent. Not a lot of structure, there is some structure worth probing along the campground shoreline. Many tournament bass anglers seek out the smallest underwater structure in hopes it holds fish. Crappie anglers find success along shoreline using live bait---minnows, worms, crickets, redworms.

Saugeye were introduced in 1989, long after walleye planting of the 1960's failed. The saugeye is best found in the tailwaters below the lake as well as in the reservior. Jig a minnow right on the bottom when fishing for saugeye. Catfish, best caught on stink baits, are abundant.

Occasionally, there are good spring runs of white bass in the lake's tributaries, the Olentangy River and Whetstone Creek. Bluegill are only "good" at Delaware.

Hiking: Seven miles of hiking trails are concentrated in the campground area. Easy walking, the mostly wooded trails connect amenities. The Mink Run Trail connects to the Marina, Briarpatch Trail is located in camping Loop A, and Big Foot Trail connnects to Briarwood to the shoreline to Loop D. Shoreline walking meanders along coves and tiny bays of the lake.

Day-use Areas: Almost an arboretum, the pleasant tree plantings make the picnic areas popular, especially during the colorful fall season. A sled hill, ice skating areas, swimming beach east of the park office, and group picnic sites are busy on weekends---quiet on many weekdays. The neighboring wildlife area, located on the east shore of the lake, offers fishing ponds, rifle range, three small boat launches, hunting, and shoreline fishing.

Shady cabins are popular at Dillon State Park.

17   *Dillon State Park*

Land: 6,030 acres   Water: 1,660 acres

Dillon State Park is a good park, good in all aspects. It's conveniently located and there's good fishing, boating, wildlife, wildflowers, scenery, campground, and cabins. Everything there is good -- not spectacular, but good. It's the kind of place to go when you just plain want to get away and feel good. Thousands of people do just that every year.

Dillon sits on the edge of the Appalachian Plateau in an area that seems to be on the verge of deciding whether it wants to be hilly or flat. It's neither, yet it's both. The hills here are well-rounded and the valleys broad and gentle.

Here and there in and around Dillon are outcroppings of 300 million year old Black Hand Sandstone. Just twelve miles away in a sandstone outcrop was the mysterious petroglyph of a large, soot-blackened human hand that some archaeologists theorized was a guide directing Indians to Flint Ridge, an important source of their flint to be used in tools and weapons. Others believe it marked the boundary of neutral territory where no Indian was to raise a hand against another. The petroglyph, unfortunately, was destroyed in 1828 during construction of the Ohio and Erie Canal. The sandstone deposits now bear the Black Hand name as does the Blackhand Gorge State Nature Preserve which is just up the Licking River from the park. Just a few miles west of the park, off US-40, Flint Ridge is preserved as a state memorial. Several important Hopewell Indian sites are also nearby.

So Dillon has also became popular as a good place to stay because it's so close to so many interesting things. Dillon's been a good place to go since the park was officially opened in August, 1968.

Information and Activities

Dillon State Park
P.O. Box 126
Nashport, Ohio 43830
(614) 453-4377 Office
(614) 453-0442 Camp Office

Directions: Take I-70 to Zanesville area then west of SR146. Approaching the park are turn-offs to Dillon Dam and to a scenic overlook of the dam and reservoir before reaching the main entrance at Clay Littick Dr.

Information: The park office is located at the intersection of Littick and Dillon Hills Drives.

Campground: Not surprisingly, Dillon has a good campground that is nearly full throughout the summer season. Arrive as early as Wednesday before a holiday weekend to insure a site. The camp is typically 80-90 percent full on other weekends, 40 percent during the week. There are 192 sites here, all except the 12 walk-in tent sites have electric hook-ups. The sites are concentrated in three loops off Dillon Hills Drive on the lower part of the reservoir. Loop A is largest with 104 sites, pets are allowed in Loop

C. Most sites are open but the planted shade trees are maturing. Sites 40-48 have a little overlook to the reservoir. Flush toilets and showers are available as is a camp commissary with basic groceries, supplies and a laundromat. The commissary is open mid-May to Labor Day.

Cabins: Twenty-nine family cabins along two separate roads through a nicely wooded area with very limited views of the lake. Cabins 1-6 are along a winding lane crowded with second growth woods, edged in dogwood in spring. Cabins 21 and up have porches facing the lake, but still only limited views. Parking is generally not directly at individual cabins.

Boating: Dillon Reservoir was constructed by the Corps of Engineers in 1961 for flood control. Water depth averages 18 feet and is deepest at the dam, 30 feet.

Although the reservoir allows unlimited horsepower and is popular for waterskiing, many take a canoe or rowboat and simply explore the many quiet coves and inlets at a leisurely pace.

Two improved boat launches are available near the dam, one at the marina at the end of Dillon Hills Dr. and the Big Run boat ramp off SR146. The Nashport ramp on Road 7 on the shallow "no wake" section of the upper lake and the Pleasant Knob launch are both more suitable as small boat drop-offs. The cove up Poverty Run and up the cove by the main launches are no wake zones, as is much of the lake above the beach area.

The marina has 70 docks for seasonal rental and 28 courtesy docks for cabin/camping guests. Pontoons, runabouts, rowboats and pedalboats are among the boats available for rent. Dillon Water Sports, (614)453-7964, offers a variety of canoe trips on the Licking River, including several through the narrows of Blackhand Gorge. The trips, which are safe for beginners, include shuttle service.

Fishing: Fishing in Dillon Reservoir is, of course, good for panfish, largemouth bass, some walleye, and, especially, channel catfish. Fishing is excellent in the tailwaters below the dam.

Hiking/Bridle Trails: Five trails totalling seven miles are featured.

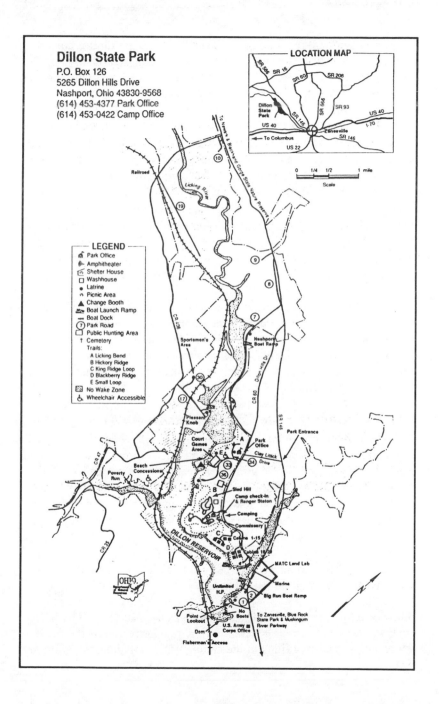

Dillon State Park

P.O. Box 126
5265 Dillon Hills Drive
Nashport, Ohio 43830-9568
(614) 453-4377 Park Office
(614) 453-0422 Camp Office

LOCATION MAP

LEGEND
- Park Office
- Amphitheater
- Shelter House
- Washhouse
- Latrine
- Picnic Area
- Change Booth
- Boat Launch Ramp
- Boat Dock
- ⑦ Park Road
- Public Hunting Area
- † Cemetery
- Trails:
  - A Licking Bend
  - B Hickory Ridge
  - C King Ridge Loop
  - D Blackberry Ridge
  - E Small Loop
- No Wake Zone
- Wheelchair Accessible

Licking Bend Trail (6.0 mi., one-way). Skirts the lakeshore connecting the beach area with the marina. Four other trails are mostly offshoots of the Licking Bend Trail: the Ruffed Grouse Nature Trail (.75 mi.) which begins at picnic area "C" and is an excellent introduction to the park's varied habitats; the Blackberry Ridge Trail (1.0 mi.), Kingridge Loop (1.1 mi.), and Hickory Ridge Trail (1.5 mi.) all begin from the camping and cabin areas. Hickory Ridge and Kingridge trails are strenuous in parts. A one-half mile easy access paved trail loop begins at the beach area, courses along the shore and through a very nice second-growth woods.

Day-use Areas:

The beach area is a focal point in summer where behind the nearly one-third mile of sand beach is a selection of tennis, basketball, volleyball, and one-wall handball courts along with a large open picnic shelter. Separate swim areas are designated for boaters and the public. Until funding increases no lifeguards will be available.

Dillon is also a very popular picnic park with four primary picnic areas. Picnic areas "A" and "C" are both small, pleasantly wooded areas above the lake but with no real views. "A" has an open play area. Tables, grills, and flush toilets are provided. Lookout Point at the scenic overlook features a modern lookng shelter that can accommodate up to 100 people. A short paved path with benches is a pleasant stroll.

Nature Notes:

The park and adjacent Dillon Reservoir Wildlife Area offer good opportunities for wildflower and wildlife viewing. Birding is very good here, especially in the fall. Sightings of immature eagles and osprey (spring and fall) aren't unusual. A healthy heron population inhabits the area. Great blue herons and green herons are very common, with lesser numbers of great egrets and black-crowned night herons. The easiest and best way to look for these and other marsh species is to take the very plesanat drive up the lakeshore on Park Road 7.

Wild turkey were introduced here in the late 1980s and are thriving. It's not unusual to see them in the cabin area.

Dillon offers nature programs in summer, but shares a naturalist with Blue Rock so check for current information. A regular feature is the fireside stories and showing of films in the campground amphitheater on Friday evening.

Hunting: Shotguns and longbows are permitted in season except in the
main public section of the park. Deer, grouse, pheasant and squirrel are
among the sought after species. Six duck blinds are available along the lake
but because the hunting is better elsewhere there's little pressure for their
use.

Dillon Sportsmen's Center maintained by the state and operated by the
League of Ohio Sportsmen on CR408 in the Pleasant Knob area offers a
public rifle, pistol, trap and skeet range open Wednesdays and weekends.
Call the center at (614)454-6784.

Dillon State Park has 192 campsites that are often full on the weekends.

18   East Fork State Park

Land: 10,580 acres   Water: 2,160

East central Clermont County's rolling hills and meandering river valleys provide a rich scenic backdrop for spacious East Fork State Park. You'll never guess that you are less than a half-hour east of busy Cincinnati, nestled among lush farmlands, and the many small tributaries to the East Fork of the Little Miami River.

The 2,160 acre reservoir was created in 1978 and surrounding park lands were developed to comprise one of southeastern Ohio's largest recreational areas. Long before modern man's development the Little Miami basin was the home of many generations of man, dating back more than 3000 years ago. Mound building people, the Hopewell and Adena Indians once occupied the area. A burial mound, located near Elklick Road on the south end of the park, is thought to be a Hopewell Indian creation.

This region of the state was settled in the early 19th century attracting settlers from the east who built grist mills, sawmills, stagecoach depots, and even two gold mines that operated duirng the 1860's. The Old Bethel Church, built in 1867 on a site first occupied in 1807, is near the park office.

Information & Activities

East Fork State Park
P.O. Box 119
Bethel, Ohio 45106
(513)734-4323
(513)724-6521 Campground

Directions: 20 miles east of Cincinnati, take SR125, the park entrance and main office is near the intersection of SR125 and SR222. Take Elklick Road north to office. The Campground office is on the north side of East Fork Lake, off Old Route 32, between Batavia and Williamsburg.

Campground: It's easy to see why the East Fork campground is usually full every weekend, and why campers travel long distances to enjoy the 12 camping loops and 416 sites that border the Buckeye Trail. A 200 yard-long beach is located at the southeast end of the popular campground. A lifeguard is on duty during the busy weekends.

With 57 miles of bridle trails that wind through fields, cool wooded acres, and over hills, horsemen also have their very own camping loop. Loop A is near the bridlepath trailhead and reserved for horsemen only. Horsemen by the hundreds trailer in their equines and RV's to enjoy leisurely trail riding and camping. For other pets, Loop B, sites 18-41 and part of Loop C, is reserved for your use.

Campground loops L and J are heavily wooded and private, while loops G, H, and I are only lightly shaded and flat. Loop F is quite sparse of shade and used less by campers than the other loops. The group camping area is particularly clean and well-clipped, located on a hill with light shade and freshly painted restrooms.

East Fork also has Rent-A-Camps for those campers without their own equipment. Showers, flush toilets, camp beach and boat launch are exclusively used by campers and their guests. There is more than one camper host in the park, offering friendly assistance, fishing tips, and local color.

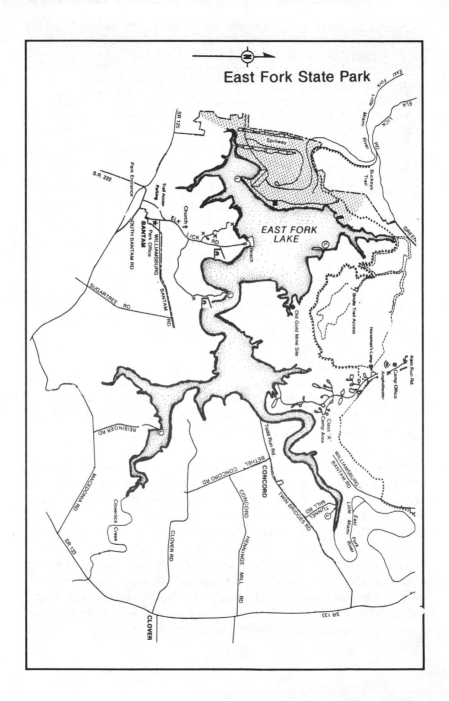

East Fork State Park

114

Horsemen have camping sites at East Fork State Park.

Day-use Facilities: Because, in part, of its proximity to Cincinnati the park offers quailty day use amenities including two picnic shelters, dozens of picnic table locations, over 55 miles of hiking trails, 57 miles of bridle paths, a 1200 foot swimming beach, small beach concession, five boat ramps, plus cross-country skiing, sledding, and ice fishing during the winter. Seasonal naturalist programs are offered.

Fishing: Bass anglers work the snags and structure that is located throughout the lake. Spring angling along the shoreline shallows is especially exciting when active fish attack topwater and other crankbaits. Jigging live bait for panfish works year-round Five quality ramps await, with the biggest east of the park office.

Hiking: Aside from 55 miles of state park hiking trails, which roam forest and valley, the popular Buckeye Trail meanders along the northern portion of East Fork. The 1200 mile-long Buckeye Trail encircles the state in a continuous loop traversing 40 of Ohio's 88 counties. The trail passes along some of East Fork's best areas, including heavily forested stretches, a small bottomland area, and near the equine pathways. Trails are well maintained and wander along the shoreline in many places, crossing public roads in places, there are resting spots, (and at least one small country store where I found and bought a cold soda)and plenty of birding and wildlife observation opportunities. Sectional maps are available from the *Buckeye Trail Association, Box 254, Worthington, Ohio 43085.*

East Harbor's campground is well known for its unique natural features.

19 East Harbor State Park

Land: 981 acres Water: 848 acres

East Harbor has always been a gathering place along Lake Erie. It was the home of the Wyandot Indians and a major junction where an early lakeshore route joined the famed Scioto Trail from the south. The area around East Harbor was influenced by the French more than any other part of Ohio because of its importance along a fur trading route that stretched into Canada's Northwest Territory. And East Harbor saw more than its share of battles and skirmishes as the French clashed with the English for access of the rich Ohio Valley and later the English with the Americans over the control of Lake Erie in the War of 1812.

Today, the peninsula is the great gathering place of campers. With 570 sites, East Harbor State Park boasts the largest campground in the Ohio State Park System. What is even more impressive is the facility is filled every weekend throughout the summer, a testimony to the growing popularity of Lake Erie among anglers, swimmers and others who simply enjoy a sunset over that endless expanse of blue.

Information & Activities

**East Harbor State Park
1169 N. Buck Road
Lakeside-Marblehead, Ohio 43440
(419) 734-4424**

Directions: East Harbor is 81 miles west of Cleveland and 45 miles east of Toledo. From Port Clinton head west on SR163 for 7 miles and then turn north on SR269. The park entrance is reached in less than a mile.

Information: A park office is located near the entrance and is open 8 a.m. to noon and 1-5 p.m. Monday through Friday. For information on site availability during the summer call the campground office at (419)734-5857.

Campground: With 570 sites spread out on more than two dozen loops, East Harbor has the largest campground of any Ohio State Park. The vast majority of them are in a grassy, open settings and all the sites are close together with little privacy from your neighbor. But Camp Area A (sites 1-91) offers more shade than the rest of the campground and sites 108-112 are right along the East Harbor shore. Facilities include paved spurs, picnic tables, dump station, rest rooms, three shower and laundry houses, commissary with a snack bar, lots of play equipment and a ball field in the middle of the campground.

Campers at East Harbor also have their own boat launch with two ramps, a loading dock, parking for 50 vehicles and trails and a fish cleaning station. The campground does lacks one amenity important to some people: electrical hook-ups.

Despite its size, the East Harbor campground fills up every weekend from Memorial Day to Labor Day by Friday evening and often by Thursday. Sites are usually available Sunday through Wednesday. There is also a youth camp area with a capacity of 50 and a group camp for up to 100 people. Interested parties should contact the park two weeks prior to their arrival.

Day-use Areas: The park has several picnic areas, two featuring shelters near the park office and campground. There are also picnic tables along the old beach on Lake Erie. The swimming area was closed after being severely damaged in a 1972 storm. The park then built a new beach to the north with bathhouses and a small commissary. The sandy beach is so popular that shuttle buses are used during the summer to ferry swimmers from the original beach parking lot.

Hiking: There are 7 miles of foot paths in East Harbor along a network of five trails that explore the unique natural features of the peninsula, including beach plant communities, marshland and the area's abundant bird life. In the beach parking lot are trailheads for the Wetlands and South Beach Trails, a 3-mile series of loops that wind along the marshes of the East Harbor. Another interesting walk is the Middle Harbor Trail which departs from near a picnic area. The mile-long loop winds along the marshy southwest corner of the Middle Harbor, a designated game sanctuary, to an observation blind used by birders to view herons, Canada geese, many species of waterfowls and shorebirds.

Boating: Separated from the rest of the park is the East Harbor State Park Marina with a two-ramp boat launch, fuel, marina supplies and rental slips. The facility is located on West Harbor, north of the main park entrance on Buck Road. The marina has a 123 slips for rent which are handed out annually through a lottery. Contact the park office to register.

Fishing: The Western Basin of Lake Erie is renown for its walleye fishery as well as perch and smallmouth bass (see South Bass Island State Park). Anglers also find East and West Harbors productive for bass, bluegill and crappie while shore anglers often park and fish the narrow strip that separates East Harbor from Middle Harbor.

Nature Notes: Though not nearly as impressive as those on Kelleys Island, East Harbor has a set of glacial grooves located just beyond the group camping areas. The park also has a amphitheater and small nature center where a naturalist is on duty throughout the summer. Programs range from slide shows and evening campfires to guided hikes and birding outings.

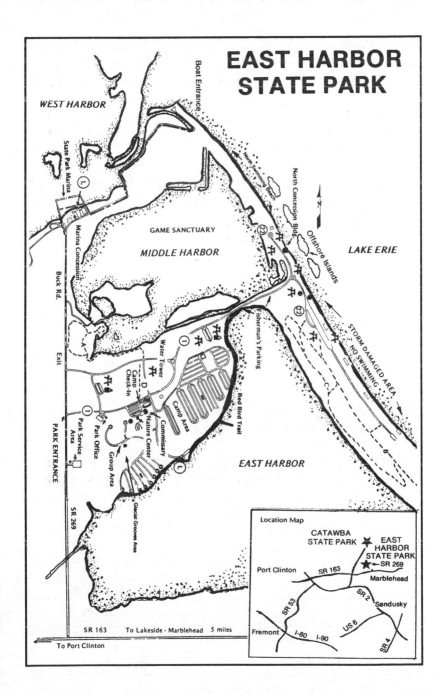

EAST HARBOR STATE PARK

WEST HARBOR

State Park Marina

Boat Entrance

Marina Concession

Buck Rd.

Exit

PARK ENTRANCE

SR 269

GAME SANCTUARY

MIDDLE HARBOR

North Swimming Beach

North Concession Bldg.

Offshore Islands

LAKE ERIE

Water Tower

Camp Check-In

Nature Center

Fisherman's Parking

Red Bird Trail

Commissary

Camp Area

Park Service Area

Park Office

Group Area

Glacial Grooves Area

EAST HARBOR

STORM DAMAGED AREA
NO SWIMMING

Location Map

CATAWBA STATE PARK

EAST HARBOR STATE PARK

SR 269

Port Clinton

SR 163

Marblehead

SR 53

SR 2

Sandusky

Fremont

I-80

I-90

US 6

SR 4

SR 163   To Lakeside - Marblehead   5 miles

To Port Clinton

Facilities for the Handicapped: At East Harbor facilities for the physically-impaired include changing booths and ramps to the beach as well as handicapped accessible sites and showerhouses in the campground.

Winter Activities: The most popular winter activity by far is ice fishing on Lake Erie. During a normal winter, anglers begin gathering on the ice from early January to the first week or two in February and many use snowmobiles to transport their shanties and equipment out on the frozen surface. The Western Basin is renowned among Ohio ice fishermen for perch as well as walleyes which often reach the 10-pound range. Jigging lures such as Swedish Pimples and Rapalas tipped with the minnows are by far the most popular technique for walleye.

Rental boats at Findley State Park means family fun.

20   *Findley State Park*

Land: 838 acres Water: 93 acres

Labeled a "quiet retreat" by the Ohio Division of Parks, Findley State Park is a quick escape outdoors for more than 500,000 visitors annually, many from the Cleveland-Akron metropolis. Located in the southwest corner of Lorain County, the 838-acre park has an excellent campground and offers opportunities to fish, swim, hike or study nature. The 200-acre Wellington State Wildlife Area adjoins it.

Its most charming aspect, however, is its mature woodlands that are stunning in the fall. Much of the park is heavily wooded with a variety of broadleaf trees, including white and red oak, black cherry, beech and shagbark hickory, as well as pines.

The area was actually a tract of farmland until purchased in 1936-37 by Guy B. Findley, a Lorain County judge. He donated the land to the state to be maintained as a state forest after the Civilian Conservation Corps planted a variety of pines and hardwoods in the area. Findley Forest was transferred to the newly created Division of Parks in 1950 and six years later an earthen dam was completed across Wellington Creek, creating the center piece of the park, 93-acre Findley Lake.

Information & Activities

Findley State Park
25381 SR58
Wellington, Ohio 44090
(216)647-4490

Directions: From US-20, just south of Oberlin, head south on SR58 and pass through Wellington. The park entrance is off of SR58, two miles south of Wellington.

Information: The park office is part of the campground check-in station and open 8 a.m. to noon and 1-5 p.m.

Campground: Findley has a large but well spread-out campground with 275 sites on six loops at the southeast corner of the lake. Coverage ranges from open sites and others in a forest of hardwoods to sites 210-272 that are situated in a scenic stand of mixed white and red pine. None of the sites are directly on the water or even in the view of the lake but most are only a short walk from the shoreline.

Facilities include fire rings and tables but not electric hookups for recreational vehicles. The campground also has vault toilets, two showerhouses with laundry facilities, a Pet Camping Area, three Rent-A-Camps, dump station, play equipment and campstore. The facility fills up holidays and is usually 80 percent full on most summer weekends.

Day-use Areas: The park maintains a beach and marina concession at the north end of the lake. The beach is mostly an open grassy area with little sand. Along with a marked swimming area there is a beach concession store that rents out canoes and rowboats.

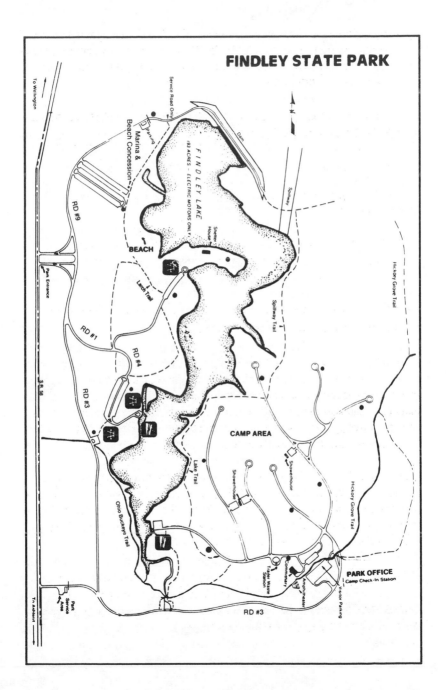

FINDLEY STATE PARK

Findley's picnic ground is a very scenic area with part of it in a stand of oaks near the boat launch. The other half extends out on a long point into the lake where it's a short walk from the parking lot to the tables, grills and a shelter. A third area called Picnic Pines has tables, grills and a posted trailhead where the Buckeye Trail enters the park.

Fishing:
Findley is a 93-acre lake with a depth of 25 feet near the dam at the north end and a ban on all motors except electric. Findley is considered a heavily fished body of water and subsequently has been selected for protected slot length limit due to the abundance of slow growing bass. All bass between 12 and 15 inches in length must be returned.

The lake is stocked periodically with largemouth bass, bluegill and crappie. Spring and fall, report anglers, is by far the most productive time to fish Findley. The park maintains a boat launch with a cement ramp, loading dock and large parking lot at the picnic area while in the campground is a smaller launch on the south end of the lake.

Hiking:
There is a 10-mile network of trails within the park, including almost 1.3 miles of the statewide Buckeye Trail that can be picked up at trailheads in Picnic Pines and near the park office where it merges with Hickory Grove Trail. Hickory Grove extends a mile from the park office to the spillway at the north end of the lake where Spillway Trail will lead you back to the campground.

Also posted near the office is the Black River Audubon Society's self-guided nature trail with 15 interpretive posts that correspond to a brochure available at the park. This is a 1.2-mile trek that returns along a portion of Hickory Grove Trail. Finally, you can link together portions of the Buckeye Trail, Hickory Grove and Larch Trail to form a 3-mile circuit around the lake from Picnic Pines.

Facilities for the Handicapped:
Flush toilet restrooms and showerhouses are barrier free in the campground.

Nature Notes:
Findley employs a naturalist during the summer. At the north end of the park is the Duke's Skipper Butterfly Sanctuary, a small preserve for the extremely rare insect. Butterfly collecting is prohibited.

21 Forked Run State Park

Land: 815 acres   Water: 102 acres

Head darn near as far southeast as you can and still be in Ohio, look for the Long Bottom near the Big Bend and there, just a big old cornfield away from the Ohio River, is Forked Run.

That's "For-ked Run," buddy, say it in two syllables or, like it as not, they'll have you pegged as being from Columbus or, worse, even further north.

It seems West Virginians have discovered Forked Run but for the most part it has been kept a secret from Ohioans. Pity, because it's a great place to discover. George Washington did when he surveyed the Ohio River way back when and dubbed these rich wide-open bottomlands the "long bottom."

The river was different then, flowing uninhibited by modern locks and dams. It was a wild powerful river through a wild unforgiving land where Indians hid on the high ground to ambush pioneer flatboats. Not far away Morgan's Raider's crossed the Ohio River in a desperate last Confederate gasp in the Civil War.

Approaching the river on SR681, a roller coaster of a road over knobby overgrazed hillsides, you can feel the river approaching. And then, suddenly, the hills are behind you and you're in the long bottoms where today tomatoes and sweet corn grow succulent in the rich soil (be sure to pick some up at a local produce stand).

At the park you can enjoy the long bottom and, in the evening, climb to the campground in the hills where, perhaps, Indians once waited for invading pioneers.

Information and Activities

Forked Run State Park
P.O. Box 127
Reedsville, Ohio 45772
(614) 378-6206

Directions: From Columbus take US-33 south to US-50 east at Athens until it intersects with SR7, then SR7 south to SR681 at Tuppers Plains. Follow SR681 until it deadends at Reedsville, then SR124 west three miles to Forked Run. Also, I-77 to Marietta, take SR7 south out of Marietta to SR124.

Information: The park and campground office is located on the main park entrance drive at the campground entrance.

Campground: 198 sites including four Rent-A-Camps that are booked all summer. No electric hook-ups available but two showerhouses are located on the five loops. The showerhouse on loop 1 is open through the end of December, while the one on loop 2 closes in September. Pets are allowed on loop 2 sites 59-82 and loop 3 sites 98-127. All the camp areas are up high, loop 2 is the highest with nice views of the river when the foliage is down. Sites on loop 3 are level, nicely spaced and shaded -- good for tents and fold-out campers. Loop 5 is the oldest loop and has very good grassed tent sites in a semi-open setting. Families like this loop because the beach is right down the hill and children can easily travel back and forth. The sites aren't as level on Loop 4 so that area is last to fill. Forked Run can accommodate RVs up to 35 foot in length, bigger vehicles should check out the pull-through sites between 31 and 39 on loop 1. It's a pleasant family campground with everything in walking distance.

You should always be able to find a spot here. The campground has never filled, although it comes close on the summer holidays. Steer clear of the skunks in the area.

Boating: A recent land purchase gave Forked Run frontage on the Ohio River which the park has used to build a new boat launch, the only launch for miles on this section of the river above the Racine locks. The free 24-hour lighted launch is a two lane concrete ramp with courtesy docks. Parking and portable restrooms also provided.

Two boat ramps are provided on Forked Run Lake, a paved ramp at the dam and concession area and a small gravel ramp on T272 serving the upper lake. The concession is open May 1 though September and offers canoes, rowboats and pedalboats as well as refreshments, bait and ice.

Horsepower is unlimited, of course, on the Ohio River but there is a 10hp limit on Forked Run Lake.

Fishing: Forked Run's new Ohio River launch now opens up all the opportunities on the Ohio River in addition to some pretty good fishing on the park lake. On Forked Run Lake, Largemouth bass in the five to six pound range are fairly common as are some lunker flathead catfish generally caught on bank lines and jigs near the dam. The lake is stocked annually with a mix of rainbow, golden and brown trout, and with saugeye in 1990. Crappie fishing is popular in spring and the kids love going for bluegill.

Hiking Trails: There are only two trails here but be sure to check them both. The Lakeview Trail (2.5 mi. loop) begins at the beach, drops to the lakeshore and follows through a wild woodland setting with some excellent

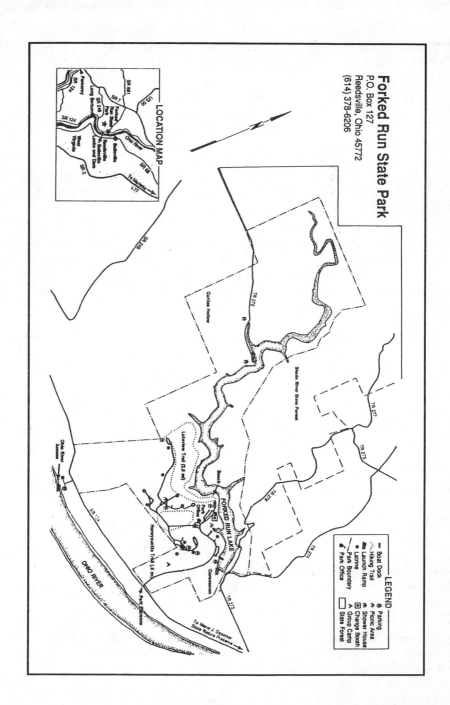

Forked Run State Park
P.O. Box 127
Reedsville, Ohio 45772
(614) 378-6206

LOCATION MAP

LEGEND
- Boat Dock
- Hiking Trail
- Launch Ramp
- Latrine
- Park Boundary
- Park Office
- Parking
- Picnic Area
- Shower House
- Charge Booth
- Group Camp
- State Forest

lake views, nice rock formations, some large oaks, and within view of some cascades in some of the coves. The trail is moderately difficult on the backside of the loop as it climbs a steep incline to campground loop 3. The Honeysuckle Trail is a self-guiding one-half mile loop that begins from the park office. Numbered markers along the trail correspond to a guide available from the office. Check for pawpaws and persimmons along both trails.

Day-use Areas: The well-shaded 500 foot sand beach below the campground is the only public beach around and, therefore, always busy in the heat of summer.

Two picnic shelters are provided, one in the lower picnic area before the beach parking, another in the open flatlands along the entrance drive. Picnicking is also available above the beach and in a small very nicely wooded area along the road to the campground which has the additional appeal of easy access to a lake cove where the fishing is good.

Nature Notes: In addition to the commonly found but nevertheless exciting to see species of animals and wildflowers, there's an aura of wildness here that's difficult to describe. The area is sparsely populated and West Virginia right across the river is even less so and more wild. In recent years a bald eagle has been commonly seen on the upper lake. In 1990 a black bear cub wandered across the river and created considerable excitement in the campground. Somehow Forked Run seems like the kind of place that sort of thing should happen.

Hunting: No hunting is allowed in the park but the campground is popular as a staging area for hunters pursuing whitetail deer and wild turkey in the adjacent Shade River State Forest.

22   *Geneva State Park*
Land: 698 acres   Water: Lake Erie

Lake Erie, the shallowest of all the Great Lakes, can also be the meanest at times. In a matter of hours, the lake can change from a calm setting and flat water to a raging boil where 12-foot waves are being driven ashore by 70-mile-per-hour winds. Such severe storms and treacherous conditions have taken their toll as more than 100 shipwrecks dot the bottom of Lake Erie.

Nowhere is this lake's fury seen better than at Geneva State Park. Located along the Great Lake's Central Basin, the Ashtabula County park was acquired from 1964 through 1972. Geneva is so exposed to Lake Erie's turbulent nature that in the mid-1970s the park was part of a federal study on erosion prevention. A variety of protective devices and vegetation were installed and some of them worked. Others obviously didn't. In 1991, the park staff was forced to close the beach in the Chestnut Grove Picnic Area because Erie's constant pounding uncovered objects submerged in the surf.

Today you can swim at another beach, camp or rent a cabin. You can enjoy the extensive picnic grounds or search the shoreline for rare plants. But many like to stroll along the east breakwall of the marina where on a calm evening they can enjoy a stunning sunset over Lake Erie. And on a stormy night, they can witness the mad rush of anglers and sailors returning to the docks of a safe harbor along this suddenly wicked lake.

Information & Activities

Geneva State Park
P.O. Box 429, Padanarum Road
Geneva, Ohio 44041
(216) 466-8400

Directions: Geneva State Park is an hour east of Cleveland. From I-90, depart at exit 218 and head north on SR534. Pass through the town of Geneva and in 7 miles you come to the posted entrance of the park on Lake Road West. Continued north on SR534 to reach Chestnut Grove Picnic Area.

Information: The park office is at the corner of Lake Road West and Padanarum Road and is passed on the way to the marina. Hours are 8 a.m. to noon and 1-5 p.m. The campground check-in station is also staffed daily during the summer.

Campground: Geneva has 91 campsites with electric outlets spread along two loops. The first loop (sites 1-37) is an open field with no shade and sites that are mowed regularly during the summer. The second loop is in a wooded area. Campers are still close together here with little privacy but most sites are well shaded. Geneva has three Rent-A-Camps and a Pet Camping Area. Other facilities include paved spurs, fire rings and tables while between the loops is play equipment and a washhouse with showers, modern restrooms and laundry facilities. A dump station is located near the campground entrance.

Traditionally Geneva fills Memorial Day weekend and then every weekend from July through Labor Day. Sites are usually available Sunday through mid-week.

Cabins: Situated in an open grassy area along Lake Erie near the campground are 12 cabins, each with three bedrooms, a full kitchen and a screened-in porch overlooking the water. There's no beach in front of the units but a path leads through the woods to the park's Breakwater

Swimming Beach nearby. In June, July and August the cabins are rented for a week at a time, from Saturday to Saturday with a maximum stay of 14 days. Rentals by the week in May and September are from Friday to Friday but weekend applications are also accepted.

As with many other parks, the cabins are extremely popular. Geneva holds a public cabin lottery the second Monday in February from applications that are sent in between Jan. 1 and Jan. 31. Interested parties can either pick up an application at the office or send a self-addressed, stamped envelope requesting one. All applications mailed in must be sent in by certified mail and post marked by Jan. 31.

Boating: Built by the U.S. Army Corps of Engineers and the ODNR in 1989, the Geneva State Park Marina is not only one of the newest facilities on Lake Erie, it's one of the most impressive. The marina has seasonal slips for 383 boats as well as a number of transient slips. The boat ramp has six lanes and four loading docks that are illuminated for night launches and day parking for 200 vehicles and trailers. Other facilities include restrooms with showers, fish cleaning station, full service boat repair, fuel service and a ship's store that stocks ice, food, camp supplies, bait and tackle and fishing licenses.

Even if you're not a boater, the marina is an interesting place. A grassy bank with a few benches and tables overlooks Lake Erie while many people stroll along the breakwaters. The extensive docks inside harbors a flotilla of sailboats, cruisers and other vessels and at night the charter captains can be seen cleaning a day's catch of walleye.

Fishing: The Central Basin of Lake Erie, though not as well known as the Port Clinton area, is still walleye country. Anglers troll crankbaits on planer boards and sometimes head more than 12 miles out into the lake in an attempt to locate schools of walleye. The lake also supports a steelhead fishery as well as yellow perch and smallmouth bass. A number of charter captains work out of the marina and charter information is available at the ship's store. Shore anglers will gather along the east breakwall of the marina while some sections of the harbor inside is open to anglers.

Day-use Areas: Passed on the way to the campground is Breakwater Swimming Beach. The facility features a large gravel parking area and

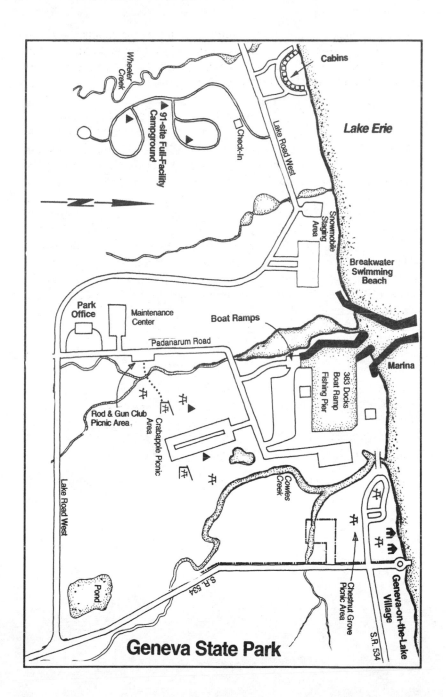

Geneva State Park

133

lifeguard services along with a sandy strip that's 30 yards wide, 300 feet long and bordered by the surprisingly clear Lake Erie.

Near the marina is Crabapple Picnic Area with tables, grills and two shelters that are pleasantly tucked away into the surrounding woods. A short trail leads from one shelter across a creek to the Rod and Gun Club Picnic Area on Padanarum Road. A bridge also links Chestnut Grove Picnic Area to the marina. This is a popular day-use area, located in an old woodlot of white oak and chestnuts on a bluff that gives way to a scenic view of the Great Lake. You'll find changing booths here but no longer a safe beach.

Nature Notes: Geneva offers the naturalist and others an opportunity to study an undeveloped shoreline of Lake Erie. The middle and western beaches of the state park contain plants that are much more common on the Atlantic seacoast than Ohio. These include sea rocket, seaside spurge, beach pea and silverweed. You'll also find interesting marsh areas at the mouth of Cowles Creek where the foot bridge to Chestnut Grove crosses Wheeler Creek near the cabins.

Grand Lake is the largest man-made lake in Ohio.

23   Grand Lake St. Marys State Park

Land: 500 acres   Water: 13,500 acres

Grand Lake, the largest man-made lake in Ohio, the largest in the world until Hoover Dam, was built by1,700 German laborers for 30-cents a day and a jigger of cheap whiskey during the mid-1800s.

A feeder lake to the Miami and Erie Canal, this 300 mile link between the Ohio River and Lake Erie, used many lakes to supply water. Grand Lake helped keep the five foot depth of the canal level. Feeder lakes, 32 miles of feeder streams, 106 locks, 19 aqueducts, and three reservoirs were built completely by hand.

Boating on the vast lake is a pleasure for thousands annually, the huge lake supports significant recreation activities and was one of first ten state parks in 1949.

Information & Activities

Grand Lake St. Mary's State Park
834 Edgewater Drive
St. Mary's, Ohio 45885
(419)394-2774

Directions: About ten miles west of Wapakoneta, from US-33, which crosses the Buckeye Trail near SR66, go straight on US -33 to 29 then go south at state park exit to the park entrance on Edgewater Drive.

Information: For historic information contact the Lake Improvement Association, P.O. Box 118, Montezuma, Ohio 45866. Grand Lake has one of the most interesting histories of all the lakes and state parks in Ohio. The park headquarters is located at the northeast shore of the lake just off SR 364. It is open most days 8 a.m. - 5 p.m.

Campground: Complete with 206 campsites on six loops, five latrines, two bathhouses, laundry, and play area, Grand Lake's campground has asphalt pads, and many shady sites. The middle section of the six loop camping area is quite open, with sparse shade. The group camping area can accommodate 125 people by reservation only, is located on a knoll near the small nature center.

A small beach for campers is located at the end of lane #1. The most requested campsites according to staff are 70, 71, 96, 97, 98. Site numbers 7-12, 169, 181, 194, 201 and 33-37 are on the water. Lanes 1-3 do not have elecricity.

Boating: The lake has 52 miles of shoreline, a lighthouse, and is over nine miles long, and is extra popular with all type of boaters. Dishpan shaped, the deepest parts of the lake are only 7-8 feet. St. Mary's has an active sailing club, private marinas abound, and dozens of sailboats line the docks and bob-about offshore. Boats may have unlimited horsepower, and comply with the 300 feet from shore no wake and ski zones. Watch for stumps and buoys that identify channels and zones. Boats can be rented from the St. Mary's Marina, at the east end of the lake, call (419)394-2198.

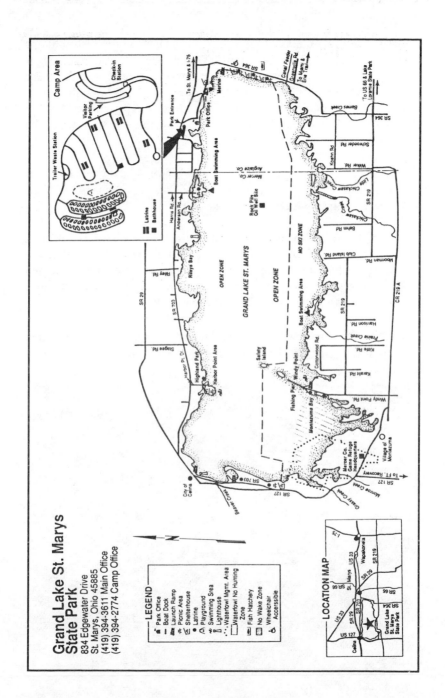

Grand Lake St. Marys State Park

834 Edgewater Drive
St. Marys, Ohio 45885
(419) 394-3611 Main Office
(419) 394-2774 Camp Office

LEGEND

- Park Office
- Boat Dock
- Launch Ramp
- Picnic Area
- Shelterhouse
- Latrine
- Playground
- Swimming Area
- Lighthouse
- Waterfowl Mgmt. Area
- Waterfowl No Hunting Zone
- Fish Hatchery
- No Wake Zone
- Wheelchair Accessible

LOCATION MAP

Fishing: With excellent shoreline fish habitat structure, many stumps create a wealth of angling opportunity. Grand Lake is considered the best large crappie lake in the state. Smart crappie anglers probe the feeder streams and channels after ice-out, and during April and May, the action heats up again in mid-autumn. Locals use a lead head jig with bobber and tip it with a waxworm or minnow. Fish slow and move to find fish or the structure that they are holding in.

Ten times more crappies are caught than largemouth bass in the lake, but bass anglers are enjoying increasing catches. There are plenty of excellent shoreline fishing spots around the large lake.

Interestingly a state fish hatchery is operated at the east end of the lake that is open to the public. Dozens of rearing ponds are controlled and used to raise saugeye, bass, and northern pike. The rearing ponds are maintained to help the state assure adequate fish populations. Staff is sometimes available to answer questions about the rearing facility.

Hiking: There are no designated hiking trails but there is considerable walking area along the shoreline, at Windy Point, and near the campgrounds.

Ohio's only inland lighthouse.

138

Day-use Areas: The lake is surrounded with full-time homes, stores, small communities, farmlands, rural developments, party stores, villages, and resort-like housing developments. There's lots to do in the area. At the park there are many picnic areas with tables and grills and some shelters. The Windy Point area, located on the southeast shore off SR219, offers a boat launch, shoreline fishing and lakeside picnic areas.

A small lighthouse in Celina, constructed in 1986 by the Celina Rotary club, is a fun side trip. Swimming beaches at Windy Point and the two swimming beaches near the park headquarters offer sandy beaches, lifeguards, and picnic tables. A restaurant and busy marina are also in the area. Two boating beaches and two outlying beaches are also operated by the park.

Nature Notes: As already mentioned the fish hatchery is a wonderful opportunity to see and learn about fisheries management. The Mercer Wildfowl Area, located at the southwest end of the lake, is sportsman funded to provide nesting and resting places for migratory waterfowl. The sparkling white barn and in the nearby pond is a terrific place to observe geese and maybe bluebirds that routinuely nest in the area.

There's a lot of waterside camping at Grand Lake St. Marys State Park.

139

24   *Great Seal State Park*

Land: 1,864 acres

Anyone who has driven across the flatlands of glaciated Ohio, through Columbus and south toward Chillicothe has marveled at the seemingly sudden appearance of a cluster of high knobs looming on the horizon rising out of acres and acres of rich farmland.

William Creighton, an early Ohio Secretary of State, marveled at them as well. He is credited with designing the Great Seal of the State of Ohio, a design inspired by these very knobs, now preserved, in part, by Great Seal State Park.

Although Great Seal State Park was appropriately dedicated in 1980 to the wilderness spirit of early Ohio, there is equal fascination here with learning about those who walked this land before us. The area was once the home of the Shawnee Indian Nation. Bordering the park is the Sugarloaf

Mountain Amphitheater where the spectacular summer outdoor drama, "Tecumseh!," is staged. The drama depicts the life of the legendary Shawnee warrior who nearly succeeded in uniting the Indian nations.

In 1800 Chillicothe became the first capital of the Northwest Territories and, just a few years later, the first capital of Ohio.

Before the Shawnee and the European settlers were the prehistoric moundbuilders whose works are preserved nearby in the Mound City National Monument. Twenty-three Hopewell Indian burial mounds are concentrated there on a 13 acre site surrounded by an earth wall. Further to the southwest are the Serpent Mound State Memorial, and Seip Mound State Memorial.

Great Seal is a park of great beauty with a fascinating past.

To really appreciate the setting that inspired the Great Seal --the sun rising behind the rolling hills with a field of shocked wheat in the foreground -- you have to move out of the park to the west side of US-23. I had fun exploring the countryside and finally found a spot at the intersection of SR104 and SR207 that seemed to fit the bill. Check it out.

Information and Activities

Great Seal State Park
825 Rocky Road
Chillicothe, Ohio 45601
(614)773-2726

Directions: US-23 to Delano Rd. north of Chillicothe, follow Delano Rd. east to Marietta Rd., turn right onto Marietta Road and head south to the main park entrance which will be on the left.

Information: The park office is well off the beaten path. Follow Marietta Road south past the main entrance to Rocky Road, then a mile on Rocky Road to the park office.

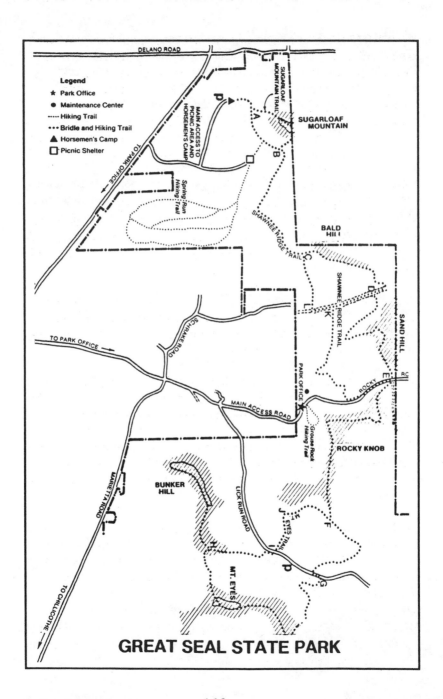

GREAT SEAL STATE PARK

Campground: Although the surrounding scenery is beautiful, the 15-site primitive campground is small and rather uninviting. The camp sits in a tight loop on a small open knob in the northwest corner of the park. Sites have gravel pull-ups, fire rings and tables with nearby drinking water, vault toilets and a shelterhouse capable of holding perhaps 70 people. Pets are permitted in the camp. Sites 1-5 are reserved for horsemen. Self-register or by park staff at the camp. The appeal here is the surrounding natural area and the proximity to the trail system, not the camp itself.

Hiking/Bridle Trails: Twenty-one miles of rugged to gently rolling trails are available here, seventeen miles are shared hiking/bridle trails. Two trails, the Grouse Rock Trail which begins at the park office and the gentler Spring Run Trail at the picnic area total four miles and are strictly footpaths. The Spring Run Trail is open to cross-country skiers when snow conditions are inviting.

Horses and hikers should be well-conditioned to venture onto the longer trails, which do interconnect and can be combined for one long ride or hike. No drinking water is available on the trails, although there is generally limited water in streams for horses.

Sugarloaf Mt. Trail (2.1 mi. loop) climbs up from the campground through a dense maple-dominated forest to the crest of Sugarloaf Mt. Although this is a short loop it rises almost 500 feet in less than one-fourth mile.

Shawnee Ridge Trail (7.8 mi. loop) can also be accessed from the camp. It traverses a long ridge known as Bald Hill, Sand Hill and parts of Rocky Knob so it incorporates several steep trail sections along with longer, more gradual climbs.

Mt. Eyes Trail (6.4 mi. loop) has a separate parking area on Lick Run Road off Rocky Road not far from the park office. The trail winds to and along the top of Bunker Hill and Mt. Eyes and provides views of the surrounding features including the Scioto River Valley. The trail tackles a number of ridges and is very strenuous.

Day-use Areas: A nicely shaded picnic area in a rolling setting is provided at the end of the entrance road with access to several trails. A very nice new picnic shelter is also available for use.

Special Note: Advance reservations are recommended for "Tecumseh!" which shows each year from mid-June to early September. Call (614)775-0700 for information.

To get a feel for the scene that inspired the seal -- the sun suspended over rolling hills with a field of shocked wheat in the foreground --you have to move back from the park to the west side of US-23. Try the intersection of SR104 and SR207

Hunting: Hunting is permitted in some sections of the park, in season, as well as in the nearby 1,124-acre Ross Lake Wildlife Area.

Group picnicking is popular at many of Ohio's state parks.

Group picnicking is popular at Guilford State Park

25 Guilford Lake State Park

Land: 92 acres   Water: 396 acres

Guilford Lake State Park in Columbiana County began as swamp and, later, became a canal reservoir before it was drained by farmers. Eventually it was returned to being a 396-acre lake and became a shoreline state park with an interesting history.

Originally, the lake was created in 1834 as a reservoir for the Sandy and Beaver Canal. The 73.5-mile canal was unusual because it was a privately financed project and involved two tunnels, 30 dams, 90 locks and a 400-foot long aqueduct. The chief engineer of the canal company was E. H. Gill and a town named in his honor, Gillford, was plotted nearby. But when the town applied for its Grange charter in 1874, its name was misspelled Guilford. Rather than delay the important charter, the locals accepted the new name.

By then the private canal had long since gone bankrupt, leaving landowners uncompensated for the land that became Guilford Lake. The lake was subsequently drained and its bottomland used for farming.

Information & Activities

**Guilford Lake State Park
6835 East Lake Road
Lisbon, Ohio 44432
(216)222-1712**

Directions: The state park is 28 miles east of Canton and seven miles west of Lisbon. From I-77 in Canton head east on US-30 and then in 5 miles continue east along SR172. Posted roads to the various areas of the park are reached in 23 miles.

Information: The park headquarters is located at 6835 East Lake Road at the northeast corner of the lake and half-mile north of SR172 via Baker Road. Summer hours are 8 a.m. to noon and 1-5 p.m. Monday and 9 a.m. to 3 p.m. Tuesday through Friday. Winter hours are 8 a.m. to noon and 1 p.m. to 5 p.m. Monday through Thursday.

Campground: Guilford Lake has a campground on an arm off the north side of the lake, reached by turning west on County Road 411 (Teegarden Road) from East Lake Road. The 42 sites are located in an old pine plantation and feature tables, and fire rings but not electric hook-ups. Many sites are located right on the lake with a scenic view of Pine Island located at the mouth of the inlet while sites 7-9, 31 and 33 are for tent camping only. The facility also features vault toilets, play equipment and a boat launch. Guilford Lake fills up on holidays and occasionally on a nice weekend in July but usually has available sites the rest of the summer.

Day-use Areas: The park has four day-use areas with the largest located on the north shore from the west end of the lake to the beach area off Camp Boulevard. The area is accessed from SR172 by turning north on CR411 and features tables, grills and a shelter overlooking the water. The beach has a marked swimming area and a large bathhouse as well as a 600-foot long and wide sandy beach that provides excellent swimming and sunbathing. Smaller picnic areas with tables and grills are located off Lakeview Road just off SR172, on Spillway Drive and Baker Road at the southeast corner of the lake.

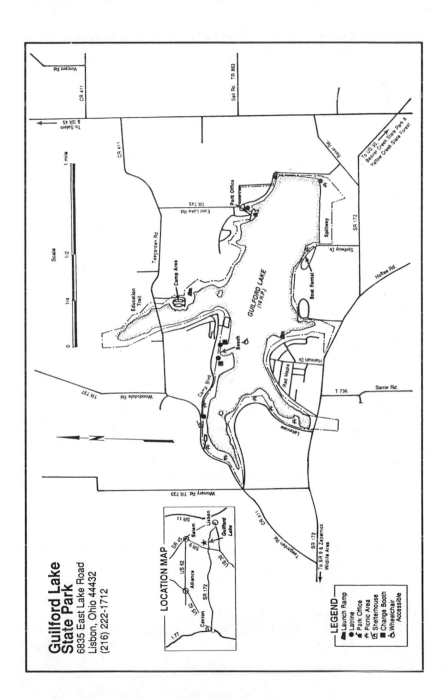

Guilford Lake
State Park
6835 East Lake Road
Lisbon, Ohio 44432
(216) 222-1712

LOCATION MAP

LEGEND
Launch Ramp
Latrine
Park Office
Picnic Area
Shelterhouse
Change Booth
Wheelchair
Accessible

GUILFORD LAKE
(10 H.P.)

Scale

1 mile

0   1/4   1/2

Fishing: Guilford Lake is stocked annually with largemouth bass and channel catfish. The 396-acre lake is heavily fished during the summer with anglers targeting bluegill, crappie and northern pike as well as bass. Boat motors up to 10hp are permitted and launches are located in the campground, near the park office on East Lake Road and at the end of Shore Lane on the south that is reached from SR172 by turning north on Hanna Drive. Shore fishermen gather along the dam at the east side of the lake along East Lake Road while most of the north shore is also accessible to bank fishing.

26 Harrison Lake State Park

Land: 142 acres   Water: 105 acres

Harrison Lake may have been a Michigan State Park, but in 1836, Congress, in its infinite wisdom, agreed with Ohio's claim for the current border location. For years Ohio and Michigan argued over---and both claimed ---the eleven-mile strip of land that extends from the mouth of the Maumee River to the Ohio-Indiana border. Today, Harrison Lake is an island of recreational opportunity amid lush farmlands that track to the horizon.

In a lightly populated portion of Ohio, Harrison Lake is, in part, the result of massive efforts to reclaim and drain what used to be called the *"Great Black Swamp."* Once wet, virtually impassible, and mosquito infested, the state park now serves the needs of visitors from southern Michigan, northern Ohio and travelers crossing the Midwest. Visitors find the park to be intimate, clean, and fun. Thousands of campers, day-users, and outdoor lovers visit year after year.

Information & Activities

Harrison Lake State Park
Route #1
Fayette, Ohio 43521
(419)237-2593

Directions: Two miles south of US -20/127, and two miles west of SR 66. Four miles south of the Michigan/Ohio border.

Information: The park **LOCATION MAP**
office is on the north side of
the lake east of CR 27. Open
Monday - Friday, 8 a.m. - 5
p.m.

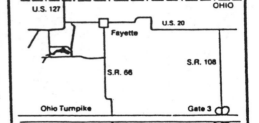

Campground:

Harrison Lake offers three
overnight camping areas.
The group camping area is
near the water and requires
advanced registration, the
Class B campground is on
the south side of the lake
near CR26. There are 52
rustic sites, no electricity or showers, and it's rarely full. Sites number 5, 7, and 10 are on the highbanks overlooking the 105-acre lake and often highly sought after by knowledgable campers.

The Class A campground has 126 sites, paved pads, and electricity with a modern showerhouse. Loop 1-51 has moderate shade, sites 23-30 are lightly shaded. Sites 6-15 are very nice, with site #51 having a view of the lake. Larger RV rigs will find plenty of space in this loop. Pet sites are 110-126 and optional pet sites are also 103-109. Rent-A-Camps are popular, sites 94-96; while handicapped sites 84-85, 63 and 64 get steady use. Sites 74-82 are shady, and the end of the loops overlook rich farm fields. Sites with light shade also include 89-126. A small beach is at the south end of the campground.

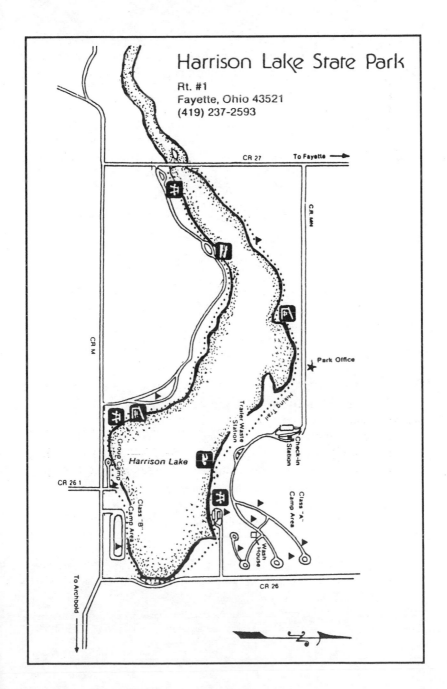

Harrison Lake State Park

Rt. #1
Fayette, Ohio 43521
(419) 237-2593

CR 27   To Fayette →

C.R. MN

Park Office

CR M

Trailer Waste Station

Check-in Station

Hiking Trail

Group Camp

Harrison Lake

CR 26 1

Class "B" Camp Area

Class "A" Camp Area

Wash House

To Archbold

CR 26

151

Boating: A small, quiet lake, only electric motors are allowed. Some car-top boats are used to cruise the wooded shoreline and scout fishing areas. A small launching ramp is located on the southwest shoreline with access off of CR27.

Fishing: Springtime crappie fishing along the rustic campground shoreline is fair to good. Anglers will also find the westside of the lake under the trees and among underwater structure productive during the spring and fall. Largemouth bass, some pike, and bluegills are taken by small boat. Catfish at night are often taken in good numbers during the summer season.

Hiking: The three-mile long trail around the lake is easy to moderate in difficulty. Two highbanks areas require some climbing along the partly wooded trailway.

Day-use Areas: The 50-yard long beach is at the bottom of a small shoreline bank. Near the campground, the private, bouyed-off beach is under the water tower and staffed by a lifeguard on weekends during the summer.

A horseshoe pit, 370 picnic tables and 70 grills, plus open space areas and shelters, offer day-users many amenities in the rural state park. The rangers often patrol the park astride mountain bikes always ready to answer questions about the dam and footbridge, trails and campgrounds.

Nature Notes: Seasonal naturalist programs are offered on the weekends only. Hikes, demonstrations, and nature talks are scheduled for campers, but the general public is also welcome to attend. Films are regularly shown in the Class A campground on Saturday nights.

Hit the beach at Headlands State Park.

27 Headlands Beach State Park

Land: 125 acres · Water: Lake Erie

Headlands Beach State Park on Lake Erie preserves the largest natural beach in Ohio, a mile-long sandy strip that is more than 150 yards wide in places. This impressive beach led to the purchase of the land by the state in 1948 and the designation of Headlands as state park in 1953. Today, with the improving clarity of Lake Erie, due in part to the zebra mussels, the park has become a popular day-use area, attracting more than a million visitors annually who come for both the sugar-like sand and the clean surf.

153

Information & Activities

Headlands Beach
9601 Headlands Road
Mentor, Ohio 44060
(216) 257-1330

Directions: The park is two miles north of Painesville in Lake County. From I-90, depart at exit 200 and head north on SR44, which ends at the park entrance.

Information: A park office is part of the concession stand on the west side of the beach.

Day-use Area: Most of Headlands is a mile-long beach and the adjacent parking area. The parking lot holds 3,900 cars but it still occasionally fills up, forcing the staff to turn away cars the rest of the day. Concession stands and restrooms are located along the beach while a shaded picnic area with tables and grills splits the parking lot in half.

Hiking: Headlands is the northern terminus for the Buckeye Trail. A posted trailhead is at the east end of the service road and from here the statewide trail heads south and quickly leaves the park. More foot trails are located in the Mentor Marsh State Nature Preserve just south of the park and also traversed by the Buckeye Trail.

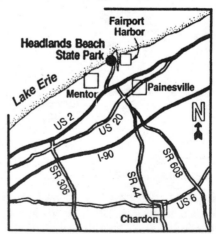

Fishing: In the southwest corner of the park is a large pond with a fishing dock on its north side. Anglers can reach it from the parking lot by following the road past the maintenance building. Others fish it from the steel bridge on Headlands Road that crosses the water.

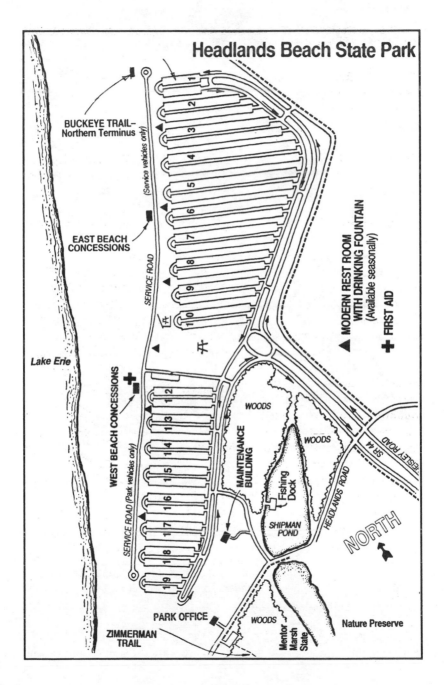

Headlands Beach State Park

BUCKEYE TRAIL–
Northern Terminus

(Service vehicles only)

EAST BEACH
CONCESSIONS

SERVICE ROAD

Lake Erie

WEST BEACH CONCESSIONS

SERVICE ROAD (Park vehicles only)

◄ MODERN REST ROOM
WITH DRINKING FOUNTAIN
(Available seasonally)

✚ FIRST AID

WOODS

WOODS

MAINTENANCE
BUILDING

Fishing
Dock

SHIPMAN
POND

HEADLANDS ROAD

SR 44

WESLEY ROAD

NORTH

PARK OFFICE

ZIMMERMAN
TRAIL

WOODS

Mentor Marsh State

Nature Preserve

155

The rock ledges, waterfalls, and rugged outcrops are unique to the Hocking Hills State Park.

28 Hocking Hills State Park

Land: 2,331 acres   Water: 17 acres

Hocking Hills is *the* destination park in Ohio. Other parks can make an argument, but they're just pretenders to the crown. It is, I think, the best known state park in the system.

And with good reason. Each of the six sites that make up the park have a unique natural attraction. Among them are waterfalls, deep gorges, and huge recess caves set in beautiful woodlands. Whether walking through the gorges or picking your way along the rim of a cliff, the beauty here is awesome. There's nothing else like it in Ohio.

It's all carved out of Blackhand sandstone. The sandstone isn't all the same, some layers are much more resistant to the timeless effects of erosion than others. Generally, what you'll find here are harder top and bottom layers sandwiching a softer middle zone. The recess caves, for example, are carved out of this softer middle zone, with the cave roof and floor made of the more resistant sandstones. Cross-bedding and the honeycomb weathering which gives some cliff faces a pitted appearance are very evident, as are slump blocks, sometimes huge rocks which have broken away from the main cliffs to the streams below.

The glaciers never scoured this area, but their impact is evident, nevertheless. As the glaciers pushed south they cooled the climate ahead of their advance, pushing with it the plants and animals of much more northern areas. When the glaciers retreated and the normal climate returned, so did the warm weather species. But here in Hocking Hills, in the damp cool of the deep gorges where it seems sunlight hardly penetrates, some species you'd expect to find much farther north survive. That's why you'll find the native hardwoods on the clifftops but Canada yews, yellow birch, black birch, huge specimens of eastern hemlocks, and other glacier-seeded species surviving in mini-ecosystems below.

Archaeologists have found evidence of humans using this area as far back as the Adena culture 7,000 years ago. It was then, as it is now, an excellent hunting and foraging area, and the recess caves provided ready-made shelters. In the mid-1700s the Wyandot, Delaware and Shawnee were known to inhabit and travel through the area. Their name for the main river in this region, "Hockhocking" or bottle river, gave the region, the county and the park their names.

Settlers began moving into the area in numbers after the Treaty of Greenville in 1795. The various areas that now comprise the park were already popular picnic and resort areas shortly after the Civil War. In 1924, the State of Ohio purchased the first tract of forest, 146 acres that included Old Man's Cave. Today, over 11,000 acres of the Hocking Hills is preserved in the park and surrounding state forest.

Information and Activities

Hocking Hills State Park
20160 SR664
Logan, Ohio 43138
(614) 385-6841

Directions: Hocking Hills is comprised of six non-contiguous sites, the most popular of which is Old Man's Cave. To reach Old Man's Cave take US-33 to SR664, follow SR664 south approximately 12 miles to the Old Man's Cave Area entrance and the visitor center.

Information: In addition to the visitor center, information is available at the park office located inside the Dining Lodge at the end of the Old Man's Cave drive. Also at the campground office which is open from May through October.

Campground: The year-round main campground is up on a wooded ridge, a nice place to be from the moment you take your car across the stream ford at the base of camp. It has 172 sites, all with electric hook-ups except 13 sites (#81-93) on an offshoot loop and the group camp. Showerhouses are available from April 1 to October 31. A swimming pool in the camp is open Memorial Day through Labor Day.

The pool, amphitheater, dump station, a playground and a showerhouse are all located in the same area. Sites 24-30 are shaded and right next door, as are 76-80. The most popular area seems to be sites 37 and up on that loop. Sites 94-107 are also nicely shaded, but my choice would be the more quiet, secluded loop with taller hardwoods, sites 164-172. Sites 121-123 are also shaded and somewhat isolated from other sites. Reservations are required for the ten tent sites in the group camping area, also located near the pool. Another youth group camp which can accommodate 160 people is located off SR374 north of SR56.

The main camp is in great demand and fills on summer weekends, generally by 6 p.m. on Friday evening. For holiday weekends and during fall color arrive mid-week to be assured of a spot. If the camp is full, two private campgrounds only ten minutes away offer full services and hook-ups.

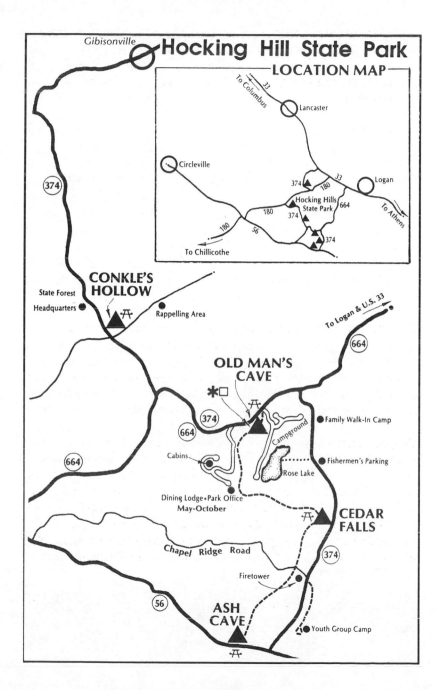

Hocking Hill State Park

Gibisonville

LOCATION MAP

To Columbus
33
Lancaster

Circleville

374 180 33 Logan

Hocking Hills State Park

To Athens

180 664

180 374

56 374

To Chillicothe

CONKLE'S HOLLOW

State Forest Headquarters

Rappelling Area

To Logan & U.S. 33

664

OLD MAN'S CAVE

374

664

664

Cabins

Dining Lodge • Park Office
May-October

Campground

Family Walk-In Camp

Fishermen's Parking

Rose Lake

CEDAR FALLS

374

Chapel Ridge Road

Firetower

56

ASH CAVE

Youth Group Camp

159

A very pretty, more primitive alternative to the main camp is the off-the-beaten-track Family Walk-In Camp, 30 tent sites scattered 30 to 40 yards apart to maximize privacy and the feeling of being outdoors. Camping fees here are less than half the rate of the main camp. Vault toilets, drinking water is available in the parking area. Parking is not permitted at the sites. You can tell the campers who've used this camp before, they're the ones who bring a wheelbarrow or child's wagon to haul supplies to their camp. The last site is about a one-half mile walk. But darn well worth it.

Cabins: Forty family cabins, reservable through the park office, and now through the state-wide reservation system. are as busy as the camp-ground. All are in the Old Man's Cave area at the top of the drive opposite the Dining Lodge. They sit on a pine-forested ridge that deer often wander through. The cabins, like those in most state parks, are available only by the week in summer. To be safe, book them a year in advance. They take reservations for June, for example, in May of the year before. October weekends are among the first to go.

Dining Lodge: The dining lodge with its charming Swiss Chalet atmosphere is open from April through October with full service dining along with a snack bar that serves up burgers, hot dogs, and fries at the lodge's outdoor swimming pool. That pool is open free to cabin guests and to the general public at a small charge. Also available are a meeting room that can accommodate up to 300 persons, a TV room and game room. There are no overnight accommodations here. The restaurant and pool are wheelchair accessible.

Fishing: Rose Lake is a 17 acre natural spring-fed lake accessible only by walking an easy one-half mile trail. Fishermen's parking is on SR374 just south of SR664 and the Family Walk-in Camp. It's actually the water supply for the park but it's a pretty good little fishing hole that's stocked annually with golden and some rainbow trout. Bank fishing is favored, mostly for the natural abundance of largemouth bass, bluegill, and catfish.

Hiking Trails: If you don't take a trail at Hocking Hills you will have missed the essence of the park. Some parks you can drive around and get the gist of what's going on, others can be appreciated from the water, but here the magic is on the trails, down in the hollows and gorges where waterfalls plummet and massive cliffs rise, and kids find their way back into the deepest reaches of recess caves. Most of the trails are short and the rewards are obvious.

A word of caution: this is cliff country and almost every year someone gets careless, is on a trail after dark, or wanders off the trail and falls to their death. Most parks are open until 11 p.m. The trails in Hocking Hills close at dark and there's a good reason for it. Remember if you walk the clifftop trails that the soil there is thin. It's not uncommon for someone to lean over the edge for a look while holding onto a small tree for balance, only to have the shallow-rooted tree rip right out at its roots. Use common sense, keep small children off the rim trails.

That said, let's have a look at the terrific selection of trails here. Don't try to do them all in one day, allow two days at least.

Old Man's Cave. Without a doubt the Old Man's Cave Area is the best known destination in the state park system. The size of the parking lot itself stands as testimony to its popularity, and with good reason. It is the heart and soul of Hocking Hills State Park.

Old Man's Cave is a recess cave, a large cavity protected by a huge shelf of overhanging sandstone. No doubt prehistoric peoples used the area, but it was a more modern human, a hermit named Richard Rowe, who inspired the name that the cave and gorge now carry. Rowe reportedly made his home there shortly after the Civil War and remained there until his death.

Start at the Visitor Center and quite literally make the trail as long or as short as you like. A simple 100 yard walk takes you to the bridge over the gorge for a nice view, less than one-fourth mile which includes negotiating some steps and a tunnel takes you to the base of the cave itself. Or you can walk the entire bottom of the gorge, or around much of the gorge rim, or both. Or follow the trail to the lower gorge and pick up a section of the Buckeye Trail which will take you to nearby Cedar Falls, a distance of about three miles.

There is an upper falls at the head of the gorge. Devil's Bathtub is a pothole in the sandstone created by sand and gravel swirled by the stream. Below the cave is the Sphinx head which is a formation that looks, well, like an

Egyptian monument. At the Lower Falls the stream plunges forty feet into a pool. It's worth the extra walk to a side hollow where Broken Rock Falls tumbles over a sandstone cliff and picks its way through a jumble of massive boulders to the main stream.

Ash Cave is the largest recess cave in Ohio, an awesome overhang that stretches in a 700 foot horseshoe 90 feet above the valley floor. A small waterfall stretches in a long sparkling ribbon from overhang to valley. Below, the cave reaches 100 feet from rim to the deepest recess. Early settlers found huge mounds of ashes on the cave floor thought to be evidence of ancient campfires used by the early Indians who sought shelter there. The ashes gave the cave its name.

Located on SR56 just west of SR374, it's an easy one-fourth mile walk to the cave. The park has taken advantage of the easy grade by paving the trail for wheelchair access.

Cedar Falls

In my opinion, Cedar Falls is the most beautiful waterfall in Ohio. It's not just the waterfalls which is pleasing enough as it rushes over a sandstone cliff, twisting and splaying as it rides the smoothly contorted surface to a plunge pool below. Situated at the head of a steep-walled, hemlock-choked gorge carved out of the sandstone, the walk to the falls is inspiring in itself, as is a very short side trip up a small hollow just to the right of the approach to the falls. The scene here is especially magnificent when all the seeps and falls are frozen into icicles -- wintertime stalactites and stalagmites.

Cedar Falls was named by early residents who mistook the large hemlocks in the gorge for cedars.

From the Cedar Falls parking area located on SR374, the falls is a short trail of little more than one-half mile down into a gorge with switchbacks and steps to minimize the effort. It is also accessible via the Buckeye Trail from either Old Man's or Ash Caves, walks that are well worth the effort if you have the time.

Conkles Hollow

Hocking Hills State Park

163

I've included Conkles Hollow in the state park description even though, like Sheick Hollow and Little Rocky Hollow, Conkles is now under the jurisdiction of the Division of Natural Areas and Preserves. But everyone still thinks its part of the park, the Conkles Hollow Picnic Area is still maintained by the Division of Parks, and it's a fantastic spot, so I think you should know about it.

Conkles Hollow is easily one of my favorite spots in Ohio. It's a deep narrow gorge crowded by sandstone cliffs that tower 200 feet over hikers on the gorge trail. The gorge trail is a very easy one mile walk (round-trip) along the stream at the base of the hollow. The trail crosses the stream several times on its way through the stands of large hemlocks which shade the hiker and an undergrowth of ferns and wildflowers. The rock outcrops and huge cliffs are very evident from this trail which eventually deadends at a small waterfall at the head of the hollow.

The Rim Trail is a very different trail, one which requires extreme caution because it can be dangerous even in summer. But the views up and down the hollow from this 2.5 mile loop trail are absolutely spectacular. Enough said, except yet another reminder to stay away from the cliff edge -- what looks like solid ground may not be -- and be sure to time yourself so you're off the trail before dark. I'd also recommend thinking twice before taking small children on this trail. Once you're on top of the rim the trail is relatively easy, but it's a long, strenuous climb up from the base of the hollow (steps and landings are now provided, so it's better than it once was) to the rim. You'll find it a bit easier if you start the trail to the west and return off the east rim.

Rock House

On my first visit I was initially appalled at my first glimpse of the graffiti carved into the face of the sandstone cliff at Rock House. That disgust turned to reluctant fascination as I realized that most of the damage was done back in the 1800s, putting a slightly different face on the "vandals." Perhaps they were guests at the 16-room hotel and ballroom that once stood where the picnic shelter is today.

Rock House entices exploration, seven windows in a cliff of Blackhand sandstone opening into rooms that connect in a "house of rock." It's a geologically interesting site where one can easily see the series of cracks and joints that caused the phenomenon.

It's less than one-fourth mile back to Rock House with a number of steps provided to make the climbs and drops easier. From there the trail loops back another one-fourth mile to the fire tower and then along a drive to the parking area. The trail passes through one of Ohio's best examples of a mixed mesophytic forest, that is, a forest with many different kinds of trees in which no one species dominates.

Rock House is located about ten miles northwest of Old Man's Cave on SR 374.

Cantwell Cliffs

The least known and least used section of the park due to its 17 mile distance north of Old Man's Cave on SR374. Nevertheless it's a beautiful area well worth your time.

A variety of trail options are available here from very short to healthy walks, along the rim and through the gorge, up hollows and along streams. Created by the eroding power of Buck Run, Cantwell Cliffs is an area dominated by several large recesses, deep woods and towering cliffs. Don't forget to test your girth at "Fat Woman's Squeeze," a narrow passage between a slump block and cliff face which is a challenge to larger hikers (there is an alternate route that avoids the squeeze).

Day-use Areas: Picnic areas and vault toilets are provided at each of the six areas. Picnicking is very popular here -- 634 tables are scattered among the sites. Shelterhouses are available at Old Man's Cave, Ash Cave, Cantwell Cliffs, and Rock House. The new Old Man's Cave Visitor Center has a snack bar that serves up hamburgers, hot dogs and fries.

Nearly 100 acres of the surrounding Hocking Hills State Forest have been set aside for rock climbing and rappeling. The area is located on Big Pine Road, east of Conkles Hollow. For more information call the state forest at (614)385-4402.

Nature Notes: Nature walks and programs are offered year-round here. During summer months naturalist aide programs for 7-9 year olds and ages 10-14. Many programs begin from the naturalist cabin at Old Man's Cave. Slide and movie programs are presented in the campground amphitheater every Friday and Saturday night.

A naturalist is on duty in the Old Man's Cave visitor center on weekend afternoons in the busy season.

Hunting: Due to the heavy year-round public use and the size of the park sites, no hunting is allowed on the park or in the three state nature preserves. However, hunting is allowed in season in the 9,238 acre Hocking State Forest.

Winter Activities: Hocking Hills is a popular destination in winter as well as summer. The scenery is gorgeous after a snowfall or when the ice falls form in the gorges.

Probably the single most well-known and popular event held each year is the Old Man's Cave winter hike. Held rain or snow or shine the third weekend in January each year, the walk begins at the upper falls in Old Man's Cave gorge and follows the segment of the Buckeye Trail known as the Grandma Gatewood Trail, past Cedar Falls where refreshments are served, and on to Ash Cave. Buses return participants from Ash Cave. Last year nearly 5,000 hikers participated.

Wildlife, nature trails, golf, cabins, pool, and more at Hueston Woods.

29 Hueston Woods State Park

Land: 3,596   Water: 625

One of the oldest, busiest, and most developed parks in the Ohio system, Hueston Woods history actually dates back to 1797 when Matthew Hueston began to buy land in the area. Hueston, one of the state's first conservationist, and his family that followed, perserved the land until the 1930's. The state purchased the vast land holdings in 1941, by the mid-1950's the dam was completed, and the following year Acton Lake was impounded. Shortly after, the park was dedicated as Hueston Woods State Park.

From family and standard cabins and lodge to Class B camping, Hueston Woods has a variety of amenites that will please families, hikers, horsemen, and water enthusiasts. Sailing, golfing, a historical pioneer museum, nine picnic areas, nature center, and wildlife rehabilatation center are part of the huge park.

Acton Lake is a recreational haven for anglers, boaters, swimmers, and sailors, the lake is over two miles in length with coves and inlets that make a scenic backdrop for all of the park's activities and facilities.

Information & Activities

Hueston Woods State Park
Rt. 1
College Corner, Ohio 45003
(513)523-6347

Directions: About 45 miles west and slightly south of Dayton, Hueston Woods is only four miles from the Indiana/Ohio border. There is good signing from 732 to the park office.

Information: The park office is located at the end of Butler-Israel Road and open 8 a.m. - 5 p.m., Monday - Friday. Located next to the nature center, the office has complete information about the lodge, cabins, boating, and so on.

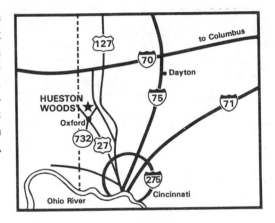

Campground: The Class A camping area makes up more than half of the total 490 campsites at Hueston Woods. The 255 Class A sites have electricity, laundry facilities, flush toilets, and space for up to 30-foot RV's. Showers, a good number of mature trees, and a camp store near the campground office makes the Class A area heavily used on weekends, often filling up by early evening on Fridays.

Row B has pull-through sites designed for RV's. Rows D and E are island-like with light shade and less privacy. The south side of Row C has good shade and is used mostly by tents. The north side of Row G is hilly, shady, and has a water view. For pet owners, Row G is designated for your use. Hueston Woods also has four group camping areas.

Hueston Woods State Park

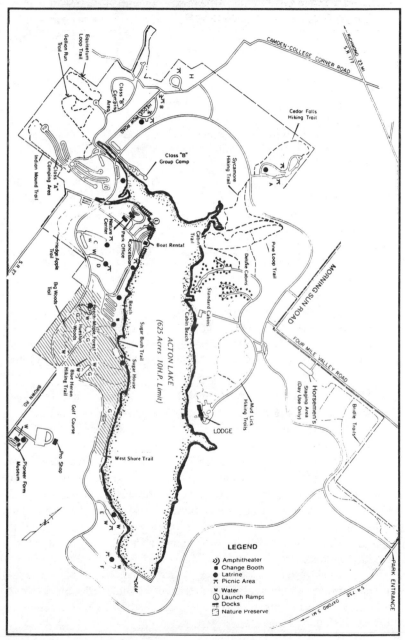

LEGEND

)) Amphitheater
Change Booth
Latrine
Picnic Area
W Water
Ⓛ Launch Ramp
Docks
Nature Preserve

The Class B camping area, which offers fewer amenities, is rarely full, even on holiday weekends. No showers, rustic, and offering plenty of room for tent and large campers, the B-area is popular with families and those campers that enjoy mature trees---plenty of trees----and privacy.

Area N has a large playground area and is somewhat secluded, an ideal area for kids. Area O is large and shady, but there is no electricity on individual campsites. The most secluded and private sites in this area are 175-185. There are plenty of day-use areas including open spaces for ball games and volleyball, while picnic tables and grills are also scattered about.

Lodge:
Hueston Woods Resort and Conference Center is located on the north side of Acton Lake, five miles north of Oxford. Originally a council site for the Western Ohio Indian tribes, the beautiful center continues as an important conference and meeting facility. The lodge, complete with a 100-foot tall sandstone fireplace and 94 guest rooms also has two pools, and six meeting rooms that can accommodate groups of 300 people. The lake view is terrific!

Game rooms, indoor and outdoor pool, tennis, shuffleboard, volleyball, courtesy docks, horseshoes, playground equipment, giftshop, and a nearby 18-hole golf course is available to guests. During the summer season the lodge also offers a wide variety of recreation programs for youth and adults.

Cabins:
Hueston Woods' cabins are located on the north side of the lake about one mile from the lodge. There are two loops, one loop has 25 two-bedroom family cabins, the other 35 one-bedroom standard cabins.

The two bedroom cabins are snuggled into a shady loop. They consist of a kitchen/dining area, living room with daybeds; two bedrooms with two twin beds in one room and one double- bed in the second bedroom (cabins #36-58 and 60); bathroom and screen porch. These cabins sleep six. The cabins, heated for year-round use, are often booked many months in advance, call (513)523-6381 for reservation information. Cabins 40-50 have the best location.

The standard cabins feature one room efficiency, with one double bed, two day beds, kitchen area and bath. Each is equipped for light housekeeping

Heated pools, game room, golf, and leisure at the lodge.

and are available April - October. The simple, but fun, cabins can sleep four and are heated with propane.

Cabins are rented on a weekly basis only begining in June until Labor Day. During the rest of the season cabins can be rented for as short as two days at a time. Each cabin is equipped with basic linens, blankets, towels, dishware, silverware, cooking utensils, and so on. You may want to bring a window fan, lawn furniture, portable grills, or extra towels for the beach.

Boating: Acton Lake has a ten horsepower motor restriction. A sailing association operates on the lake, and many small sailboats are busy on the horizon. The launch ramp is located on the south side of the lake near the park office, with docking nearby, the eight-hole ramp is busy with small boats and fishermen. The marina (tel. 513-523-8859) is open seven days and offers a snack bar, bait, and boat rentals. From pontoons to canoes and sailboats, visitors can spend a quiet afternoon exploring the shores of Acton Lake.

Fishing: If you are over 16 years old you must possess a valid Ohio fishing license which may be purchased at the marina or park office. The good habitat of Acton Lake and limitation on boat size offers good fishing, especially during the spring and fall.

Although crappie angling is poor, it has improved since the late 1980s. Other than crappies, the overall fishing on Acton Lake is considered excellent. Bluegill fishing is good, catfish are plentiful, and tiger muskie are occasionally taken by trolling. According to fisheries biologists, who constantly survey the lake, largemouth bass are very plentiful. You just have to find them. Once you get on the fish, crankbaits, spinner baits, and artifical worms work well.

A slot limit is in effect on the lake.

This new regulation effective in 1990, and the control of agricultural runoffs will greatly help to improve the lake's fishery. Some small largemouth bass tournaments are conducted on the lake, but the best time to fish the lake is on weekdays.

Hiking: Over 12 miles of hiking trails are marked and maintained in the 3600-acre state park. There are 13 hiking trails at the park, all described, complete with maps, in the Hueston Woods Trail Maps and User Guide.

Mudlick Trail - three small loops through a mature beech-maple forest.
Pine Loop- 0.6 miles along a stream and through a floodplain forest.
Cabin Trail - 0.7 miles in length is a popular birding route along an old farm field, also an Acton Lake overlook.
Cedar Falls- 0.9 miles through a lush floodplain forest featuring mature black walnut and oak tree canopy. You will ford a creek and see a small waterfall, 450 million year old bedrock, and many wildflowers.
Sycamore Trail- 0.8 miles along a floodplain with many sycamore trees.
Hedge Apple Trail- 0.7 miles through a once cleared farm field that now is returning to a natural forest. Look for the apple trees.
Big Woods Trail- 1.8 miles of majestic forest, one of the few 200 year old virgin forests left in the state. The beech-maple forest is a tiny reminder of the forests that once covered Ohio. Impressive and a National Natural Landmark.
Blue Heron Trail- 0.7 miles, a more leisurely trail into the Big Woods, towering beech trees overhead, pawpaws and spicebushes, which bear red fruit in the fall.

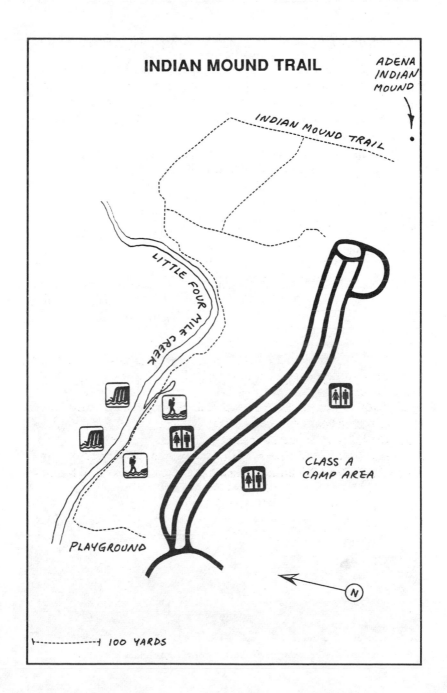

INDIAN MOUND TRAIL

ADENA
INDIAN
MOUND

INDIAN MOUND TRAIL

LITTLE FOUR MILE CREEK

CLASS A
CAMP AREA

PLAYGROUND

N

├----------┤ 100 YARDS

Sugar Bush Trail- 0.8 miles complete with lots of sugar maples that are used in the Sugar Maple Festival each March.

West Shore Trail- 1.5 miles along the western banks of Acton Lake. Through a small virgin beech-maple forest, and along the lake, bring your panfishing rod and tackle.

EquestrianTrail- one mile hike through a bottomlands that has many elms, sycamores, and walmuts.

Gallion Run Trail- .7miles through three distinct habitats. From the Class A campground you begin a decline into a beautiful valley, then dry hilly areas, diverse forest of oak and other species much different than the Big Woods area.

Indian Mound Trail- three short loops near the Adena Indian mound. Along Little Four Mile Creek, through a meadow, and across exposed limestone outcrops.

Day-use Areas: An 18 hole golf course, dozens of secluded picnic areas complete with grills and table, shoreline fishing, a fishing pier, boat rentals, and a beach near the park office complete with bathhouse on the south side of the lake.

The pioneer farm offers interpretive history programs and tours.

The Pioneer Farm Museum is located on the southeast part of the park at the corner of Doty and Brown Roads. The museum was the Doty farm homestead for 125 years until it became part of the developing Hueston Woods State Park in the mid-1950s. As Acton Lake was created, the Ohio Division of State Parks and Recreation renovated the old brick farmhouse for use as a park office. In 1959, the house was leased to the Oxford Museum Association and opened to the public.

Today, the museum features the renovated house and furnishings, and a towering Pennsylvania Bank-style barn. Complete with well, root cellar, the old homestead is open weekends in season and offers an interpretive program. Contact the Oxford Museum Association at P.O. Box 184, Oxford, Ohio 45056.

Nature Notes: Maybe the most impressive feature of Hueston Woods is the nature center and Raptor Rehabilitation Education Project, a program dedicated to the preservation of all birds of prey. The nature center and the rehabilitation center are located next to the park office on the south side of the lake.

Inside the nature center, which is open daily, April 1 to Nov. 1, Tuesday - Sunday, are a number of live animal exhibits including snakes, aquatic life, kestrel and short-eared owl, opossum, and many interpretive displays about our natural world. Naturalists conduct regular, year-round interpretive programs in the park. Programs on snakes, morning-time strolls, visits to natural areas, films, pioneer farm tours, fossils, night hikes, Ohio animals, and camp gatherings are offered.

The raptor center concentrates on the rehabilitation of injured and orphaned bird of prey. There is a large flight pen, six perches/shelters, one enclosed cage. You will be able to see many birds of prey up close, due to injury most will never be released back into the wild.

Located behind the nature center, Cooper's hawks, golden eagle, turkey vulture, barn owl, barred owl, and others reside while recovering from injury.

30 Independence Dam State Park

Land: 604 acres   Water: river/canal

Independence Dam State Park lies between six unbroken miles of the historic Miami and Erie Canal and the Maumee River. The parkland is actually between the canal and the river, in some places only 30 yards wide. The marina and park office were constructed in 1971 nearly 35 years after the Civilian Conservation Corps completed construction of the roads, shelter houses, and other park facilities.

The entrance to the park is over the ruins of Lock No. 13, once a vital part of the canal system that once brought economic vitality to this area of the state. A walk along the 2.5 mile stretch of the canal within the state park is a quiet moment with history; a history that changed quickly when modern transportation rumbled through the state. The scenic road along the canal offers walkers and bicyclists a year-round opportunity to walk between two great bodies of water---one manmade---the other natural and mighty.

Information & Activities

Independence Dam State Park
Rt. #4, SR424, Box 27722
Defiance, Ohio 43512
(419)784-3263

Directions: Independence Dam is located in Defiance County on SR 424, three miles east of the city of Defiance.

Information: The park headquarters is west of Independence Road on SR424. The office is staffed as much as possible Monday - Friday, 8 a.m. - 5 p.m.

Campground: The linear park offers 40 unmarked rustic campsites all located between the canal and the river. The campground has no electricity or flush toilets, but that doesn't stop many family campers seeking a quiet retreat. The campground is rarely full.

Boating: The Independence Dam Marina is located on SR424 and features a two ramp launch into the wide Maumee River. A restroom, park office, pop machines, and scattered picnic tables offer boaters a place to launch and picnic. There are no horsepower restrictions on the river.

Fishing: Anglers often fish the dam area where deeper waters attract a variety of species, but along much of the park's shoreline, topwater bait for bass are usually the rule due to thick vegatation and snags. Smallmouth, Northern pike, crappie and catfish are caught in the spring, with poor to fair panfishing after spring.

Hiking: The three mile long Tow Path, once used by men and mules to pull barges and other craft along the canel, is located at the very east end of the park. Like the 2.5 mile roadway between the canal and the river, it is easy flat walking.

Day-use Areas: With close proximity to Defiance, many walkers and day-use visitors enjoy the quiet park that offers four picnic shelters, 40 grills, 125 picnic tables, and eight vault toilets. About 300,000 people visit annually.

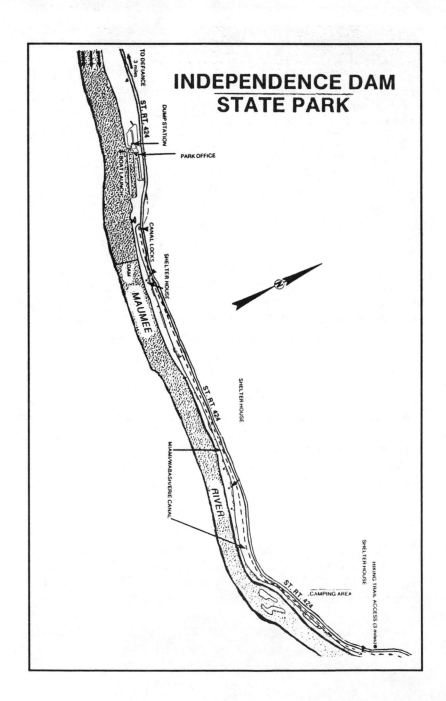

INDEPENDENCE DAM
STATE PARK

TO DEFIANCE
3 miles

ST. RT. 424

DUMP STATION

PARK OFFICE

BOAT LAUNCH

CANAL LOCKS

SHELTER HOUSE

DAM

MAUMEE

SHELTER HOUSE

ST. RT. 424

MIAMI/WABASH/ERIE CANAL

RIVER

SHELTER HOUSE

HIKING TRAIL ACCESS (3 miles)

ST. RT. 424

CAMPING AREA

Bring your boat and camp next to the water at Indian Lake State Park.

31   Indian Lake State Park

Land: 648 acres   Water: 5800 acres

At one time Indian Lake was known as the "Midwest's Million Dollar Playground." The original Indian Lake was built in 1851 as part of the canal program, by 1898 the Ohio General Assembly dedicated the lake as a state park. The region was---and is today---a popular resort area. At the turn of the century due to its central location on the old Toledo and Ohio Central Steamline and the Ohio Electric Railway, the area bustled with activity and resort development.

Today, Indian Lake State Park is at the heart of a resort area complete with marinas, restaurants, nearby Ohio Caverns, fast food, shopping, Mad River ski mountain, cottages by the hundreds, golf, motels, and lots more. Water skiers, boaters, speedboats and drifting pontoons help make the lake itself a busy place.

One of the busiest boating lakes, jet skis, small craft, and fishermen share this popular body of water that is blessed with many coves, miles of shoreline, and plenty of places to explore.

Information & Activities

Indian Lake State Park
12774 SR235N
Lakeview,Ohio 43331
(513)843-2717
(513)843-3553 camp office

Directions: The park office is located 15 miles northwest of Bellefontaine on SR235N. There is also easy access from I-75 by taking US-33 exit east. Other major routes to the park are SR235N, 117, and 274. The park office is located one-half mile north of US-33 on SR235N.

Information: The park headquarters is open 8 a.m. - 5 p.m., sometimes closed during the lunch hour depending on staffing.

Campground: Indian Lake has 443 Class A campsites (370 with electrical hook-ups) for tents and trailers off SR235 on the north shore of the lake. The large campground has 16 loops, heated showerhouses with flush toilets, coin-operated laundry facilites, a modern commissary (two pool tables, video games, bait, newspapers, simple foods, cold pop, etc.), playground, nature center, dump station, beach, boat launch ramp, pet area sites D43-72 and A3-31, two Rent-A-Camps (sites C, 6 and 7), twenty dock spaces with electricity for those that want to camp on their boats, and a small amphitheater.

Area C doesn't have much shade, so area B, which is very shady, is the first to fill-up and is the most popular camping area in the park. The first two legs of area C, sites 2-59 are great. Waterside sites are along the channel, sites 30-55, 56-60, 62-64, 66, 68-72. Sites at the end of area B's four loops, site numbers 16, 46, 47, 71, 72, 73, 101, 102, 103, are near the water. The campground fills up on all holiday weekends, but you can usually get a spot on other summer weekends if you can get there by mid-afternoon on Friday.

Boating: A popular boating lake for unlimited horsepower boats, many types of watercraft share the 5800 acre lake. Public boat launch ramps are located at Lakeview Harbor on US-33, Moundwood (near the park headquarters), Blackhawk near the campground, and Chippewa Marina.

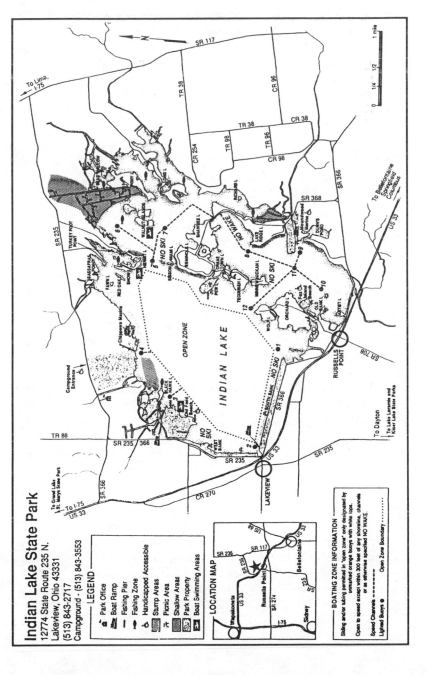

Indian Lake State Park

12774 State Route 235 N.
Lakeview, Ohio 43331
(513) 843-2717
Campground - (513) 843-3553

— LEGEND —

⚓	Park Office
🚤	Boat Ramp
⊢	Fishing Pier
	Fishing Zone
♿	Handicapped Accessible
▨	Stump Areas
🏕	Picnic Area
▨	Shallow Areas
🏊	Park Property
🏊	Boat Swimming Areas

LOCATION MAP

BOATING ZONE INFORMATION

Skiing and/or tubing permitted in "open zone" only designated by unmarked orange buoys with white tops.

Open to speed except within 300 feet of any shoreline, channels or as otherwise specified NO WAKE.

Speed Channels ------
Lighted Buoys ●   Open Zone Boundary ....

The park rents season docking, contact the park office at (513)843-2717. Although there is no horsepower limits on Indian Lake, there are many fishing and channel areas marked "NO WAKE." All lake area within 300 feet from the shoreline is no wake. Skiing and tubing is permitted only in the large "Open Zone" area. Indian Lake is the only inland lake in Ohio with lighted buoys for night navigation. There are many large commerical marinas that also operate around the lake that offer boat rental, repairs and fuel.

Fishing: Area bait and tackle shops specialize in assisting anglers with the challenges of busy Indian Lake. According to staff, spring and fall, when the hectic summer wanes, is the best time for serious fishing on the lake. Largemouth bass (early April), bluegill, yellow perch, catfish, white bass, crappie (in the shallows), and walleye are commonly taken in the spring along the riprap. Full limits are rare in the summer season.

With improving water quality due to newly installed waste water treatment facilities around the lake, fish planting is hoped to increase, and overall angling is improving rapidly. Slow drift/troll for walleye using a small jig and minnow, bass can be taken around structure using artifical lures, locals also like to jig for crappies using a bobber. Channel catfish are often taken with bologna or doughballs.

In the late 1980's millions of saugeye were planted and they are thriving.

Hiking: There are four miles of trails at Indian Lake. But lots of walking can be done along the large beaches and along shorelines.

Day-use Areas: Two popular swimming beaches highlight day-use amenities at Indian Lake. Oldfield Beach is located off 235, with a sandy beach about 300 yards long and 30 yards wide, is complete with new bath houses, pop machines, lifeguards, plenty of parking and lots of people when it's warm. The Fox Island Beach is smaller and older, but equally busy. Off 33, near the McDonalds restaurant, there's plenty of picnic tables and sunny places. Pew Island, off Cranetown, has a small hiking trail and there is a great blue heron rookery at Walnut Island.

32 Jackson Lake State Park

Land: 242 acres   Water: 92 acres

Jackson Lake is a nice, quiet place, a get-away with really special appeal if you like to fish. It's also earned a place in our history books.

Jackson Lake is in the famous Hanging Rock Region, a region of rich iron ore deposits which coupled with vast stands of hardwood forests to use as fuel made it a center which once produced much of the nation's iron. The region stretched from Vinton County, Ohio, southward into Kentucky.

In the park, along the shore of Jackson Lake at Laurel Point, are the remains of the old Jefferson Furnace. There the Welsh-operated Jefferson Iron Company under the trade name of Anchor made Jefferson iron the standard for quality and value. It was the Jefferson Furnace that produced the iron for the Monitor, the Union ironclad that met the Confederate ironclad, the Merrimac, in a famous Civil War battle.

The furnace averaged about ten tons of iron a day -- except Sunday, the company's by-laws forbade Sunday labor -- that was valued for car wheels and heavy machinery, as well as by the military for artillery. It ran about six to seven months a year, allowing time to replenish wood and charcoal and make repairs. The furnace, the last of the Hanging Rock furnaces to remain in operation, made its last cast at the end of 1916, 62 years after it began. The iron industry shifted to Lake Superior ores smelted with coke.

The great forest, which was cleared by woodcutters frantically trying to keep the furnaces supplied with charcoal, is returning and Jackson Lake stands in the midst of a very picturesque region. The land owned by the Jefferson Iron Company was eventually deeded to the state. The lake was dug by hand and scrapers by Depression-era CCC crews, and, although public improvements were added gradually over the years, Jackson Lake wasn't officially dedicated as a state park until 1979.

Efforts to restore the furnace have been unsuccessful so eventually the stone furnace may go the way of the buildings that once surrounded it, adding to the mystique of the site. Somewhere, it's said, under Laurel Point there still exists an old secret mine where Indians mined for ore. It's still there, so the legend goes, under the waters of Jackson Lake.

Information and Activities

Jackson Lake State Park
P.O. Box 174
Oak Hill, OH 45656
(614) 682-6197

Directions: Take US-23 to US-35, east to SR93, then head west of SR279 out of Oak Hill.

Information: SR279 bisects the park on a causeway. To find the park office look for the first road to the right after crossing the causeway. Follow Tommy Been Road past several small picnic sites to the campground. The office is located at the campground entrance.

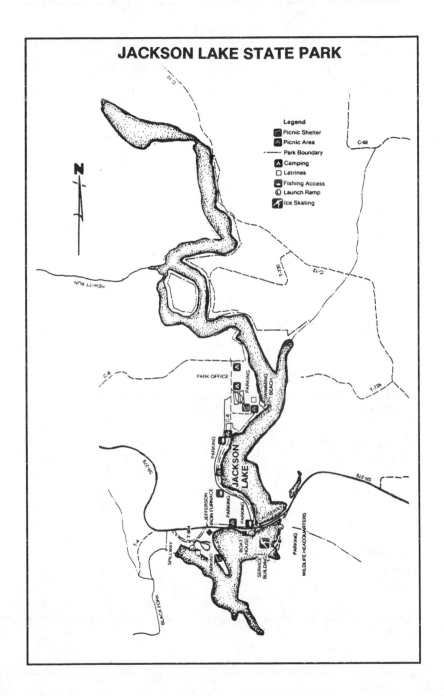

JACKSON LAKE STATE PARK

Legend
- Picnic Shelter
- Picnic Area
- Park Boundary
- Camping
- Latrines
- Fishing Access
- Launch Ramp
- Ice Skating

Campground: An extremely well-kept 36 site campground near the swimming beach that opened in the early 1980s. Pets permitted. Ten sites are tent only. Drinking water and lighted vault-type toilets are located at each end of the camp. Dump station and faucet for refilling RV tanks provided. Although the campground is pleasantly rolling, all sites are level with little to partial shade. The best sites for RVs are 19-22 which are close to the beach and lake. Tent sites 32-36 are right over the water with nice views. Site #5 also has a nice view worth checking. Camp usage peaks in June and July, but the camp has never been filled. The tent sites, however, do fill. Camping supplies are available two miles away in Oak Hill.

Between the office and camp are a half-dozen apple trees that produce what locals call the best cooking apples in the state. It's a believable claim, Jackson County is noted for its apple crop. The deer seem to agree, check the trees morning and evening when the apples are on the ground and you'll likely see them.

Boating: There's a 10hp limit here with three small public launches spaced along SR279. The lake was formed by constructing an earth dam across Black Fork in 1938. Although Jackson Lake is long and narrow it has a bathtub-like bottom, the deepest spot is only about 16 feet.

Fishing: Jackson is a fishing lake. People travel long distances to try for it's big bass, some approaching the ten pound range, four to five pounders are common. Try your luck, especially in the early spring and late fall when they seem to hit hardest on lime-tailed spinner baits. Most seem to be caught in the old stream bed and around Rhodes Island, a large island in the upper end of the lake owned by former Ohio Governor James Rhodes. Some have had luck with tiger muskie and muskie, as well as northern pike. The lake is also good for catfish, bluegill and crappie. Both boat and bank fishing are popular here. There is a fifty foot wide fishing easement all around the lake. The three shoreline fishing accesses along Tommy Been Road can start to look like a carnival with all the lights of the night fishermen.

Johnboats can be rented from a private concessionaire on the lake outside the park.

Day-use Areas: Jackson Lake is very much a day-use park, very popular for fishing, leisurely boating, and, especially picnicking. It's not unusual to find eight to ten family reunions underway on any given summer weekend.

Picnic Area 1 is located among some large trees on a hillside overlooking the lake and beach next to the campground. A large open picnic shelter is provided high on the hill, a smaller shelter is available as well. Picnic Area 2 is located on Laurel Point above the old Jefferson Furnace with a combination of open to well-shaded sites. Both sites have vault toilets.

Winter Activities: Sledding and ice skating are available here when the weather permits. The park offers a well-maintained area for ice skating just south of the causeway.

Nearby Attractions: Jackson Lake is well-situated for visiting other nearby sites of interest including the Buckeye Iron Furnace State Memorial where the Ohio Historical Society restored a furnace and appropriate buildings. Buckeye Furnace is north of Jackson Lake off SR124. Off US-35 is the Leo Petroglyph State Memorial, a 12 acre site with over forty well-preserved prehistoric carvings in sandstone. Also nearby is Bob Evans Farms about 12 miles east of the park on US-35.

The 4,300-acre Cooper Hollow Wildlife Area is approximately six miles east of the park.

Jefferson Lake State Park Dam.

33 Jefferson Lake State Park

Land: 906 acres Water: 20 acres

Located in the foothills of the Appalachian Mountains is Jefferson Lake, a lightly used but rugged gem in the state park system. Just driving to the park is a scenic experience as you pass rolling farms and hillside fields, enjoy expanded views of the surrounding countryside from the edge of a ridge and catch a glimpse of wooded hollows and ravines. Then the county road begins its steep descent to the park and you end up on the edge of 20-acre lake whose shoreline is composed of steep forested hills and ridges.

The lake was a National Park Service project during the Great Depression when the Civilian Conservation Corps dammed the Town Fork of the Yellow Creek in 1934. In the middle of these rugged hills of oak and hickory a lake was formed and eventually was turned over to the Division of Parks in 1950 to be administered as a state park.

Jefferson Lake draws only 80,000 to 90,000 visitors a year making picnicking one of its most attractive features. Others like its spacious campground that always seems to have an open site, even on Saturday afternoons.

Information & Activities

Jefferson Lake State Park
Rt. 1, P.O. Box 140
Richmond, Ohio 43944
(614) 765-4459

Directions: From US-22, west of Steubenville, depart north on SR43 and follow it 5.5 miles through the town of Richmond to C54 where the park is posted. C54 passes through the park.

Information: The office is in the north end of the park near the campground and accessed off of C54. Hours are 8 a.m. to noon and 1-5 p.m. The campground check-in station also has information on Jefferson Lake.

Campground: Expanded to its present size in 1978, the campground features 100 rustic sites on a wooded ridge above the lake. The first loop (1-53) is a mix of open and wooded sites well separated with tables, fire rings and paved spurs for recreation vehicles. The lake is not within view from your camp but in the back of the loop is a posted trail the descends directly to the bathhouse and beach. The second loop is actually on the wooded crest of the ridge and includes group sites (54-100) in a stand of oak-hickory trees. The entire campground, but especially the second loop, is a pleasant area to pitch camp and rarely fills during the summer.

Day-use Areas: The park has three separate picnic areas and two of them, along the west side of the lake and in the southwest corner of the park at the end of T219, have shelters and play equipment, tables and grills.

More tables are scattered along the lake's north shore while ball fields are located where C54 enters the park on the east side. Also along the west side of the lake is a bathhouse and small beach with a marked off swimming area.

Fishing: Jefferson Lake is 25 feet at its deepest point but most of it is less than seven feet. Largemouth bass are plentiful though lacking overall in size while others fish the impoundment for channel catfish, bluegill and redear sunfish. The lake has also been stocked with grass carp that must be released if caught.

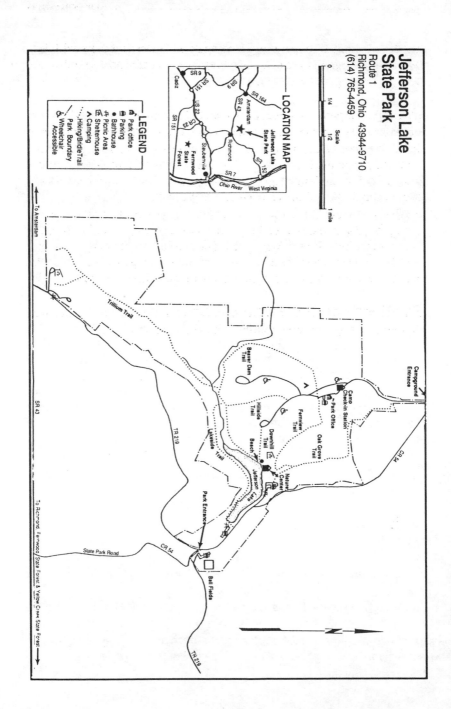

Jefferson Lake
State Park

Route 1
Richmond, Ohio 43944-9710
(614) 765-4459

LOCATION MAP

Scale
0   1/4   1/2   1 mile

LEGEND

🏠 Park office
🅿 Parking
● Bathhouse
🖾 Picnic Area
🏚 Shelterhouse
⛺ Camping
••• Hiking/Bridle Trail
—•— Park Boundary
/ Hiking/Bridle Trail
♿ Wheelchair
     Accessible

The lake is limited to non-motorized boats and electric motors with less than a 4hp rating. A paved boat launching area is located on the north shore near the parking lot for day visitors.

Hiking: The park features approximately 15 miles of foot trails that wind around the lake and over the surrounding ridges and hills. The longest route is the Lakeshore Trail, a 2-mile walk that begins with a posted path in the southern picnic area off T-219. You begin with a sharp descent into a wooded hollow and then follow the valley to Town Fork and eventually skirt the south side of the lake, ending at the dam.

Fernview Hollow Trail, somewhat shorter, is posted near site 5 of the campground and descends to the picnic area near the beach before looping back into the hills. Beaver Dam Trail is posted near site 16 of the first loop and descends to Town Fork where it heads both east to emerge at the bathhouse and west to form a junction with the Lakeshore Trail.

Facilities for the Handicapped: Jefferson has barrier-free facilities in its picnic area, campground and park office.

Rustic camping only at John Bryan.

34   *John Bryan State Park*

Land: 750 acres

John Bryan State Park's history is "written in the rocks" of the Little Miami River gorge. The gorge drops 130 feet through layers of bedrock, each telling a story of the times. Springs feed small waterfalls and cascades are common, while erosion resistant dolomite and limestone are undercut and form unusual rock formations.

John Bryan, an ambitious businessman, was responsible for the preservation of much of the area as a state reserve. In 1896, Bryan purchased 335 acres along the gorge, in 1918 he deeded the wilderness area to the state, by 1949 the state created the park in his name.

Even more impressive is the neighboring Clifton Gorge, 255-acre portion of the state park that was dedicated as a scientific and interpretive nature preserve. This is one of Ohio's most unusual natural areas featuring a wonderful opportunity to study geology, and a place of considerable plant and animal diversity. Only a portion of the preserve is open to the public, but the overlooks are terrific. The gorge is located on the east end of the state park, information is available at the park headquarters.

Information & Activities

John Bryan State Park
3790 St. Rt. 370
Yellow Springs, Ohio 45387
(513)767-1274

Directions: South of Springfield about 10 miles, depart US-68 at 343 and travel east to 370, then south to the park entrance. The park is three miles southeast of Yellow Springs, Ohio.

Information: The park headquarters is located before the campground in a small brown building bordered by a stone wall on the right side of the road. Open by chance due to the small staff, there is usually a ranger available from 8 a.m. - 5 p.m.

Campground: John Bryan has 100 rustic sites nestled under a canopy of mature trees. The rolling campground has no camp site numbers so campers may set-up more leisurely, usually around fire pits and picnic tables. No showers and vault toilets, but maybe one of the most pleasant of the smaller older Ohio state parks. A great family camping park offering playfields, newer play equipment, open spaces, and quiet.

Mostly tent campers and small RVs use John Bryan. All camping is by self-registration and the park is rarely filled, except for holiday weekends. John Bryan is one of the last to fill up in the region, often getting overflow from the more modern and higher energy campgrounds. There is a small dump station connected to the one vault restroom.

Fishing/Boating: There is no lake at John Bryan, but the Little Miami River does meander through the park. Campers often try their luck angling for smallmouth bass and panfish.

Hiking: With ten trails totalling ten miles of hiking, John Bryan trails connect to the impressive gorge-side trails of the neighboring Clifton Gorge State Nature Preserve. Inside the state park the trails range in length from the 0.3-mile long Popular Trail to the easy walking 1.2 miles Arboretum Trail

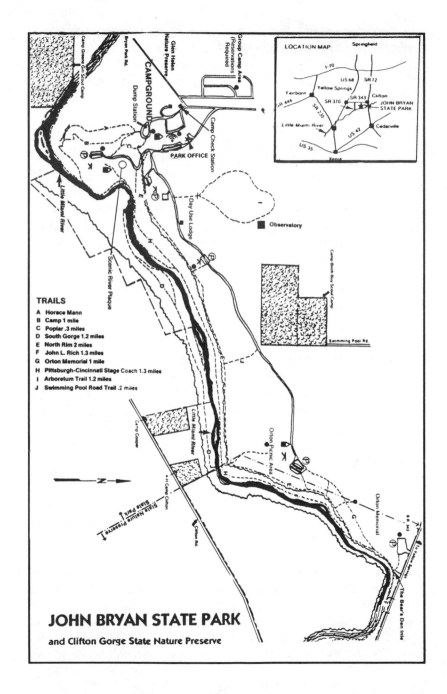

TRAILS

A Horace Mann
B Camp 1 mile
C Poplar .3 miles
D South Gorge 1.2 miles
E North Rim 2 miles
F John L. Rich 1.3 miles
G Orton Memorial 1 mile
H Pittsburgh-Cincinnati Stage Coach 1.3 miles
I Arboretum Trail 1.2 miles
J Swimming Pool Road Trail .2 miles

JOHN BRYAN STATE PARK

and Clifton Gorge State Nature Preserve

Three trails leading from the campground area will take you over to the Clifton Gorge. Follow either the North Rim Trail(two-miles), South Gorge Trail (1.3-miles), or the Pittsburg-Cincinnati Stage Coach Trail (1.3) miles. The trails are moderate in difficulty passing through wooded areas and a great spring wildflower area.

West of John Bryan is the Glen Helen Nature Preserve, operated by Antioch University. This natural area, bordering the state park also offers 12 miles of hiking trails (tel. 513-767-7375). A covered bridge, swinging bridge, mills, and more are in the area.

The Buckeye Trail, totally over 1200 miles in length, passes the park at the western edge, offering biking and hiking on a well-marked trail system. The Buckeye Trail wanders through the small pleasant college town, Yellow Springs, only two miles from the park entrance.

Day-use Areas: Two picnic shelters, plenty of tables and grills, play equipment, and a popular riverbank area makes John Bryan a delightful, but under-used park.

Nature Notes: The habitat diversity of this region is impressive and one of the best areas in the state for nature study and observation. More than 105 species of trees and shrubs, 343 species of wildflowers, 16 ferns and allies, plus plentiful numbers of songbirds including warblers, flycatchers, and many woodpeckers inhabit the mature forests.

Reptiles and amphibians in the region are well represented but seldom observed by the visitor. Reptiles are represented by five species of turtles, ten species of snakes, while amphibians include eight species of salamander and seven species of frogs and toads. Most notable are the Butlers garter snake and the long-tail salamander sometimes seen in the Clifton Gorge area.

Mammals of the area include the common ground dwellers, with lesser seen species including mink, weasel, skunk, short-tailed shrew, red fox, and small rodents.

A variety of interpretive programs are offered by the Clifton Gorge State Nature Preserve including hikes of two hours, and themed presentations.

35 Kelleys Island State Park

Land: 661 acres Water: Lake Erie

During the Pleistocene Ice Age, glaciers crossed Canada and pushed their way south into the United States. At one point they almost reached the Ohio River in the Cincinnati region but nowhere in Ohio is the glaciers' presence more dramatic than at Kelleys Island State Park.

The island's limestone bedrock was deeply gouged by the Wisconsinan, the last glacier that retreated 12,000 years ago and a massive sheet of ice, more than a mile thick at times. The advancing ice sculptured long, rounded grooves in the rock that have long since become renown among geologists and tourists alike as the Glacial Grooves of Kelleys Island.

In the 19th century, some grooves were more than 2,000 feet long. But most of these "great grooves" were lost to a limestone quarry operation that reached its peak in 1918. What was left was a mere 35 feet of grooves until

1971 when geologists conducted a test dig into the surrounding hillside of glacial tilt. They discovered the glacial footprints continued into the soil and a full excavation the following year exposed a set 396 feet long, 25 to 30 feet wide and 15 feet deep.

Some geologists believe these are largest and most extensive set in the country. Others say due to the location and ease of accessibility, the Kelleys Island grooves are surely the most famous in the world. The state park also features a lakeshore campground, beach, boat launch and hiking trails but no doubt the majority of its 120,000 annual visitors arrive to see the Glacial Grooves and to study the tracks of their geological past.

Information & Activities

Kelleys Island State Park
Kelleys Island, Ohio 43438
(419) 746-2546

Directions: Kelleys Island is the largest American island in Lake Erie and located due north of Sandusky. Three ferry companies provide transportation from the mainland to the island from April through November. Neuman Boat Line (tel. 419-798-5800) departs from its Frances Street dock in Marblehead with hourly and half-hour service. Kelleys Island Boat Lines (tel. 419-798-9763) has the largest auto/passenger ferries and departs from both a dock at Marblehead and Sandusky. Sandusky Boat Line (tel. 800-426-6286) provides service from Sandusky as well as an inter-island service between Put-in-Bay and Kelleys Island.

You can bring your car to the island or rent bicycles or golf carts once you arrive. From the downtown area of Kelleys Island head north on Division Street which ends on the state park on the north shore.

Information: A park office is located in the campground and doubles up as the check-in station for campers. It's open daily during the summer. During the off-season call Catawba Island State Park at (419)797-4530. For

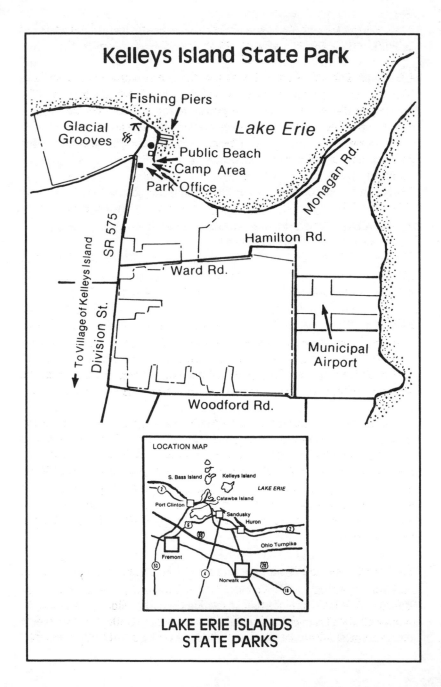

Kelleys Island State Park

Fishing Piers

Glacial Grooves

Lake Erie

Public Beach

Camp Area

Park Office

Monagan Rd.

SR 575

To Village of Kelleys Island

Division St.

Hamilton Rd.

Ward Rd.

Municipal Airport

Woodford Rd.

LOCATION MAP

S. Bass Island

Kelleys Island

LAKE ERIE

Catawba Island

Port Clinton

Sandusky

Huron

Ohio Turnpike

Fremont

Norwalk

LAKE ERIE ISLANDS STATE PARKS

more information on the hotels, bicycle rentals and other island facilities call the Kelleys Island Chamber of Commerce at (419) 746-2360.

Campground: Kelleys Island has 129 sites overlooking Lake Erie. Sites 112 to 129 are for tents only and located in a lightly shaded area. The majority of the rest are in an open grassy setting and 15 sites are situated on the edge of the lake for a spectacular view of the lake. There are 17 pet camp sites while in the middle of the campground are showers, restrooms, play equipment and a picnic shelter.

The campground fills up most weekends from Memorial Day to Labor Day either by Friday evening or Saturday morning. Signs are posted at all mainland ferry docks when the campground is filled.

Day-use Areas: Near the campground is a small sandy beach with changing booths and latrines. The park also has picnic tables and grills scattered in the campground and near the boat launch.

Hiking: There are more than five miles of foot trails on Kelleys Island. Departing from near the quarry is the North Shore Trail, a 1.5-mile loop with 10 interpretive posts that correspond to a brochure available at the park office. The trail passes the remains of the quarry operation as well as the shoreline where you can enjoy views of other Lake Erie islands.

The majority of the park, more than 500 acres, is located in the middle of the island between Ward, Monagan and Woodford roads. In the middle is East Quarry and most of the park's trail system. Trailheads are located on every road but a numbered interpretive route begins at the Ward Road trailhead across from the 4-H camp. The east end of the quarry is scenic Horseshoe Lake while the rest is a rocky, moonscape terrain that is a haven for fossil hunters. A brochure to the East Quarry Trail is also available at the park office.

Fishing: The park has a two-ramp boat launch with a loading dock and additional parking for vehicles and trailers but no slips for overnighting. The launch is located in a small bay protected on one side by an L-shaped breakwall that has been paved for shore anglers. Kelleys Island offers anglers opportunities for perch, smallmouth bass and walleye in Lake Erie (see South Bass Island State Park). If the Great Lake is too rough, try Horseshoe Lake in East Quarry. Anglers catch smallmouth bass, often in the two to three-pound range, as well as several species of sunfish.

Biking: Like South Bass Island, Kelleys Island has a limited amount of paved road that is ideal for short biking adventures. Bicycles can be rented in town at a number of liveries. Two especially scenic stretches are West Lakeshore form downtown to the State Park and the north end of Monagan Road.

Nature Notes: Located across from the campground is the Glacial Grooves State Memorial, where you will find the grooves preserved in a fenced area. A short interpretive path leads around the area and features six stops that correspond to a brochure available at the park office.

Nearby is North Quarry, which like East Quarry, attracts fossil hunters who search the limestone for 18 different types of fossils, including corals, brachiopods, gastropods and pelecypods. You can see several types of fossils from the "D" post on the Glacial Grooves walk but if you want to collect fossils from the floor of the abandoned quarry you need a permit from the Ohio Division of Parks.

Located in the downtown area on East Lakeshore Road and separate from the rest of the park is Inscription Rock. Between 300 and 400 years ago pre-historical Indians carved numerous pictographs on the large limestone rock that were discovered by Army Captain Seth Eastman in 1850. Eastman carefully measured and copied the stone drawings and today there is an accurate relief of them at the monument even through the original cravings have been nearly obliterated by natural elements.

Kiser Lake State Park

36 *Kiser Lake State Park*

Land: 474 acres   Water: 396 acres

"Kiser Lake was only a dream in 1932, but an exciting one to the residents of Champaign County," says the brochure. Today, the small stream that is known as "Mosquito Creek," is a busy recreational area that draws visitors from around the state and Midwest.

Hundreds of proud workers from the WPA and CCC cleared the land which was to become the lake bottom. Unlike most dams in the state, the Corps of Engineers didn't build this one. In fact, the former State Highway Department constructed the dam, altered the roadways, and installed the spillways in the late 1930s. The 2.5 mile long lake is named after John W. Kiser, who donated much of the land used to develop the state park.

Although an old park in Ohio's system, Kiser is one of the cleanest and best designed. A shiny new park office building, carefully maintained buildings, boats, and amenities, makes Kiser Lake State Park a busy facility year-round.

Information & Activities

Kiser Lake State Park
P.O. Box 55
Rosewood, Ohio 43070-0055
(513)362-3822

Directions: North and somewhat east of Dayton about 50 miles, from I-75 depart at US-36 and go east to SR 235, go north to park entrance located at the northeast end of the lake.

Information: The park headquarters is just east of SR235, open Monday - Friday, 8 a.m. - 5 p.m. The campground office is open Noon to 8 p.m. during summer months.

Camping: Kiser Lake has a 115 site Class B family camping area that is open year-round. Picnic tables, fire rings, a trailer waste station, and latrines are provided. A group camping area is also available by advanced registration located on the south side of the lake. The main campground is located at the east end of the lake convenient to two hiking trails, fishing access and pier, concession stand and beach.

Site numbers 78 and 79 are walk-in camping areas about 50 yards back into a heavily wooded and secluded area. The playground is near site 90. Sites 90-106 are fairly shady, but are small. Campsites 111, 112, 113, 115 are on the water. There are two Rent-A-Camps at Kiser Lake.

The preferred sites are 60-90, sites 20-39 are very open with little shade. There is no electricity or water at any of Kiser's camp sites. Pet owners may report their pet and be assigned sites 1-10 only. Usually full on holiday weekends, the camp rarely fills up on normal summer weekends.

Boating: The boat concession next to the park office has a dozen or more 14-foot aluminum boats for rent. Although two launch ramps are operated, one near the campground and the other near the park office, motors are not permitted. Sailing is popular at Kiser Lake, many small sailboats glide the lake that has over five miles of shoreline.

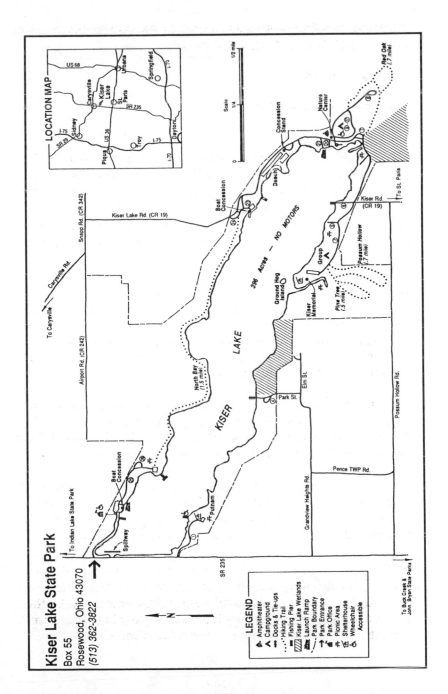

Kiser Lake State Park

Box 55
Rosewood, Ohio 43070
(513) 362-3822

LEGEND

⚘	Amphitheater
⋀	Campground
⟋⟍⟋	Docks & Tie-ups
	Fishing Trail
	Hiking Trail
▨	Kiser Lake Wetlands
⊏	Launch Ramp
	Park Boundary
↑	Park Entrance
⌖	Park Office
⚏	Picnic Area
⌂	Shelterhouse
⟁	Wheelchair Accessible

LOCATION MAP

396 Acres — NO MOTORS

KISER LAKE

Fishing: A fishing map showing depths, the streambed locations, structures, and other useful information is available from the park or campground office. The quiet retreat-like lake offers excellent shoreline panfishing. Anglers line the shore from the park entrance past the fishing pier to the east. Small poppers, plastic lures, and live baits under a bobber, especially in the evening, are killers on pan and sunfish.

During the spring, bass anglers can use topwater crank and spinner baits with success around the stumps. Small jigs tipped with some form of live bait will help anglers fill their creel with bluegill, crappies or walleye. Many channel catfish are taken on chicken liver and other stink baits. The lake is quite clear, even during the spring. Try the north shore area!

Hiking: Five hiking trails are located at the park providing 4.5 miles of walking and wildlife observation opportunities. Red Oak (0.7 mile) trails are near the family camping area at the east end of the lake. At the group camping area are the Pine Tree (0.5 mile) and Possum Hollow (0.7 mile) trails. The North Bay Trail traverses the shoreline of the lake for over 1.5 miles. All of the trails are easy to moderate, following well-worn paths along lightly wooded areas, open fields, and along the rambling shoreline.

Day-Use Areas: The popular fishing pier, walking trails, and plenty of open spaces furnished with picnic spots, offer day-use visitors plenty of opportunity to enjoy the quiet lake. From the Putnam Picnic Shelter located off of SR235 at the southwest end to three other picnic sites located near the shoreline. The 600-foot swimming beach is open Memorial Day to Labor Day, with lifeguard on duty from 11 a.m. until dark daily. The concession stand is nearby and open daily. Scuba diving is permitted in Kiser Lake as long as you mark your diving area and dive with a buddy.

Nature Notes: Naturalists offer interpretive programs on the trails, at the wetland nature preserve, and at the tiny nature center and amphitheater located in the campground. The Kiser Lake Wetlands Preserve consists of two separate areas on the south side of the lake. The area is a remnant of a 300-acre bog, once called Mosquito Lake Bog. Both areas support interesting flora and fauna typical of bogs including, fringed gentian, shrubby cinquefoil, and other plants found in wet prairies, like queen-of-the-prairie. Ask at the office about use of the preserve.

Lush woodlands, wetlands, rolling hills, and natural areas at Lake Alma.

37   Lake Alma State Park

Land: 323 acres   Water: 60 acres

Ohio State Parks have flourished along the shores of lakes created for flood control, for community drinking water, for maintaining water levels in the old canals, and simply for water recreation.

Lake Alma is a breed apart. The 60 acre lake was created in 1903 when C.K. Davis, a wealthy local resident, dammed Little Raccoon Creek, named the resulting lake in honor of his wife, and opened the area as an amusement park.

The seven-acre island now reached by a footbridge alongside SR349 was once home to a large dance pavilion, concession stand, outdoor theater, a merry-go-round and other amusements. The merriment didn't last long, by 1910 the amusement park had faded. Today, virtually all signs of the old amusement park has disappeared and nature has reclaimed the island. The island's shores are kept open and are very popular for walkers and fisherman.

In 1926, Lake Alma stepped back into a more traditional role when the City of Wellston purchased it as a reserve water supply. Soon after, it was leased to the Ohio Department of Conservation and then passed to the Division of Parks when it was created.

Although Lake Alma is smaller than most state parks, it has proven to be very popular both as a day-use park for nearby towns and for overnight use.

Information and Activities

Lake Alma State Park
Rte. 1, Box 422
Wellston, Ohio 45692
(614) 384-4474

Directions: Follow US-93 to Wellston, then two miles north on SR349 to the park.

Campground: A pretty campground up several ravines that open up on the lake. Sixty sites, all with electricity, heavily shaded with sycamores, maples, and oaks, but many sites are grassy. Pets are permitted on sites 28-41, a campground spur up a narrow, heavily wooded ravine. Drivers with large vehicles or towing trailers should exercise caution pulling into this area. For those pet owners with a large RV, contact the park office for special arrangements. Sites 17-27 are up another ravine, sites 1-9 back up to a hillside and are very shallow. Two vault toilets service the camp-ground, no showerhouse or flush toilets.

Self-register at the information station located near site number 51---close to the first vault toilet. A playground is at the camp entrance and a dump station is located nearby.

The campground is typically three-quarters full weekends and weekdays throughout the summer, and full or nearly full on holiday weekends.

Boating: Lake Alma is restricted to electric motors only. A small launch ramp is located just beyond the second of the two swimming beaches. This ramp is greatly improved over the steep gravel ramp that it replaced.

Fishing: Lake Alma is an excellent fishing lake for largemouth bass in early spring and for crappie in spring and fall. The lake is only 15 feet at its deepest location and averages eight to nine feet. Several bass in the eight pounds-plus range have been caught in recent years on plugs. The best crappie fishing is from the pedestrian bridge to the island. Bluegill fishing is popular in summer.

The lake is choked with coontail and lilies which makes for great fish habitat but is hard on electric trolling motors. The lake has been stocked with over 300 white amur (grass carp) to bring the aquatic vegetation under control. If caught, an amur must be released unharmed.

Hiking Trails

Two trails totalling about 1.5 miles combine to provide a trail through the north, east and south sections of the park. Plans and work is underway to use an old railroad right-of-way in the west section of the park across SR349 to enable walkers to complete the circuit and minimize walking along roadsides. When completed, that new section of trail will open up a view of a great wetland area.

Old Pine Nature Trail (0.5 mi, one way) Connects the swimming beaches with the campground. Begins from the beach area and climbs steeply to a ridge through a white and red pine forest. Once on the ridge it's a nice walk along the top through a deciduous forest. The trail drops gradually back to camp.

Acorn Trail (1 mi. one-way) Climbs a hillside up and out of the campground from near site 25 and connects to the south picnic shelter. The trail travels back through a hollow and makes a gradual climb to the ridge, follows the ridge to a nice overlook of the lake and park, and then drops through a rich hollow where showy and fringed orchids, among many other wildflowers, can be seen.

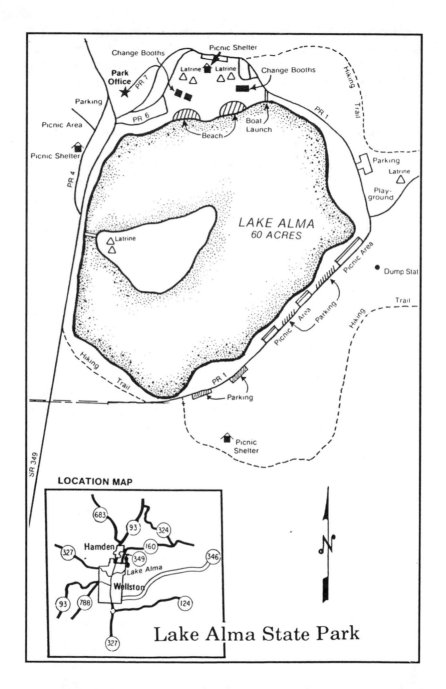

Change Booths

Picnic Shelter

Park Office

PR 7

Latrine Latrine

Change Booths

Hiking Trail

Parking

PR 6

PR 1

Picnic Area

Beach

Boat Launch

Picnic Shelter

PR 4

Parking

Latrine

Play-ground

LAKE ALMA
60 ACRES

Latrine

Picnic Area

Dump Stat

Parking

Trail

Picnic Area

Parking

Hiking

Hiking

Trail

PR 1

Parking

Picnic Shelter

SR 349

LOCATION MAP

683

93

324

327

Hamden

160

349

346

Lake Alma

Wellston

93

788

124

327

N

Lake Alma State Park

Jogging/Bikeway (1.0 mi. loop) A level paved path along the section of park roadway designated for one-way traffic. The trail begins at the Pine Hill Shelter near the swimming beaches and follows a separate lane on the left-hand side of the roadway around to SR349 where trail users can either turn back or follow SR349 to the park entrance.

Day-use Areas: Summertime is swimming and picnicking time at Lake Alma. Picnic areas are well-spaced along the lakeshore. The best of these, for those who like picnicking on the water, are three relatively small sites, each with several tables and grills, on the southeast shore of the lake. Just down and across the road from these areas is a large picnic area set in an ash woods with a large open shelter and vault toilets. Across SR349 from the main entrance to the park is a larger more open picnic area and shelter below the dam where picnic sites are scattered among large sycamores. Yet another small shelter and table sites are set in a pine plantation on a hillside above the swimming beaches.

Two small swimming beaches, the first about 100 yards long and the second somewhat smaller, are located just inside the main park entrance. There is a lifeguard on duty at the first beach on Friday, Saturday and Sunday through the summer.

Nature Notes: Movies are shown in the campground at the VIP campsite every Friday and Saturday evening, Memorial Day through Labor Day. An amphitheater is in the park's future plans.

Lake Hopes gentle waters are great for family activities.

38   Lake Hope State Park

Land: 3,103 acres   Water: 120 acres

People and lightning are drawn to Lake Hope. It takes more than its share of lightning strikes presumably because of the high iron content in the sandstone hills. Why people come requires more explanation.

They come because of its great natural beauty on what geologists call the maturely dissected Allegheny Plateau. Translated that means millions of years ago Lake Hope was a plateau but streams have cut extensive valleys creating the hill country of today. People come to backpack and walk the trails that follow these rugged contours, and they like its accommodations -- no park in the state has more or better or more unique cabins. They come to fish, canoe, hunt, swim, observe wildlife, to see the Hope Furnace, and because it's a nice place to bring the family.

Actually, it's a perfect place to bring the family. It's quiet and secluded, no big boats roar on the lake, it's easy for kids to pull in some fish, and it's an excellent natural and scenic park.

There's some history there, too. Hope Furnace is in the heart of the Hanging Rock Iron Region which in the 1800s supplied much of the nation's iron needs. In 1853, sandstone was cut from a nearby hillside to form the furnace's outer shell. It was built below a hillside so the top of the furnace was at the same level as the sheds storing the charcoal, iron ore and limestone. At the base of the furnace was the casting shed where the iron was drawn off into molds. In its heyday Hope Furnace produced about 15 tons of iron each day and its hunger for charcoal to fuel the hearth decimated the surrounding 4,000 acres of virgin timber. As you look at the furnace today, the now-collapsed opening in the front was the hearth and the smaller opening on the left-hand side was the air blast.

Though poor for agriculture, the Lake Hope area was rich in natural resources. Thousands of acres of big timber provided fuel for industry. The surrounding hills contain large deposits of iron ore, coal, clay, and sandstone for building stone along with enough oil and natural gas to merit drilling. Indians once quarried the tough Zaleski black flint that crops out northwest of the lake and cherished it for the projectile points which are found extensively throughout the region. Another of the local flints which was too porous for projectile points but perfect for dressing into millstones was the basis for the first Lake Hope area business back in the early 1800s.

Lake Hope itself lies serenely in the valley where Sandy Run flowed through the Washington Keeton farm. The Keeton Cemetery near the sleeping cabins and the pioneer cemetery on Olds Hollow Nature Trail are reminders of those who have wandered these hills before us.

Today, one of the most industrious area residents is the beaver who occasionally leaves his mark by flooding SR278. SR278, by the way, is a beautiful drive to the park, winding through beautiful countryside, and in its last miles approaching the park from the north, following the deep-cut valley of pre-glacial Zaleski Creek, a route now followed by the picturesque Sandy Run.

Information and Activities

Lake Hope State Park
Zaleski, Ohio 45698
(614)596-5253

Directions : US-33 to Nelsonville, south on SR278 13 miles to park. From the west try US-35 or US-23 to Chillicothe, then US-50 east to SR278.

Information: The park reservation office is located in the dining lodge located at the end of the Lodge/Cabins entrance drive. The park headquarters is located on SR278 between the lodge entrance and the beach entrance.

Campground: All 223 campsites are located on Park Road 17 just north of the Hope Furnace. The road climbs up and away from SR278 to the wooded ridge where the camp is stretched along the road with several spurs as well. Two showerhouses provide only vault toilets. A laundry is available near the northwest end of the camp. Forty-six sites are equipped with electric hook-ups. The camp is excellent for tent camping with only a few sites capable of accommodating the larger RVs. Three Rent-A-Camps and two camper cabins are available.

Sites 43-45 are very secluded tent sites down the hill form the road in deep foliage, sites 53-54 are popular because of their proximity to the play area, and 61-67 are down a hill and are the most popular pet areas. Pets are also permitted on 27-37. Sites 81-85, 88-96, and 98-104 are the most popular sites with electric hook-ups as they are close to a showerhouse and the laundry. Site 105 lacks a hook-up but is nicely isolated at a showerhouse. Sites 178-184 are in a flat area that's excellent for setting up several tents, good for groups and family reunions.

Up to 100 people can be accommodated in the Group Camp at the end of Park Road 20 west of the lake.

Some camp supplies are available at the beach concession, others in stores south of the park on SR278.

Cabins: Sixty-nine cabins are available at Lake Hope, the most in the park system. More than just the number, though, is the uniqueness of the sleeping cabins located at the Lake Hope Lodge. There's nothing else quite like them. Situated on a heavily forested ridge that drops to Lake Hope on one side and to the deep shade of ravines on the other, the 23 sleeping cabins range in size from one to four bedrooms. Each has a beautiful stone fireplace, central heat, small kitchen (no utensils provided), living/dining area, and bath with shower. Ask for them by name: Buckeye, Black Oak, Basswood -- they're named after the locally milled wood that was used to finish the interior. These cabins, built back in the late 1940's, are the only fireplace-equipped cabins open year-round other than the new cabins at Maumee Bay State Park. These are the most popular cabins in the park, and can be rented on a daily basis, year-round. Other cabins may only be rented by the week in the summer season. No firewood is supplied.

Twenty-five modern year-round family cabins are provided along with 21 standard cabins. Eighteen family cabins are located near the dining lodge, the other seven up the Beach Entrance road near Oak Point Picnic Area. Twenty-one standard cabins, open from mid-April though October, are also located on the Beach Entrance road and have the advantage of being closest to the boat concession and beach. The sleeping cabins, built in mid 1930's and named after area iron furnaces, have fireplace heat only but are otherwise well-equipped. Kitchens have utensils and dishes, living/dining areas are separated either by curtain divider or wall.

The rustic Laurel Lodge is also a one-of-a-kind facility, a group lodge with eight sleeping rooms and bedspace for 22 people. Large kitchen and sitting/ dining area with massive stone fireplace. Located near the dining lodge. The lodge is in great demand, be sure to call early for reservations. Reservations are accepted 12 months in advance.

Dining Lodge: The Stone Terrace Restaurant reopened in 1991 and should be a required stop on any Lake Hope visit. Located in the Lake Hope Lodge, the sandstone-walled interior, fireplace, and oak furnishings create a perfect atmosphere for dining and quiet conversation. Not only that, the food's excellent -- it's a favorite with local residents -- and reasonably priced as well. Open weekends year-round, weekday schedule varies with the seasons. Call (614) 596-4117 for reservations.

The Sycamore Room located on ground level of the dining lodge can seat up to 100 people. You can reserve its use through the Stone Terrace Restaurant.

Boating: Only electric motors up to 3hp are allowed on Lake Hope, a restriction which keeps the lake quiet and preserves the wild feeling of this park. A boat launch is located off SR278 near the beach entrance road.

Canoes, rowboats, electric motorboats, and pedalboats are all available for rent by the hour or day at the Lake Hope beach concession, as is bait and tackle, ice, camping supplies and a variety of food and refreshments. The concession is open daily from 8 a.m. until sunset, May through September, and as demand warrants through November.

Fishing: The water quality has improved steadily in Lake Hope since the Big Four Hollow Project sealed off the iron and sulfur contaminants draining from some area coal mines. With the improved water has come better fishing. Some 20-plus pound catfish, several eight pound largemouth bass, and a bunch of crappie and bluegill have come out of the lake. Most of the locals like to use minnows or purple plastic night crawlers, fishing the banks and the hollows for bass. Nightcrawlers and chicken liver for catfish. The upper lake is loaded with weed and lily beds.

Hiking/Bridle Trails: Thirteen miles of trails in the park range from a one-quarter mile stroll to four miles. People come from all over the U.S. to hike the challenging 23.5 mile backpack trail in the adjacent Zaleski State Forest.

Olds Hollow Trail (1.5 mi. loop) is the best trail for diversity. It begins across SR278 from Hope Furnace, crosses a bridge into a deciduous woods that includes a musclewood grove, up an incline and into a pine plantation, opens into a pioneer cemetery that is all that remains of the town of Hope, then drops to Olds Hollow Cave (actually a sandstone overhang), and swings on a boardwalk across a marsh that includes bald cypress knees. It's a moderate trail with a good chance of seeing beaver near the beaver dam and lodge.

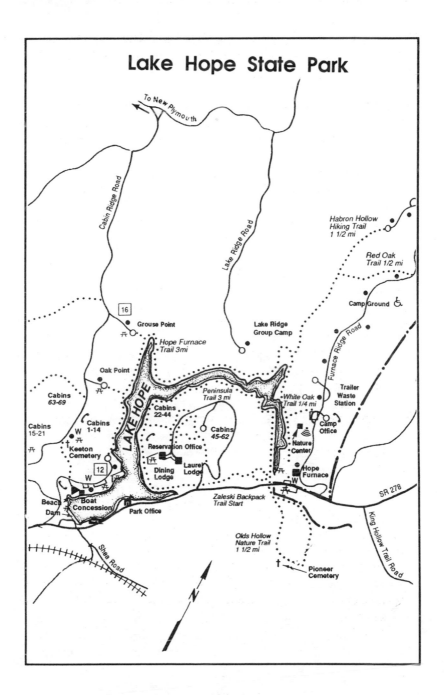

Lake Hope State Park

To New Plymouth

Cabin Ridge Road

Lake Ridge Road

Habron Hollow
Hiking Trail
1 1/2 mi

Red Oak
Trail 1/2 mi

Camp Ground

16

Grouse Point

Hope Furnace
Trail 3mi

Lake Ridge
Group Camp

Furnace Ridge Road

Oak Point

LAKE HOPE

Cabins
63-69

Peninsula
Trail 3 mi

White Oak
Trail 1/4 mi

Trailer
Waste
Station

Cabins
15-21

Cabins
1-14

Cabins
22-44

Cabins
45-62

Camp
Office

Keeton
Cemetery

Reservation Office

Nature
Center

12

Dining
Lodge

Laurel
Lodge

Hope
Furnace

Beach
Dam

Boat
Concession

Park Office

Zaleski Backpack
Trail Start

SR 278

Shea Road

Olds Hollow
Nature Trail
1 1/2 mi

King Hollow Trail Road

Pioneer
Cemetery

N

Hope Furnace Trail (3.5 mi. one-way) connects Hope Furnace with the main picnic shelter near the beach. It's a very well-maintained moderate trail that skirts the outside of Lake Hope, similar to the Peninsula Trail except it has bridges over areas of intermittent water. On this and the Peninsula Trail watch for Eastern hemlocks, the easily recognized gray-white bark of the stands of white oak, and for beaver and signs of beaver activity.

Peninsula Trail (3.0 mi. loop) along the inside of the lake with access at the cabin area below the lodge and at the lodge entrance. Some fishermen like to use this moderate trail for access to the lake. May require walking through intermittent streams.

Little Sandy Trail (2 mi. one-way) connects SR278, where trail parking is provided, with the family cabins area and with Grouse Point Picnic Area on the west side of the lake. Even a short walk up this trail can be rewarding, a beaver dam can be seen right at the road, and successive dams can be seen stair-stepping back up the hillside. As you proceed further up the trail it enters some excellent grouse and wild turkey habitat.

Hebron Hollow Trail (1.5 mi. one-way), the **Red Oak Trail** (0.5 mi. one-way) which connects to it, and the **White Oak Trail** (0.25 mi. one-way) are connectors between the camp area and the lake. Hebron Hollow follows an intermittent stream from the northernmost section of camp. **Buckeye Nature Trail** (0.5 mi. loop) begins at the service center on Park Road 15 just off SR278.

Zaleski Backpack Trail (23.5 mi. loop) begins at Hope Furnace on SR278 and follows a route mostly in the adjacent 25,000 acre Zaleski State Forest. There are two major inclines on the way to the first camp (1.8 miles in) but the rest of the trail mostly follows ridges. Most people tackle it as a weekend trail, starting in the afternoon and hiking to the first camp. A 9.9 mile loop is a great option for an all-day hike.

Day Use Areas: The beach area with its swimming area, docks, boat rentals concession, and large picnic area is the focal point for day-use facilities. Lifeguards are on duty at the 600 foot beach just above the dam. Two picnic shelters, one above the boat rental, are open to the public. Drinking water and vault toilets are available there and at all picnic areas.

Also located on the Beach entrance road (Park Road 9) is the Keeton Cemetery Picnic Area which is a small picnic area near a township cemetery with markers going back to the Civil War. Oak Point Picnic Area, and Grouse Point Picnic Area are an overgrown scenic overlook. A small picnic area is also provided at Hope Furnace.

Bridle trails are available in Zaleski State Forest. Private horse liveries are available in the area, call (800)221-1122 or (614)385-8361.

Nature Notes: Lake Hope is an excellent natural area blessed with abundant and varied flora and fauna, including some rare species. The woodland wildflowers of spring are outstanding, as are the fall colors in October.

A widely varied offering of nature walks and programs is offered through the summer, including Friday and Saturday evening campfire programs in the campground amphitheater.

Hunting: There's no hunting in Lake Hope State Park but the surrounding Zaleski State Forest is widely considered to be the best place to hunt wild turkey in Ohio. Squirrel, grouse and whitetail deer hunting is also very good.

39   Lake Logan State Park

Land: 300 acres   Water: 417 acres

Lake Logan is the park most people know only as the dam spillway on SR664 that they pass on the way to Hocking Hills State Park. But there's a lot more to Lake Logan than that.

To be sure, Lake Logan is a far cry from the wilderness-type setting of the larger hill-country parks. Except for the upper end of the lake, it has the look of a resort lake, with cabins and homes crowding much of its shoreline, swimmers splashing at the beach, and pontoon boats plying the waters. But it lacks the bustle and roar of big ski and bass boats. It's a quiet, relaxing atmosphere.

The focus here is the lake and water activities, especially fishing, swimming and boating.

When the dam was completed and the waters stocked with fish in 1955, the lake was originally known as Hocking Lake and administered by the Ohio Division of Wildlife. Jurisdiction was transferred to parks in 1964. The lake was renamed Lake Logan to prevent confusion with nearby Hocking Hills State Park and to honor the rich Indian heritage of the region.

Information and Activities

Lake Logan State Park
30443 Lake Logan Rd.
Logan, Ohio 43138
(614)385-3444

Directions: Located just off SR33 two miles west of Logan, Ohio. From the north take the SR180 exit, from the south, SR664. Off either road turn on Lake Logan Road which follows the northern shore of the lake where most park facilities are located.

Information: The park office is located above Lake Logan Rd. at the beach area.

Campground: No overnight accommodations are provided in the park. Two private campgrounds are located nearby with electric hook-ups and flush toilets but no showerhouses. Also, see Hocking Hills State Park.

Boating: A 10hp, 10 mph limit is enforced on Lake Logan, preserving a quiet atmosphere on the lake for fishing, relaxing lake cruises, and for sailboating which is popular here. Two boat launches are provided. The main launch, located off Lake Logan Road at the east end of the lake, has two ramps and a walk-out. Also at the east end of the lake is the boat rental which offers packaged snacks in addition to rentals of pontoon boats, rowboats, canoes, pedalboats, and two-person bass boats with electric motors. The second launch is a single ramp just northwest of the beach.

Fishing: Lake Logan is an excellent fishing lake known for producing record fish. The former state record largemouth bass, a nearly ten pound beauty caught in 1970, was caught here, as was the current state record saugeye, a 31-inch, 11 pound, 9.6 ounce lunker taken from the lake in February, 1992. That saugeye, at this writing, was under consideration by the International Game Fish Association as a new all-tackle world record.

The lake has good populations of bluegill, crappie, bass, muskie, catfish and northern pike. Saugeye were first stocked here in 1984 but because growth rates weren't considered satisfactory, stocking was discontinued. Saugeye stocking resumed in 1990.

There's good structure in the lake which is only 25 feet deep at most. From the dam and spillway back halfway in the lake, the drop-off from the bank is steep. From there the lake bottom levels off to the upper ends of the lake where it is very marshy at Clear Fork and Duck Creek. The lake near the main launch, off fishing piers at mid-lake and in the upper lake off Lake Logan Road are all good spots for catfish -- channel, flathead and yellow-belly catfish are all present and, this year at least, shrimp seems to be a popular bait. Saugeye fishing is very good from late February through March, plastic jig heads and minnows work best at the beginning of the season but, as the water warms, plugs that imitate minnows are favored. Crappie fishing, though best in spring, can be done year-round with minnows and bobbers over brushy structure. Bait stores are located near each boat launch.

Hiking Trails: The Pine Vista Trail (1.0 mi. loop) begins above the beach area angling up a gradual hillside with the aid of steps. The area is abandoned farmland that is reverting to natural area through succession. It also passes through a stand of red pines and provides glimpses of the lake along the way.

Walking around the lake -- the park owns a strip of land that varies in width all the way around -- is easy and popular. It's ten miles to walk the entire lake. Also, a one-mile segment of the Buckeye Trail passes through the wild areas at the western end of the park.

Day-use Areas: Picnic tables are spaced at frequent intervals all around the lake with picnic areas above the beach, in a very nice, well-manicured setting below the dam spillway, and on the south side of the lake on Blosser Road. The Blosser Road area has a narrow line of trees along

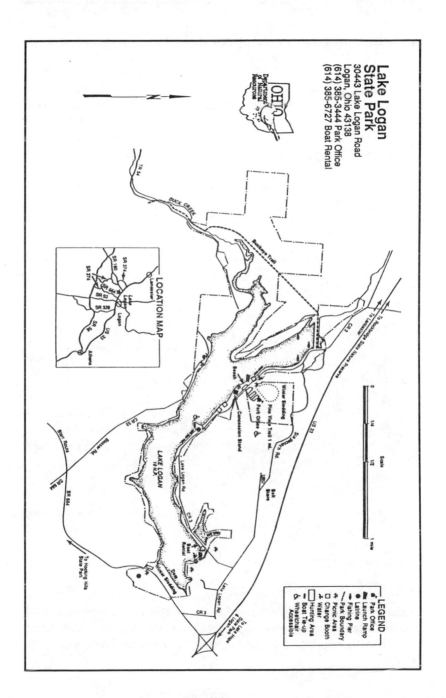

Lake Logan
State Park
30443 Lake Logan Road
Logan, Ohio 43138
(614) 385-3444 Park Office
(614) 385-6727 Boat Rental

LOCATION MAP

LAKE LOGAN
18 K.A.

LEGEND
Park Office
Launch Ramp
Latrine
Fishing Pier
Park Boundary
Picnic Area
Change Booth
Water
Hunting Area
Boat Tie-up
Wheelchair Accessible

the bank that separates picnickers from the lake and views across to the beach.

A very pleasant 500 foot sand beach is located at the lake's mid-point on Lake Logan Road. Lifeguards are on duty and a concession stand serves snack bar food and refreshments from mid-May through Labor Day.

Hunting: Hunting is permitted, in season, in the wild areas at the west end of the lake. Deer, wild turkey, ruffed grouse, and small game hunting are available. Woodcock are present in the marshy areas and there is also restricted waterfowl hunting on the upper arm of the lake at Duck Creek.

Winter Activities: Ice skating and ice fishing are popular when weather permits, as is sledding when snow is on the hills behind the park office and at the dam where, unquestionably, you can get a good head of steam going by the time you hit bottom.

Lake Logan State Park

222

Canoeing is popular along the natural-like east end of the lake.

40 Lake Loramie State Park

Land: 400 acres   Water: 1655 acres

Once a missionary, Peter Loramie came to the area in 1769 ready to preach, but quickly had to trade with and teach the Indians after being cutoff from the church. His famous trading post was burned to the ground by an over-zealous Gen. George Rogers Clark in 1792. Loramie escaped with the Indians and moved west.

In 1794, a fort was built on the site, which finally gave way to the western movement of settlers and the construction of lakes and canals to supply goods and services to the increasing population. By 1840 the Ohio canal system was completed, along with five lakes, including Lake Loramie, that were used to feed the canal system. Within a few years the canal system was replaced by other forms of faster transportation and by 1917 the state legislature decided to make Lake Loramie a state park.

Lake Loramie, the most attractive of the five lakes, was developed in 1949 by the state and lake association. The care shows!

Information & Activities

Lake Loramie State Park
11221 St. Route 362
Minster, Ohio 45856-9311
(513)295-2011

Directions: From I-75, depart at 119 and then head west on Luthmann Road, then go south to Ft. Loramie-Swanders (SR362) and turn right or west, and continue to the park entrance at the west end of the lake.

Information: The park headquarters is located on 11221 State Route 362. The office is open 8 a.m.- 5 p.m., Monday - Friday.

Campground: Lake Loramie has a total of 165 camp sites, 130 have electricity, and all sites have a paved pad. Two new showerhouses complete with flush toilets and a nearby waste station has been constructed in the middle of the Class A campground. Shaded by mature trees, Lake Loramie is often full on the weekends by Friday afternoon. Over 200 picnic tables, dozens of grills, a small nature center building, movie screen, and playground are featured.

Campsite numbers 16-36 and 96-118 are on the water, while sites numbered 55-60 and 72-77 are good tent sites near the showerhouse. The two group campgrounds require advanced registration and are designated for tents only. The group camping areas can accommodate up to 112 campers. There are three Rent-A-Camps sites.

Boating: Lake Loramie allows unlimited horsepower, but high speed boats are restricted to speed zones located at the west end of the lake at the tip of Blackberry Island. A launch ramp is located off SR 362 at Black Island, north of the park office. The Luthman Road launching ramp is located at the east end of the lake south of SR119 on Luthman Road, it has 24 parking spaces and two ramps all located near good fishing.

Canoeists enjoy the relatively quiet lake, especially the natural areas in the eastern part of the park.

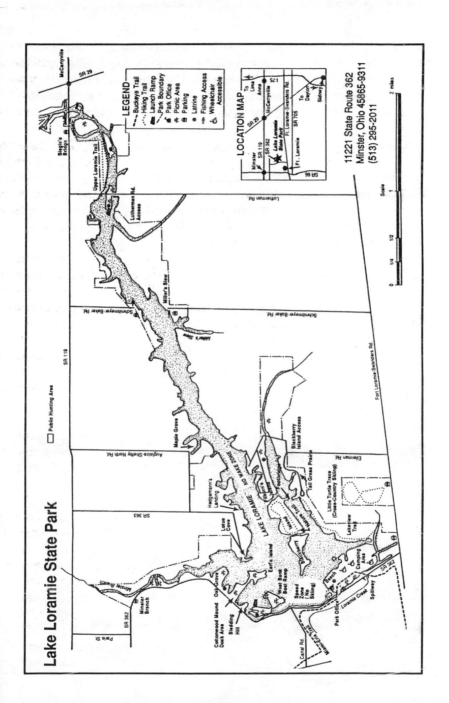

Lake Loramie State Park

LEGEND

- – – – Buckeye Trail
- .... Hiking Trail
- Launch Ramp
- Park Boundary
- Park Office
- Picnic Area
- Parking
- Latrine
- Fishing Access
- Wheelchair Accessible

LOCATION MAP

To Lima
Anna
I-75
McCartyville
Ft. Loramie-Swanders Rd.
SR 705
To Dayton
Sidney
SR 29
Minster
SR 119
SR 362
Lake Loramie State Park
Ft. Loramie
SR 66

11221 State Route 362
Minster, Ohio 45865-9311
(513) 295-2011

Scale
0   1/4   1/2   1   2 miles

☐ Public Hunting Area

SR 29
McCartyville

Siegle's Bridge

Upper Loramie Trail

Lutherman Rd. Access

Lutherman Rd.

SR 119

Schmitmeyer-Baker Rd.

Millar's Slew

Miller's Slew

Schmitmeyer-Baker Rd.

Maple Grove

Auglaize-Shelby North Rd.

Hedgemann's Landing

Lotus Cove

SR 363

Minster Branch

Oak Grove

Minster Branch

SR 362

Minster Mound Dock Area

Cottonwood Mound Dock Area

Sledding Hill

Paris St.

West Bank Boat Ramp

Earl's Island

Blackberry Trail

Island

NO WAKE ZONE

LAKE LORAMIE

Footbridge

Wilson's Island

Tall Grass Prairie

Blackberry Island Access

Little Turtle Trace (Cross-Country Skiing)

Lakeview Trail

Elsman Rd.

Fort Loramie-Swanders Rd.

Speed Zone (No Skiing)

Beach

Camping Area

Park Office

Loramie Creek

Spillway

SR 362

Canal Rd.

Fishing: Lake Loramie is a good to excellent fishing lake. The lake is shallow and occasionally hosts regional bass tournaments. Anglers should fish the brush piles along the west shoreline which has lots of cover. Bass fishing, especially springtime bass angling is very good. The professionals look for structure, using spinners, plastic worms, and crankbaits. Area tackle and bait shops have up-to-the-minute fishing reports, what's hot, and what's not.

Crappies run in the 10-14-inch range, with bluegills running 6-8-inches. Fish live bait, some small jigs and tiny spinners can also entice panfish. The many coves and small bays, combined with shallows and merging wetlands make Lake Loramie an attractive and interesting fishing lake. Anglers will enjoy the challenges and diverse habit.

Hiking: The popular Buckeye Trail/Miami and Erie Trail crosses the spillway at the east end of the park. The park's hiking network includes a two-mile hiking and cross-country ski trail. There's also a 1.5 mile trail along the lake from the main area to a 1.5 mile nature trail on Blackberry Island.

The 48-mile Miami and Erie Canal Trail, part of the Buckeye Trail, follows the old canals all the way to Delphos. Trails are flat and easy, along fields and thinly forested areas.

Lake Loramie is a gentle family-type lake.

Day-use Areas: The large "Center Playground," located in the middle of the campground is popular with youngsters. And so is the beach! The 600-foot long sandy beach is north of the camping area near the small park office. Lifeguards are on duty every weekend during the summer season. Visitors will also find over 400 picnic tables, most complete with grill and trash barrels. During the winter young and old enjoy sledding, ice fishing, ice skating, and cross-country skiing. The footbridge to Blackberry Island is a wonderful excursion for day visitors. The shallow, calm and quiet water, ample shoreline, open spaces, and wandering geese makes Lake Loramie one of the finest family campgrounds in the system.

Nature Notes: A Recycling Station for campers is an good example of the parks committment to a quality environment. A small bluebird trail, complete with nesting boxes, and the other trails offer excellent spring and summer birding. The park has also restored a prairie area in the early 1980s which is now gaining maturity. Bluestem, and a number of other prairie flora species are abundant.

On the south portion of the lake, on the north side of Blackberry Island, is an active and successful great blue heron rookery. Dozens of birds congregate annually to breed and nest in the protected area. The huge wading bird's rattling call and deep wing-beating flight can be seen and heard throughout the park. Quietly canoeing in this area during the mid-spring season can be a wonderful experience of sight and sound. Some birds also nest east of Filburns Island, but the public access is restricted.

Convenient shoreline fishing at Lake Milton State Park.

41 Lake Milton State Park

Land: 1000 acres   Water: 1685 acres

Ohio's newest state park actually has a very long history as a recreation destination. In 1910, the city of Youngstown acquired 3,416 acres in Milton Township to build a reservoir and solve its water supply needs. A 2,800-foot dam was completed three years later and formed a 1,685-acre impoundment along the Mahoning River.

Named Lake Milton, the area soon featured an amusement park at Craig Beach on the west side that included a roller coaster, boats trips and a bustling midway. On the east side of the lake there were taverns, a dance hall and a skating rink. By the 1970s the dam had structural damage and when funds for its repair couldn't be found, the gates were opened in 1986 and the lake drained.

Eventually the state legislature reconstructed the dam and in 1988 spring rains and melting snows the following years filled the impoundment. Lake

Milton was officially dedicated as Ohio's 72nd state park. Unfortunately the drought that summer left the lake with little water.

Information & Activities

Lake Milton State Park
16801 Mahoning Ave.
Lake Milton, Ohio 44429
(216) 654-4989

Directions: Lake Milton is located in Mahoning County, 15 miles west of Youngstown. From I-76, depart at Lake Milton Exit (exit 54) and head south on SR534. Follow Mahoning Avenue west as it curves to the left. Mahoning Avenue becomes SR18 and will swing past the park headquarters before crossing the lake on a causeway. On the west side turn north on Grandview Road to reach the day-use area at Craig Beach in 2 miles.

Information: The park headquarters is located on Mahoning Avenue on the east side of the lake. Hours are 8 a.m. to noon and 1-5 p.m. Monday through Friday.

Day-use Areas: Lake Milton presently has two picnic areas. The main one at Craig Beach features a wide, 600-foot sandy beach and swimming area along with changing booths, volleyball courts and showers. In a lightly shaded area overlooking the lake are tables, grills, a basketball court and play equipment. Just up Northeast Road on the east side of the lake is a second picnic area with tables, grills, play equipment and four shelters, all overlooking the lake or park marina.

Boating: The 1,685-acre lake is designated for unlimited horsepower but there are no wake zones 300 feet from the entire shore, between the bridges and where the lake narrows in the south end to re-enter Mahoning River. The park maintains two boat launches. Miller's Landing Launch is off Mahoning Avenue opposite the park headquarters on the east side of the lake. Facilities include a cement ramp and parking for vehicles and trailers. A mile north along Grandview Road, Robinson's Point Launch is reached from Jersey Street and has similar facilities.

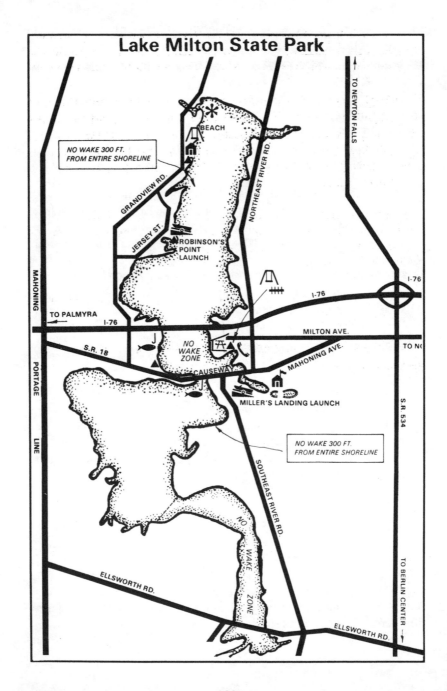

Lake Milton State Park

TO NEWTON FALLS

BEACH

NO WAKE 300 FT.
FROM ENTIRE SHORELINE

GRANDVIEW RD.

JERSEY ST.

NORTHEAST RIVER RD.

ROBINSON'S
POINT
LAUNCH

I-76

I-76

MAHONING

TO PALMYRA

I-76

MILTON AVE.

S.R. 18

NO
WAKE
ZONE

MAHONING AVE.

TO N(

CAUSEWAY

PORTAGE

MILLER'S LANDING LAUNCH

NO WAKE 300 FT.
FROM ENTIRE SHORELINE

S.R. 534

SOUTHEAST RIVER RD.

LINE

NO
WAKE
ZONE

ELLSWORTH RD.

TO BERLIN CENTER

ELLSWORTH RD.

230

The marina is located just off Northeast River Road and has 75 seasonal slips. Requests for the slips are taken during August and a lottery is held on the third Saturday of September to hand them out for the following year.

Fishing: Since the ODNR took control of the park, Lake Milton has been stocked with more than 3.2 million walleyes as well as yearling channel catfish, muskies, smallmouth bass and largemouth bass up to seven inches in length. In recent years the bass fishery has improved to the point where annual stockings were discontinued. The legal length to keep both walleyes and bass is 15 inches.

The park maintains shoreline fishing areas on both sides of the Mahoning Avenue Causeway. Here you'll find parking, vault toilets and stairways to a cement ledge just above the water where anglers often catch bass, bluegill, white bass and crappie.

Hiking: There is a quarter-mile long interpretive trail located behind the park headquarters.

Facilities for the Handicapped: Robinson's Point is a barrier-free boat launch.

Unlike most state parks, much of the shoreline at White Lake State park is privately owned.

42 Lake White State Park

Land: 21 acres   Water: 337 acres

It's worth the visit to Lake White if for no other reason than to hear the kids snicker as they pass the Pee Pee Gas signs at the SR104 turn-off from US-23, and again as they see the Pee Pee Creek signs approaching the park.

In fact, for the kids greater delight, it could be said that Lake White itself is full of Pee Pee because the lake was created during the Great Depression by damming Pee Pee Creek.

The unusual name has it's roots in the pioneer days, or so the story goes, when Peter Patrick carved his initials in a tree at the juncture of Crooked and Pee Pee Creeks below the dam. Today, souvenirs from sweatshirts to

232

coffee mugs carry the name of the creek that Peter Patrick inadvertently named.

Lake White is both literally and, in terms of how the public enjoys using it, a water park. Unlike most state park lakes where the state owns most, if not all, the shoreline, the only park-owned land at Lake White is the 21 acre site where the headquarters stands. And, though it controls the lake, the state doesn't own the land under the lake.

It is, nevertheless, a scenic spot nestled between two southern Ohio ridges dotted with lakeshore homes. Be sure to enjoy the views afforded by the shelterhouse, the headquarters balcony and from the roadways that ring the lake.

Information and Activities

Lake White State Park
Box 2767
SR 551
Waverly, Ohio
(614)947-4059

Directions: US-23 to Waverly, then two miles southwest on SR104 to SR551.

Information: Park headquarters is located on SR551 at SR104.

Campground: While Lake White has other attributes, the campground is not one of them. The 22 site campground (not 38 sites as some sources read) sits in an open mowed lowland --actually the bed of the old Ohio and Erie Canal -- along and below SR104. The nearly shadeless sites in this self-register campground are crowded around in a small, tight loop. No electric hook-ups, no paved pull-ups, no dump station. Drainage in the campground, however, was improved in 1992. No programming is provided for campers.

Unless there is a clear reason for staying at Lake White, would-be campers

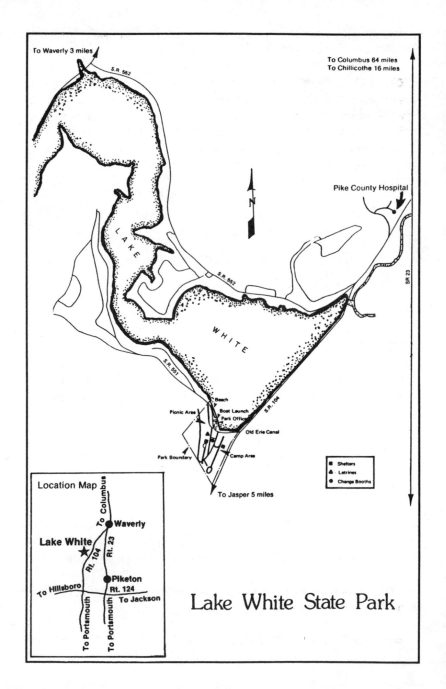

To Waverly 3 miles

S.R. 552

To Columbus 64 miles
To Chillicothe 16 miles

N

Pike County Hospital

LAKE

S.R. 552

SR 23

WHITE

S.R. 551

S.R. 104

Beach
Boat Launch
Picnic Area
Park Office
Old Erie Canal
Park Boundary
Camp Area

Shelters
Latrines
Change Booths

To Jasper 5 miles

Location Map

To Columbus

Waverly

Lake White

Rt. 104

Rt. 23

Piketon

Rt. 124

To Hillsboro

To Jackson

To Portsmouth

To Portsmouth

Lake White State Park

234

would do well to consider sites at nearby Pike Lake or at Scioto Trail State Parks, located to the north off US-23.

Boating: Lake White is an unlimited horsepower recreation lake with considerable boat traffic, both from visitors and the many residences that line the lakeshore. Waterskiing is a very popular activity evidenced by the 1/8 mile water ski slalom course located near the north end of the dam. The boat launch, located at park headquarters, is well-used and slated for improvements. Boats are prohibited in the swimming area and a no wake zone is in effect in the launch/beach area.

Fishing: In spite of the water ski traffic, Lake White is heavily fished, especially for the largemouth bass found lurking in the coves of the upper part of the lake. The lake is sporadically stocked and has yielded some nice catches of saugeye and catfish as well. Because shoreline access is limited to the park headquarters area, virtually all fishing is done from a boat.

Fuel, bait and tackle are available at a lakeside shop off SR220 while fuel and rental pontoon boats and jet skis are available at a private marina on SR552 near SR220.

Day-use Areas: Those not boating at Lake White are probably picnicking. There are some excellent sites high above the park headquarters on a terraced scenic overlook. A reservable open shelter with the best view holds 75 people. Several very nice individual sites are located on the hillside below. A larger picnic area located in the lowland adjacent to the campground has scattered grills and tables, some nice shade trees, a small playground and small open play area. Also there is a small stone and beam construction shelter.

A room on the second floor of the headquarters building opens up to a wide balcony overlooking the lake. When it's not reserved, the public is welcome to enjoy the balcony and relax on the benches provided.

Flush restrooms are available in the headquarters building, vault toilets are provided in the picnic and camp areas.

A little-used 50 foot beach is located adjacent to the headquarters.

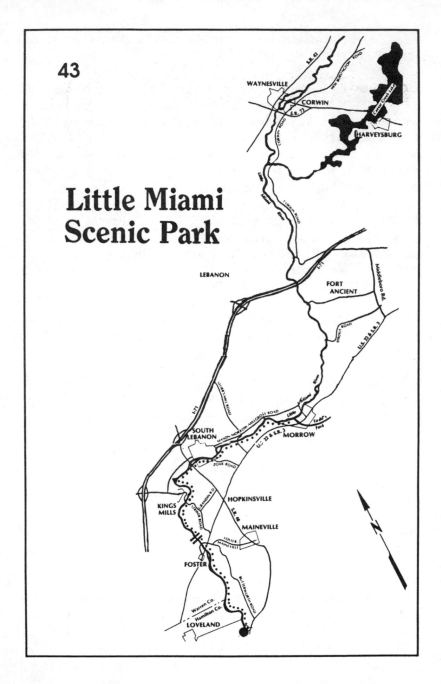

43

Little Miami Scenic Park

Shoreline fishing is popular and productive at Madison Lake State Park.

44 Madison Lake State Park

Land: 80 acres   Water: 106 acres

One of smaller state parks, Madison Lake is a tiny retreat with a quiet lake, small boat ramp, fishing (electric motor boats only), a small managed hunting areas, and plenty of picnic tables and grills.

c/o Deer Creek State Park
20635 Waterloo Road
Mt. Sterling, Ohio 43143
(614)852-2919

The day-use only park is located about five miles east of London, depart 665 at Spring Valley to park entrance.

There is no camping at Madison Lake, but pan fishermen and bass angling is considered fair to good. There has been fish habitat structure added to the lake. The 120 yard long beach has changing booths, but no lifeguard is on duty. A small boat rental is open during the summer, and the park ofice is open by chance due to the small staff.

45 Malabar Farm State Park

Land: 914 acres Water: 3 acres

Malabar Farm State Park is dedicated to more than the rolling countryside and fertile farmland that is the trademark for much of Ohio. It's a shrine to Louis Bromfield, the Pulitzer Prize winning author who was also a dedicated agriculturalist and conservationist.

Born in Mansfield, Ohio, Bromfield won a Pulitzer Prize for his novel, "Early Autumn" and went on to pen 33 books and numerous screen plays. In 1927, he moved to France but at the outbreak of World War II returned to Ohio with his wife and three children and purchased several run-down farms in Richland County's Pleasant Valley.

Bromfield raised the money to operate his farm by selling the motion picture rights to his novel, "The Rains Came" which takes place on the Malabar Coast of India. Appropriately he named his spread, Malabar Farm, and built a 32-room country home that he dubbed "The Big House." Bromfield entertained many of his Hollywood friends in his mansion, including Laureen Bacall and Humphrey Bogart, who in 1945 were married in front of the twin staircase of the Big House and honeymooned on the farm.

But Bromfield's primary interest in Malabar was not socializing but restoring the rich fertility of the fields. Developing and applying new agricultural practices to the worn-out land, Bromfield created a model farm that gained a world-wide reputation, largely through the books the author wrote on the experience. Bromfield died in 1956 and in 1972 the state of Ohio accepted the farm as a gift. It became a state park in 1976 and features not only trails, picnic areas and a rustic campground but also a variety of interpretive programs, including tours of The Big House, farm tours and sugar maple weekends.

Information & Activities

Malabar Farm State Park
4050 Bromfield Road
Lucas, Ohio 44864
(419) 892-2784

Directions: The park is located 12 miles southeast of Mansfield. From I-71, depart at exit 169 onto SR13. Just north of the interstate underpass immediately turn east onto Hanley Road. Follow Hanley for 2 miles and then turn south on Little Washington Road. Bear left onto Pleasant Valley Road and follow it for 7 miles to the posted entrance of the park at Bromfield Road.

Information: The park office is located in The Big House and is open from 8 a.m. to noon and 1-5 p.m. Monday through Friday.

Camping: Malabar Farm has a 15-site horseman camp that is available to families as well. The rustic facility has fire rings, tables, water and latrines in an open grassy area. It's located beyond The Big House and picnic area on Bromfield Road next to a classic faded barn with a *"Chew Mail Pouch Tobacco"* sign painted on the side.

Youth Hostel: Located across the farm complex is the Malabar Youth Hostel, operated by the American Youth Hostel. The home, built in 1919 from a mail order kit, is where Bromfield lived until his mansion was completed. In 1976, the hostel became the first in Ohio to open up in a state

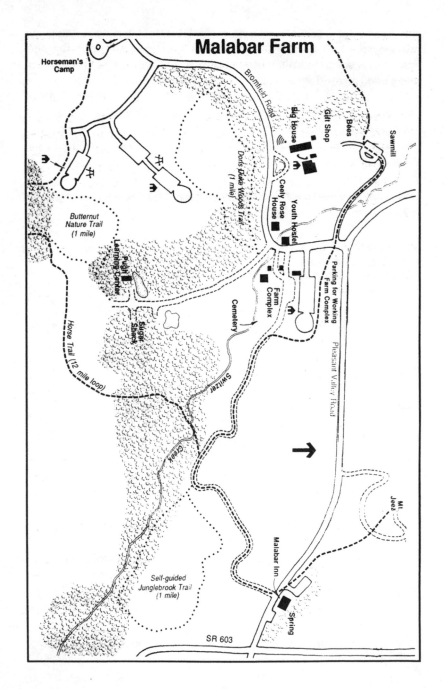

Malabar Farm

Horseman's Camp

Bromfield Road

Big House

Gift Shop

Bees

Sawmill

Doris Duke Woods Trail (1 mile)

Ceely Rose House

Youth Hostel

Butternut Nature Trail (1 mile)

Pugh Lambing Center

Parking for Working Farm Complex

Farm Complex

Cemetery

Sugar Shack

Horse Trail (12 mile loop)

Switzer

Pleasant Valley Road

Creek

Mt. Jeez

Self-guided Junglebrook Trail (1 mile)

Malabar Inn

Spring

SR 603

park. The hostel is open year-round and features 24 beds separated in male and female dormitories as well as a complete kitchen and dining area. Office hours are 7-9 a.m. and 5-9 p.m. and reservations can be made by calling (419) 892-2055.

Day-use Areas: Mt. Jeez is a spectacular high point reached from a winding dirt road off Pleasant Valley Road east of the park entrance. Upon seeing the view from the hill for the first time, Bromfield said "Jeez!" and the name stuck. From the top you are rewarded with a 360-degree panorama that includes Pleasant Hill Lake, the rugged hills of Mohican State Park and the rolling countryside of four counties. A table and trash barrel makes a picnic possible up there.

Next to the campground is a large picnic ground on a grassy hillside with vault toilets, tables, grills and a hand pump for water.

Interpretive Areas: Malabar is a working farm and the farm complex is a good spot to start any visit. The area features several barns where you can inspect the tractors and other machinery as well as a petting area with the usual chickens, calves, goats and other farm animals.

The main interpretive area of the park is The Big House, reached by immediately turning right after entering the park. The mansion is preserved as Bromfield left it in 1956 and guided tours are offered year-round for a small admission. Tours are held daily except Monday, November through April from 11 a.m. to 5 p.m. with the last one departing at 4:15 p.m. From April through October the hours are expanded from 10 a.m. to 5 p.m. Part of Bromfield's home is now a gift shop while nearby is the Malabar Farm Museum with various displays in a large barn. You can also take a 45-minute wagon tour of the farm Tuesday through Sunday at 11:30 a.m., 1:30 p.m., 2:30 p.m. and 3:30 p.m., April 1 to October 31 weather permitting.

The park maintains a rustic and charming sugar shack in a woodlot accessed from a dirt road just south of the Farm Complex. The shack is making maple sugar and open to visitors during the first two full weekends in March. Across from the Sugar Shack is the Pugh Learning Center, a day-use cabin available for rent to groups.

Hiking: Malabar has three nature trails, each a mile-long loop. The Doris

Duke Woods Trail is posted at the beginning of the dirt road to the Sugar Shack and named for the tobacco heiress who saved the woodlot after Bromfield's death by purchasing back the timber rights. At the end of the road is Butternut Nature Trail while off the Farm Complex Road is the self-guided Junglebrook Trail.

For a longer hike, follow the bridle trail, beginning in the Big House parking area. The walk is an easy three to four-hour trek that winds between stands of hardwoods, open fields and across Switzer Creek.

Bridle Trails: The park has a 12-mile designated bridle trail along with a staging area at the horsemen's campground. The network is a loop around the park with a spur to Mt. Jeez.

Fishing: Five farm ponds are open for fishing with anglers targeting mostly bluegill and catfish.

Malabar Inn: Located within the park at 3645 Pleasant Valley Road is Malabar Inn, a brick home built in 1820 after the Indians lost the Battle of the Fallen Timbers. Today the state-owned building is fully restored and offers country-style dining daily from May through October and weekends in March and April. For more information or reservations call (800) 589-8920.

Winter Activities: The park rents cross-country skies from the gift shop when there is sufficient snow. That hasn't been the case, however, since the mid-1980s.

Spring walleye fishing at M. J. Thurston State Park.

46 Mary Jane Thurston State Park

Land: 555 acres on the Maumee River

It's not hard to relive history on the way to Mary Jane Thurston State Park. Most visitors drive in on US24 from Maumee, past the Battle of Fallen Timbers State Memorial at Side Cut Metropark, one of the most important battles in opening up the Northwest Territories for settlement.

Drive on past Fort Deposit just below Farnsworth Metropark in Waterville where General "Mad" Anthony Wayne assembled his troops and supplies before pushing on to meet the Indians at Fallen Timbers; and past Roche de Bout, an unusual rock formation in the river at Farnsworth that's steeped in Indian lore and legend.

US24 from Toledo to Waterville is actually the old canal bed of the Miami and Erie Canal, at Waterville the roadway veers away from the old canal bed which from there to Grand Rapids is preserved in a series of three Metroparks of the Toledo Area -- Farnsworth, Bend View and Providence. The old canal and towpath becomes readily apparent at Providence where those heading to Thurston cross the river. There a canal restoration project is underway that by 1994 will include a completely restored 1 1/2 mile section of the canal, working canal lock, and mule-drawn canal boat for the public to ride. Already in operation is the Ludwig Mill, a 146 year old waterpower interpretive center where heritage crafts, sawmilling and grain milling are demonstrated every Sunday from 1 p.m. until 4 p.m.

The Maumee River itself was an important trade route for Indians and early trappers and traders, as well as missionaries bringing Christianity to the frontier. When the canals came it was the town of Providence located on and near the present Metropark that sat astride the main line of the canal. Across the river at Grand Rapids, then known as Gilead, a short side cut canal was constructed to enable canal boats to get around a large dam to trade in the town.

Today, only Grand Rapids remains. The brawling canal town of Providence virtually disappeared in the mid-1800s in the wake of a great fire and a cholera epidemic. Only the Ludwig Mill and two other structures remain. But both the Miami and Erie Canal and Gilead Side Cut can still be seen here, along with a lock on each canal.

Providence Metropark on the north side of the river and Mary Jane Thurston on the south are linked by an impressive concrete roller dam originally built in 1838 to feed water to the Miami and Erie Canal. The shallows below the dam are popular for fishing. The slackwater pool behind the dam is the reason for the popularity of Mary Jane Thurston's marina. An excursion steamboat plies the waters here in season leaving on weekends from Providence.

Both Mary Jane Thurston, which is named for a local school teacher who bequeathed the original 14 acres for the park in 1928, and Providence are worth visiting, for what they are and what they were.

Information and Activities

Mary Jane Thurston State Park
1-466 SR65
McClure, Ohio 43534
(419) 832-7662

Directions: Mary Jane Thurston is located 20 miles southwest of Toledo. Take I-475 (also designated as US-23 through this stretch) to US-24, take US24 southwest through Waterville and on to SR578 which is nothing more than a bridge over the Maumee River to Grand Rapids. Turn southwest (right) on SR65 and follow to the park. The total distance is about 14 miles from I-475.

Information: The park office is located off SR65 at the marina. There is generally someone on hand Monday through Friday, 8 a.m. to 5 p.m.

Campground: The campground here is new, 31 primitive grassy tent sites in a stand of mid-size hardwoods along the Maumee River. The place is truly a gem worth checking out. The campground has a separate entrance in between the entrances for the picnic area and the marina. Vault toilets are located in the camp and flush toilets are available in season at the nearby shelterhouse.

The layout of a 31 site campground expansion is readily apparent in the adjacent meadow where a gravel drive loops past what are obviously future campsites. Gravel vehicle pads to accommodate up to 32 foot long RVs will be included in these new sites along with fire rings and picnic tables. These new sites should be available in Summer, 1993. Electric hook-ups won't come immediately but are in future plans.

Boating: Unlimited horsepower boating for pleasure, sailboating, fishing, and water skiing are all popular here. There are 20 miles of navigable Maumee River punctuated by a large pool of several hundred acres that is backed up behind the Providence Dam. Caution is urged for boaters not to venture too close to the dam and to be aware of a rock hazard which is marked by a buoy.

The marina features two modern two-lane launch ramps, 116 dock slips and ten shallow-draft tie-ups which are available for rental by the season, and four courtesy docks with two-hour limits. There is no concession at the marina for gasoline and other supplies. A private marina just one-half mile upriver offers those services.

Fishing: The Maumee River is an excellent fishery including such species as channel catfish, northern pike, walleye, white bass, smallmouth bass, and crappie. Many fishermen like to wade or shore fish the shallow waters below the dam. Those who wade are cautioned to watch their footing on the slippery bottom and be aware of deeper holes.

Every April walleye spawn by the millions in the Maumee River. The biggest concentration of fish and, therefore, the most popular fishing is downstream at Side Cut Metropark in Maumee, but quite a few walleye make it to the dam to join the resident walleye that fishermen seek throughout the season. In May the white bass also have a huge spawning run and they come upriver all the way to the dam. In fall coho and a few chinook salmon collect below the dam.

In a woodland at the marina is a small fishing pond which is great for children and waterfowl. Bluegill, crappie and largemouth bass can be found there.

Day-use Areas: Picnicking is very popular here and just across the river at Providence Metropark on the other end of the dam. Mary Jane Thurston features a very attractive shelterhouse built in 1936 by the Civilian Conservation Corps. The shelter features a wonderful view of the river's wooded shores and shallows choked with water willow. If you have the chance stake out a spot there on a summer evening when the sun sets seemingly into the river channel. The shelterhouse is available by reservation through the park office for a small fee. The flush restrooms located below the shelter are open to the public.

The main picnic area is located away from the river in a heavily wooded bottomland. It's said that a skirmish between General Wayne's troops and the Indians occurred there just prior to the Battle of Fallen Timbers.

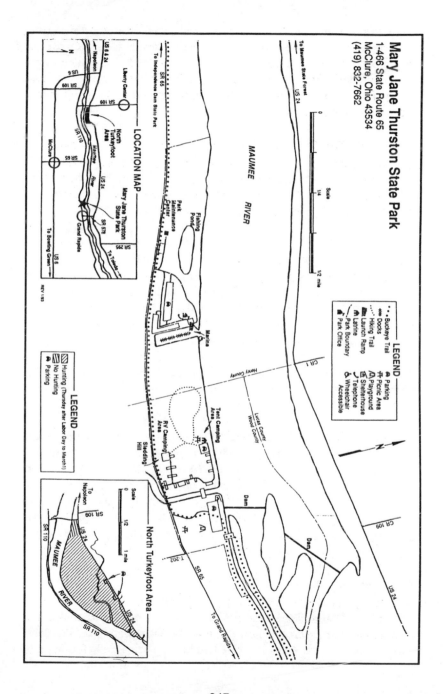

Mary Jane Thurston State Park

1-466 State Route 65
McClure, Ohio 43534
(419) 832-7662

MAUMEE RIVER

LEGEND

- Buckeye Trail
- Docks
- Hiking Trail
- Launch Ramp
- Latrine
- Park Boundary
- Park Office
- Parking
- Picnic Area
- Playground
- Shelterhouse
- Telephone
- Wheelchair Accessible

LOCATION MAP

North Turkeyfoot Area

Mary Jane Thurston State Park

Liberty Center

Napoleon

McClure

To Maumee State Forest

To Independence Dam State Park

To Bowling Green

Grand Rapids

To Toledo

REV 1-93

LEGEND

- Hunting (Thursday after Labor Day to March 1)
- No Hunting
- Parking

North Turkeyfoot Area

MAUMEE RIVER

To Napoleon

Scale
0   1/2   1 mile

Fishing Pond

Park Maintenance Center

Marina

Tent Camping Area

RV Camping Area

Sledding Hill

Dam

Henry County

Lucas County
Wood County

To Grand Rapids

Although a nice area, the view of the river and dam is obstructed by the old canal towpath where mules once pulled canal boats into Grand Rapids. A few picnic tables are spotted along the towpath and they do have nice views of the river, dam, and canal lock.

The canal lock enabled boats to enter the Gilead Side Cut for commerce in Grand Rapids. The lock remains in excellent condition and is complete with a set of reconstructed lock gates. One of the best places to enjoy the park is on a horseshoe shaped area between the lock and dam where a few park benches have been placed. They are accessible via a footbridge over the lock. A few picnic tables and four grills are scattered through the marina area for boaters to enjoy.

Hiking Trails: Gilead Side Cut Trail (0.5 mile, one-way) begins on the north side of the canal lock and follows the old canal towpath into Grand Rapids, a tastefully restored village featuring a variety of restaurants and shops. The level trail along the old canal which is still very apparent is surfaced with fine stone and is popular with joggers and walkers alike.

Mosquito Loop Trail (0.75 mi.) begins and ends at the primitive tent camp. The trail follows a small bay and the river then turns inland through a bottomland forest. It a very easy path that through floodplain that tends to be seasonally very wet. As the name implies, bring repellent along in summer.

Hunting: While there is no hunting permitted at the main park area, Mary Jane Thurston also includes the North Turkeyfoot Area, a 450 acre site on the other side of the river and five miles further upstream off US24. The site is undeveloped and popular for small upland game and whitetail deer hunting in season. Two creeks run through the property which is level and covered with about 17 years of second growth hardwoods. There are no trails on the site although some edge effect mowing is done. There is a small Maumee River fishing access parking area 1/4 mile west of the town of Texas, and two gravel lots at the main entrance located one mile west of Texas. No restrooms are provided.

Winter Activities: A sledding hill with a fire ring is provided in the campground area and cross-country skiing is popular although no groomed trails are provided. Locals like to ice fish in the marina basin for crappie.

The wetlands are abundant with wildlife at Maumee Bay State Park.

47 Maumee Bay State Park

Land: 1,850 acres on Maumee Bay

The landscape in and around Maumee Bay State Park looks innocent enough. Row after row of crops growing lush and green in the rich soils which once made Northwest Ohio the corn capital of the world. The topography is billiard table flat. About the only deviations from the pervasive flatness are the dikes that hold the lake's waters at bay and the deep drainage ditches that channel rain and floodwater off the land.

Before the days of dikes and ditches, the landscape was dominated by huge coastal marshes and, further inland off the lake and bay, the Great Black Swamp. These marshes once covered some quarter million acres and teemed with waterfowl and wildlife. Thousands of acres of wild rices grew in the pristine waters along the bays.

On the horizon of the marshes was a giant wall of trees, a vast hardwood swamp forest that stretched unbroken from Port Clinton to the Maumee River to the Indiana line and beyond. Accounts from early travelers speak of the forest appearing as a dense blue haze in the distance. Some say the name Great Black Swamp came from this darkened appearance of the forest, or from the fact that very little sunlight penetrated the thick forest canopy to the floor of the swamp. Or, perhaps, from the dark color of the soil and water of the swamp. The Black Swamp was among the last strongholds in Ohio for elk, bison, wolf, black bear and mountain lion.

In the early 1800s, the Black Swamp was considered a vast inhospitable morass, a barrier to travelers and commerce, and one of the harshest environments in the country for those early pioneers. Soldiers making their way through the area in the early 1800s wrote that it was the most desolate, forbidding wilderness in America. Today's modern SR20 was once a corduroy road -- a road surfaced with logs laid corduroy fashion -- that was so bad that it could take a horse and rider a week to travel twenty-five miles.

The great forest and swamp is history, and most of the coastal marshes are gone. The waters are too muddied now for the great stands of wild rice. The elk and the lion and wolf were gone by the 1870s. The huge hardwoods were harvested, walnut and cherry for gun stocks in the Civil War, the huge oaks were prized for use in sailing ships. Toledo, for a time, was an important lumber town. Drainage ditches and field tiles have drained the surface water and lowered the water table for agriculture.

But where pieces of the swamp and coastal marshes remain, they are incredibly rich in wildlife. The understandable temptation at Maumee Bay is to bask on the beach, play the unique and challenging golf course, and otherwise concentrate on the many amenities here. But if you want to know this land and the forces which shaped it, visit the Trautman Nature Center and take the boardwalk trail into the marsh and swamp forest east of it.

This was a wild, incredibly rich land, a land with a spirit embodied in the pair of bald eagles that occasionally can be seen surveying Maumee Bay State Park.

Remember as you travel through Maumee Bay that, while many of its facilities are available, it is a new park that still has some facilities under construction.

Information and Activities

Maumee Bay State Park
1400 Park Road One
Oregon, Ohio 43618

Park Office: (419)836-7758
Campground: (419)836-8828

Maumee Bay Resort (Quilter Lodge)
1750 Maumee Bay Park Road Two
Oregon, Ohio 43618
(419)836-1466
(800)282-7275 (Lodge/Cabin Reservations)

Directions: Located just east of Toledo on Maumee Bay. Follow I-280 to SR2 (Navarre Avenue), follow SR2 east for six miles to North Curtice Road, turn north for three miles and North Curtice runs into the main park entrance. (As you travel on Curtice note the crossing of Corduroy Road, named for its original surface of logs.)

Heading south on I-75 from Detroit, take I-280 south at the first split. Heading north of I-75 take the SR795 exit west until it intersects with I-280 then north on I-280 to SR2.

From Port Clinton follow SR2 west, approximately 30 miles.

Information: The park office is located on Park Road 1, a continuation of the main entrance drive, one-third mile from the entrance. The office is open Monday through Friday, 8 a.m. until 5 p.m. The campground office is open every day, Memorial Day to Labor Day, from 8 a.m. to 11 p.m. and reduced hours the remainder of the year. The desk in the Quilter Lodge is open 24 hours a day. Also in the lodge is a concierge desk open during busy periods.

Campground: If you're looking for a large tree to pitch your tent or park your RV under, forget it. Most of Maumee Bay was farm field until the 1970s and, although they've planted a lot of trees, there's only the promise of future shade. Bring along an awning for your RV or a dining fly if you want out of the sun.

Otherwise, the 256 site campground is nice, new, and full of amenities by state park standards. Every site has electricity, a 30 amp plug with a breaker and a 20 amp with ground fault interrupter. Four showerhouses are provided, all with flush toilets and hot showers. The northeast showerhouse is heated and has a laundromat. All of them are handicapped accessible with assistance -- they were retrofitted to the extent that the existing architecture permitted.

Three Rent-A-Camps are available (sites 122-124), one is fitted with a ramp. The most popular loop is Park Road 18 which winds around one side of the campground lake, and all the most popular sites are on the lake, both for the view and for the fishing the lake provides. Check out sites 37-44, 55-61, 99-110, and 148-152. Pets are permitted on all sites.

All sites are open and spacious. The campground is able to accommodate any size set-up that's legal on the highway. A dump station with refuse disposal and water to refill tanks is available just past the campground office.

The campground is extremely popular, filling up on one-third of the summer weekends. To insure a site, arrive late Thursday or early Friday, even earlier on holiday weekends.

Cabins: At Maumee Bay, they call them cottages because they don't look like anything else in the park system. There are twenty modern beachhouse-style cottages, the newest and arguably the nicest in the system. Each cottage is equipped with a gas fireplace, central heat and air conditioning, TVs, telephones, and microwaves. They are nicely spaced along a new road that separates the golf course from the swamp woods, offering views of one or the other or both.

Two bedroom and four bedroom cottages are available. The two bedroom also has a sleeping loft so they can easily accommodate six people. The four bedroom cottages can sleep 11. Cottages 10 and 11 each have two bedrooms and are interconnected by an elevated walkway that culminates in a picnic deck overlooking the golf course. Cottages 1 and 2 have the same arrangement but are four bedrooms each. These multi-unit cottages are very popular for larger groups.

My picks would be 16, a two bedroom which sits on a pond and meadow against the swamp woods, or 12, a four bedroom which sits on a peninsula. Numbers 13, 14, and 15 are against a woods on the golf course. Numbers 3, 7, 17, and 19 are all on the opposite side of the road from the golf course up against the swamp woods.

The cottages are booked year-round. They are offered only by the week between Memorial Day and Labor Day, on a daily basis at other times. Call well in advance for reservations. Cottage guests can use lodge facilities.

Quilter Lodge: Named for local State Representative Barney Quilter -- everybody around there knows him just as Barney -- this newest state park lodge overlooking Maumee Bay fills its expectations as a showpiece. Each of the 120 guest rooms features a balcony and easy access to racquetball courts, a game room, saunas, exercise rooms, whirlpools, indoor and outdoor pools, a snack bar, and a dining room with lounge. The lodge is also a conference center complete with catering service, meeting rooms and a large ballroom.

Twelve rooms are equipped to accommodate the wheelchair handicapped. The most popular rooms are at end of the north wing because they are more isolated and have a wonderful view of the bay. Loft rooms are available, also, and each has a refrigerator. Almost all rooms have a view of the bay and all are equipped with coffee makers and blow driers.

Weekends are heavily booked year-round. Weekly and weekend rates are offered year-round and many special packages are offered.

Boating: Sixty acre Inland Lake and 12-acre Canoeing Lake, which are connected by a channel running under PR 1, are restricted to electric motors only. No launch is provided either for these lakes or Maumee Bay. Launching beaches are provided at the first parking area west of the park office and on the west end of Canoeing Lake. The nearest launches for larger boats into Maumee Bay and Lake Erie are five miles east at Anchor Point where a public launch (with fee) is provided at Cooley Canal and several private launches are located.

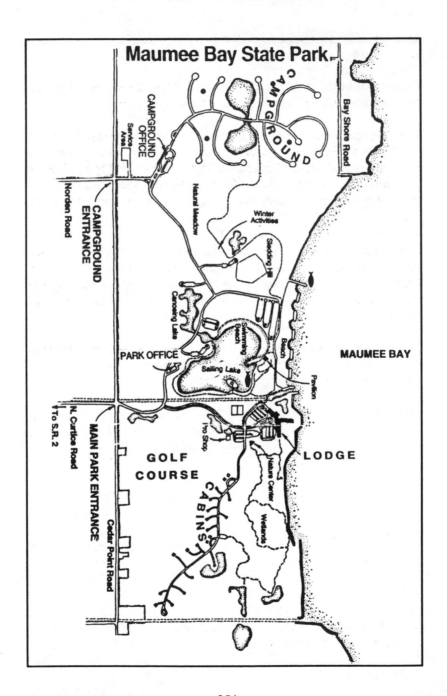

Maumee Bay State Park

Bay Shore Road

CAMPGROUND

CAMPGROUND OFFICE

Service Area

Norden Road

CAMPGROUND ENTRANCE

Natural Meadow

Winter Activities

Sledding Hill

Canoeing Lake

Swimming Beach

PARK OFFICE

Sailing Lake

Beach

Pavilion

MAUMEE BAY

N. Curtice Road

To S.R. 2

MAIN PARK ENTRANCE

Pro Shop

GOLF COURSE

CABINS

Nature Center

LODGE

Wetlands

Cedar Point Road

Jet skies, windsurfers, etc., can be hand-carried to three designated boating beaches and on into Maumee Bay.

Canoes, rowboats, several small sailboats, and paddleboats can be rented from a concession on Inland Lake near the amphitheater.

A 40-slip marina is slated for construction in 1993 at the mouth of Wolf Creek near the lodge. Thirty of the slips will be equipped with electric hook-ups. The slips are all designated for visitors and will be available on an overnight or day period basis. No fuel will be available but there will be a water hook-up and pump-out. The dockmaster will operate through the lodge.

Fishing: Most people fish from shore in the park for largemouth bass, bluegill and catfish. Numbers of small walleye are present in Inland and Canoe Lakes, a result of a connection to the bay. The smaller fishing lake west of the Big Hill was stocked in the late 1980s and its population is still maturing.

The campground lake is open to fishing for campers only and therefore doesn't get as much pressure. It is the oldest inland lakes in the park and has some very nice fish.

Hiking/Bridle Trails: All of the trails in Maumee Bay are easy. In 1993 a three mile bridle trail will be available beginning from a gravel parking area off Cedar Point Road just west of the park entrance. No stalls, water or other facilities will be available.

A six mile asphalt walkway system interconnects the campground with the amphitheater and other park facilities. It is popular with joggers and bicyclists as well as walkers. Bicycles from tandems to 16-inchers and everything in between are available at the boat rental and in the lodge. There is also a seven-mile system of grass paths that will be mowed in spring, including the bridle trail.

Mouse Trail (2.8 mi. loop) A level trail that circles the campground through a meadow being invaded by small trees. In winter this is an area to observe short-eared owls.

Boardwalk Trail (1.9 mi. round-trip) begins at the Trautman Nature Center near the lodge and pro shop and traverses swamp forest and marsh. A 1/4 mile segment of the trail will be designated for the wheelchair handicapped and have special interpretive signage.

Day-use Areas: Much of the day use activity is centered on the shores of Inland Lake. The lifeguarded 2,000 foot swimming beach and accompanying showerhouses and restrooms are there, as is the amphitheater where visitors are entertained on summer weekends by free shows so diverse they range from nature shows to the Toledo Symphony to park visitors doing solos.

Near the amphitheater is the Surfside Snack Bar which serves up burgers, fries, hot dogs, soft drinks and more all summer, and a shop selling swimming and boating souvenirs in the boat rental. Above the amphitheater, up a paved walkway, is a small sun shelter on top of a knoll which affords a fine view of the park and bay.

Picnic areas are concentrated around the beach and at the parking lot at the base of Big Hill. Additional sites are still to come, along with grills, tables, small shelters, and a large shelter with flush restrooms at the base of Big Hill.

The park has a second sand beach extending nearly a half mile on Maumee Bay. Rock barriers divide the beach into six areas, the western three are boat beaches and the eastern three are buoyed off for wading. Lifeguards are not provided.

Last, but most certainly not least, the Maumee Bay Golf Course deserves considerable attention here. The 18-hole par 72 championship course was designed by Arthur Hill and it's truly exceptional. Here at Maumee Bay the weather can be great, but sometimes the fog rolls in thick and hangs all day, or the wind howls and the rain drives on a horizontal. When it does it's not too hard to close your eyes and imagine the Scottish moors where golf originated. Appropriately, they've recreated the moors here and created a phenomenal Scottish links course with low, rolling grass-covered mounds, elegantly green bent grass fairways and tees, banks of sand bunkers, small tortured greens, and plenty of water to lose balls in. In keeping with the links theme, there are no trees on the course. Tee times are arranged through the pro shop, 836-9009, which also carries equipment, clothing, and snacks. Tee times for lodge/cottage guests are accepted with the facility reservation. Others may reserve tee times one week in advance for weekday play, and on the Wednesday preceding for weekends.

Nature Notes: The Trautman Nature Center is set to open in April, 1993, staffed by a full-time naturalist. Interactive displays on area natural history, auditorium, research laboratory and viewing windows are featured. The Telephone Pioneers of America are arranging to install and maintain video cameras set way in the marsh and remote-controlled by visitors to view wildlife. Hours and programming to be announced.

Hunting: The acreage shown for the park should technically be reduced by 400 acres. In late 1992, the Division of Parks transferred title to the easternmost 400 acres to the Division of Wildlife for management largely as a wetland. The area, now known as the Old Mallard Club Wildlife Area, will be open to hunting for all legal game species in season.

Winter Activities: Big Hill got its name from the visitors who kept asking where the big hill was until the name stuck. Hard to believe they had to ask. The huge hill is so obviously out of place here, a giant mound in a nearly perfectly flat countryside. In summer it's a terrific look-out point, in spring researchers love to watch the hawk migration from its heights, in winter it's the site of some of the best sledding in Northwest Ohio. There have been a few sledding injuries on the hill, caused mostly by sledders going down the hill striking sledders returning to the top.

Don't leave your cross-country skis at home, or, if you do, there are skis available through the lodge desk.

Cliffs, narrow gorges and ridges were cut by glaciers at Mohican.

48   *Mohican State Park*

Land: 1294 acres · Water: River

Perhaps Ohio's most unusual river is the Mohican, a "reversed stream" as a result of the glacial activity 12,000 years ago. The Wisconsinan, the last glacier to enter Ohio, ended its advance in this region, forming a glacial boundary. Not only did it create several moraines and linear ridges along the ice edge but it blocked the northern channel of the Mohican River.

The river then began to cut a new route to the south and when the glacier retreated its meltwaters carved the narrow gorge of the Mohican's Clear Fork. Some estimate the torrent was 100 times greater than the gentle flow seen today. The result was a river that flows from flat plains into deeper gorges and higher ridges, the opposite of what most people would expect.

The result was not only a reversed river but a rugged and beautiful country. The striking Clearfork Gorge is more than a thousand feet wide at the top and 300 feet deep. Its stands of towering hemlock and virgin white pine are so significant that recently the National Park Service dedicated the area as a registered National Natural Landmark. Big and Little Lyons Falls are equally enchanting and so is a paddle down the Clearfork, a designated National Scenic River.

The Ashland County park is basically a 1,200-acre corridor along the Clearfork and Pleasant Hill Lake. But it is surrounded by Mohican Memorial State Forest and adjacent to Pleasant Hill Park and Malabar Farm State Park. The entire area is generally referred to as Mohican Country, more than 10,000 acres that attract canoes, campers, hikers and a wide variety of other outdoor enthusiasts. This is central Ohio's best recreation area, the reason more than 1.5 million visitors come to the state park every year.

Information & Activities

Mohican State Park
3116 SR3
Londonville, Ohio 44842
(419) 994-5125

Directions: The state park is in southern Ashland County, almost halfway between Cleveland and Columbus. From I-71, depart at exit 165 and head east along SR97 for 17 miles. The heart of the state park, its rugged interior is reached on CR939. This county road is an extremely scenic drive as it winds along the south side of the gorge and the crosses Clearfork on a covered bridge to access the north side of the park and state forest.

Information: The business office is right off SR97 and open 8 a.m. to 5 p.m. Monday through Friday. The check-in station for the campground, near the intersection of SR97 and SR3 at the east end of the park is also a source of information and is open daily from 8 a.m. to 9 p.m. during the summer.

Campgrounds: There are 20 public campgrounds in Mohican Country, including two within the state park. A modern campground is at the east end of the park and reached from SR3 just north of the Clearfork. The riverside facility has 153 sites with tables, fire rings and electrical hook-ups. The sites vary from open grassy areas and many in a wooded setting to more than 30 situated right on the river, undoubtedly some of the most scenic modern sites in the state. The campground also includes showerhouse with laundry facilities, a dump station for recreational vehicles, a camp store, play equipment and outdoor pool.

Needless to say the campground is extremely popular. It's filled daily from Memorial Day through Labor Day and on the weekends through fall colors in late October. To check on site availability call the campground station at (419) 994-4290.

Also located within the park is Hemlock Grove Campground. The 24-site rustic facility campground is adjacent to the covered bridge and CR939 and reached from either the south state forest entrance from SR97 or the north forest entrance on CR3006. The sites are located along the river in the narrow confines of the Clearfork Gorge. It is a unique setting as there's not much room between your tent and the wall of the gorge nor do you have to walk far to reach the Clearfork. Facilities include tables, fire rings and vault toilets. The rustic facility also fills up every weekend throughout the summer but sites are usually available in mid-week. A group campground, a large grassy clearing capable of handling up to 100 people, is located off CR939 at the north side of the park.

Day-use Areas: The park maintains six picnic areas with the most impressive by far being the Gorge Overlook. Located off CR939 in the southeast corner of the park, the picnic grounds is on the edge of the Clearfork Gorge in an impressive stand of red pine and hardwoods. Facilities include tables, grills, two shelters and a stone overlook that allows you to peer deep into the gorge. Almost equally scenic is a picnic area on the banks of the Clearfork near the Hemlock Grove Campground. Tables, grills and play equipment are situated just off the bank and all within sight of the covered bridge.

On the north side of the gorge just beyond the state forest headquarters is Vista Point Picnic Area. Along shelters, tables, grills, and vault toilets, Vista Point also features views of the gorge, especially in late October after the leaves begin to drop. Other picnic grounds are located near the modern campground, just beyond the state forest headquarters on the north side of

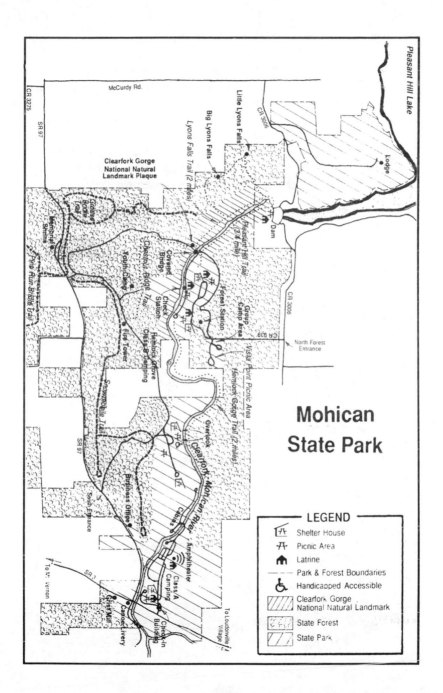

Mohican
State Park

LEGEND

- Shelter House
- Picnic Area
- Latrine
- Park & Forest Boundaries
- Handicapped Accessible
- Clearfork Gorge National Natural Landmark
- State Forest
- State Park

Pleasant Hill Lake

McCurdy Rd.

CR 3275

SR 97

Clearfork Gorge
National Natural
Landmark Plaque

Little Lyons Falls

Big Lyons Falls

Lyons Falls Trail (2 miles)

Lodge

CR 3006

Dam

Pleasant Hill Trail (3/4 mile)

Group Camp Area

Forest Station

CR 939

North Forest Entrance

CR 3006

Vista Point Picnic Area

Hemlock Gorge Trail (2 miles)

Memorial Shrine

Stump Bridge Trail

Covered Bridge

Chestnut Ridge Trail

Youth Camp

Check Station

Hemlock Grove

Class B Camping

Fire Tower

Snowmobile Trail

Pine Run Bridle Trail

SR 97

Overlook

Clearfork, Mohican River

Business Office

South Entrance

Cabins

Amphitheater

Class A Camping

SR 3

To Mt. Vernon

Grist Mill

Canoe Livery

Check-In Building

To Loudonville Village

the gorge and near the Pleasant Hill Lake Dam.

Fishing: The Mohican River is a noted smallmouth bass fishery as well as for rock bass and catfish. Most fishing activity takes place on Pleasant Hill Reservoir, however, as anglers work the 850-acre lake for saugeye, largemouth bass, crappies, bluegill and white bass. The upper portion of the lake is shallow while the lower end is deep with depths of 54 feet and features a rocky shoreline. Though best known as a bass lake, Pleasant Hill is stocked annually with saugeye and anglers do well catching the walleye cousin when they troll the deeper sections in the spring.

Hiking: More than 12 miles of foot trails wind through the more interesting sections of the state park and state forest. The most popular hike is Lyons Falls Trail, a two-mile loop that can be picked up with posted trailheads at the Covered Bridge and the dam. The trail requires some climbing but passes both Little Lyons and Big Lyons Falls. John Chapman, the famous Johnny Appleseed, visited this area so frequently that his left his name and date on the walls of Big Lyons Falls. The famous "graffiti" attracted hikers for years before erosion erased his etchings.

You can also hike through Clearfork Gorge by combining Hemlock Gorge Trail with Pleasant Ridge Trail. Hemlock is posted in the modern campground and follows the Clearfork for 2.25 miles to the rustic campground. From near the Covered Bridge you can continue along the north bank of the river on Pleasant Hill Trail that reaches the dam in 0.75 mile.

Canoeing: Mohican Country is a popular destination for canoers who can paddle a variety of rivers here including the Blackfork River from Londonville and the main channel of the Mohican River to Brinkhaven. But the most scenic stretch is the paddle through Clearfork from the Covered Bridge to the state park livery near the river's confluence with the Blackfork. This segment passes through the gorge and is a designated National Scenic River. It's an hour and half paddle but occasionally during the summer there isn't enough water for canoeists.

The Mohican State Park Canoe Livery is open daily mid-May through Labor Day and on weekends in April, September and October. Reservations are strongly recommended during the summer season and can be made by calling (800)442-2663.

Backpacking: Mohican Memorial State Forest has 10 backcountry campsites scattered throughout the area. Accessed by the bridle trails, some sites are less than a quarter mile from where you park the car, others are a two-mile trek in. Available on a registration basis only by calling the state forest headquarters at (419)938-6222.

Bridle Trails: The state forest also maintains 22 miles of bridle trails with the vast majority on the south side of SR97. A staging area is located on the state road and from there riders can access the Pine Run Trail, a 6.4-mile loop, the Grouse Run Trail, 4.7-mile loop, or the Horsetail Run, a 11-mile loop that includes riding on both sides of SR97 and passing a lookout tower. For guided rides in the park contact Mohican Riding Stables at (419) 994-3103.

Cabins And Lodge: The park features 25 family cabins located on the Clearfork in a pleasant wooded area just beyond the modern campground. Each unit has two bedrooms with twin beds, shower and bathroom, complete kitchen and a screened-in porch with most of them overlooking the river. The cabins sleep six and are rented out year-round as they are popular with skiers attacked to Clear Fork and Snow Trails ski areas nearby.

Mohican Resort is 10 miles from the main portion of the state park located on a hill overlooking Pleasant Hill Lake. The state park lodge has 96 rooms, each with a private balcony, along with a lakeview dining room, meeting rooms, cocktail lounge, Oympic-size indoor pool, sauna and a fireplace-in-the-round. Outside guests enjoy a pool with wading area, tennis courts, basketball courts and a panoramic view of the lake from a lookout point. For more information on Mohican Resort call (419) 938-5411. For reservations at either the lodge or family cabins call (800) AT-A-PARK.

Nature Notes: Mohican is the home to much wildlife including red fox, whitetail deer, box turtles and the wild turkey which can be seen here in significant numbers after almost being extirpated at one time. Of particular interest to birders is the abundance of nesting warblers in the Clearfork Gorge area. More than 15 species can be sighted including northern parula, hooded, Cerulean and American redstart.

The park also features a Log Cabin Nature Center and an amphitheater in the modern campground which host a variety of programs almost daily during the summer. Check with the campground station for time and type of activity.

Mohican State Park

Boat launches can be really entertaining.

49 Mosquito Lake State Park

Land: 3961 acres   Water: 7850 Acres

One of the largest lakes in Ohio, Mosquito Lake may not have the most attractive name but it's a popular destination for walleye anglers and boaters. The entire lake spreads over 7,850 acres in Trumbull County and was created in 1944 by the U.S. Army Corps of Engineers as the key link in a system of flood control dams and reservoirs for the Mahoning River, Beaver Creek and the upper portions of the Ohio River.

Mosquito Lake is unique, however, as it has an uncontrolled natural spillway. Throughout much of the year water flows south of the reservoir into the Mahoning Valley but when the lake reaches an elevation of 904 feet above sea level, the flow reverses. Water spills out of the north end into a tributary of the Grand River to eventually reach Lake Erie.

The park is popular with campers, boaters and anglers from Youngstown and the Cleveland area. The north portion of the lake is a designated game refuge.

Information & Activities

Mosquito Lake State Park
1439 SR305
Cortland, Ohio 44410
(219) 637-2856

Directions: The park is a 30-minute drive from Youngstown and an hour from Cleveland. From SR45 north of Warren, turn east on SR305 to reach the park entrance in 4 miles.

Information: The park office is located in the southwest corner of the lake near the campground and is open 8 a.m. to noon and 1-5 p.m. Monday through Friday.

Campground: Mosquito Lake has 234 sites on two loops situated primarily in a mature forest. Sites, for the most part, are well secluded from each other among the trees and a handful on each loop offer shoreline scenery. Sites 217-220 are right off the water. Facilities include tables and fire rings while the park plans to equip 100 sites with electricity in the near future.

The campground also has a showerhouse, a dump station and a launch area off the first loop. Call the campground office at (216)638-5700 for availability of sites but it's rare for the Mosquito Lake State Park to be filled. On most summer weekends, 60 percent of the facility is occupied.

Day-use Areas: Located adjacent to the park office is a beach and day-use area overlooking the south end of the reservoir. Mosquito Lake has a wide sandy beach 600 feet long with a marked off swimming area, changing booths and a scenic little island just off shore. Nearby in a lightly shaded area is the picnic grounds with tables, grills, play equipment and a nice view of causeway at the end of the lake. A second and much quieter picnic area is passed on the way to the beach.

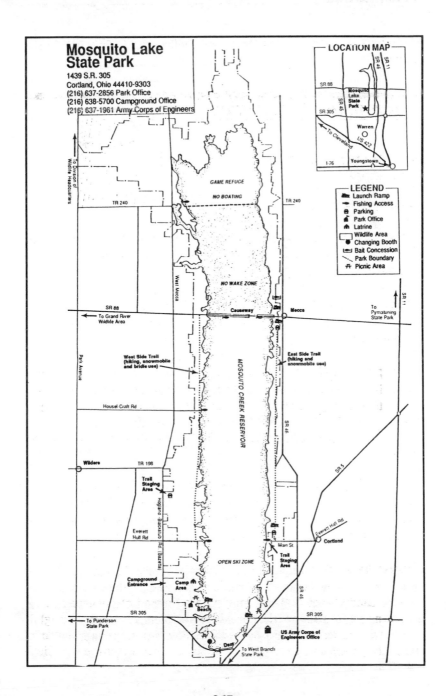

Mosquito Lake State Park

1439 S.R. 305
Cortland, Ohio 44410-9303
(216) 637-2856 Park Office
(216) 638-5700 Campground Office
(216) 637-1961 Army Corps of Engineers

LOCATION MAP

SR 88
SR 46
SR 11
Mosquito Lake State Park
SR 45
SR 305
Warren
US 422
To Cleveland
I-76
Youngstown

GAME REFUGE
NO BOATING

TR 240
TR 240

LEGEND

- Launch Ramp
- Fishing Access
- Parking
- Park Office
- Latrine
- Wildlife Area
- Changing Booth
- Bait Concession
- Park Boundary
- Picnic Area

NO WAKE ZONE

West Mecca

SR 88
To Grand River Wildlife Area
Causeway
Mecca
To Pymatuning State Park
SR 11

Park Avenue

West Side Trail
(hiking, snowmobile and bridle use)

East Side Trail
(hiking and snowmobile use)

MOSQUITO CREEK RESERVOIR

Housel-Craft Rd

SR 46

SR 5

Wildare
TR 198

Trail Staging Area

Hoagland Blackstub Rd (Bazetta)

Everett Hull Rd

Everett Hull Rd

Cortland

Main St

Trail Staging Area

OPEN SKI ZONE

Campground Entrance
Camp Area

SR 46

SR 305
To Punderson State Park

Beach

SR 305

US Army Corps of Engineers Office

Dam
To West Branch State Park

To Division of Wildlife Headquarters

Boating: Mosquito Lake is very popular with boaters during the summer and subsequently the state park has an impressive boat launch near the park office. The facility has six bays, four loading docks and parking for several hundred vehicles and trailers. Still, on nice summer weekends boaters are often backed up when trying to launch their craft. If that's the case, try the launch facilities the park maintains at the west end of Main Street in Cortland in the southeast corner of lake or the ramps on both sides of SR88 on the east shore.

The lake is rated for unlimited horsepower but because of the heavy boating traffic, there is a 10 mph speed limit after sunset and a no wake zone 300 feet from shore. North of SR88 is a 15 mph and no-skiing zone to Mahan-Denman Road where Mosquito Creek Wildlife Area begins. Boating is banned in game refuge. Boaters must remember that Mosquito Lake is a relatively large but shallow body of water that can get extremely rough when winds pick up.

Fishing: Along with nearby Pymatuning, Mosquito is often rated as one of the finest inland lakes in Ohio for walleye. The best fishing occurs spring and fall when fish move into the shallows and according to surveys, anglers catch more than 60,000 walleye a year with more than half of them being legal size. Although natural reproduction takes place, the lake is heavily stocked annually. Fishermen also take northern pike, bluegills and white and black crappies. Bass fishing is rated only fair here. Causeway fishing areas with parking are located on both sides of SR88 for shore anglers while others fish the inlet across from the main boat launch. No fishing is allowed in the wildlife area.

Hiking: The park has two miles of foot paths. Beaver Trail is a 1.5-mile loop that begins and ends off the campground boat launch road and leads to a small beaver ponds.

Nature Notes: Mosquito Creek Wildlife Area at the north end of the lake is managed by the state's Division of Wildlife and its main residents are Canada geese. But many other species of birds can be seen here including bald eagles, African cattle egret, herons and a variety of waterfowl. The Eastern massasauga rattlesnake also is found in the wildlife area.

Fishing is good near the second dam on the west end of the Mt. Gilead Park.

50 Mount Gilead State Park

Land: 142 Acres   Water: 32 Acres

Prior to settlement, Ohio was blanketed by an almost continuous forest. It's estimated that 95 percent of the state was covered by what may have been the largest deciduous forest on earth, a tract of hardwoods that stretched from western Pennsylvania to Illinois and from Michigan southward to Kentucky and parts of Tennessee. Then settlers arrived, cutting, slashing and burning the trees in an effort to clear the land and farm its rich soil.

The settlement of Ohio was nothing short of a devastating blow to the state's greatest natural treasure. By 1900, only 12 percent of Ohio remained covered in forest and a mere 700 acres of old growth forest survives today. Through reforestation Ohio extended its foliage and in places like Mount Gilead, you'll find trails that once again weave through mature stands of red oak, white ash, American beech, maple and hickory.

Mount Gilead's trees date back to 1930, when the area was preserved as Shaffer State Farm and the reservoir enlarged after Sam's Creek, a tributary of Whetstone Creek, was dammed a second time. More than 55,000 trees were shipped in and within 10 days planted on the hills and in hollows surrounding Mount Gilead Lakes. Another 30,000 spruce soon followed. The Morrow County park was eventually turned over to the newly formed Division of Parks in 1949 and today is an interesting slice of Ohio's forested past.

Information & Activities

Mount Gilead State Park
4119 SR95
Mt. Gilead, Ohio 43338
(419) 946-1961

Directions: The park entrance is off SR95, six miles west of exit 151 of I-71 and a mile east of Mt. Gilead.

Information: The park office is on SR95 at the southwest corner of the park and open 8 a.m. to noon and 1-5 p.m. Monday through Friday.

Campground: Mount Gilead's campground occupies the top of a heavily wooded ridge with a portion of the 60 sites located in a stand of red pine while others are on the edge of an open area that extends into the picnic grounds. Near site 40, a trail leads steeply down the ridge to access the rest of the park's trail system.

Facilities include fire rings, tables, play equipment, vault toilets, dump station for RVs and gravel spurs in each site but no electrical hook-ups, showers or restrooms. There are also four Rent-A-Camps while at the west end of the lake is an area designed for group camping. The only time the campground fills is on holidays or when the park holds special events. On a normal summer weekend about 40 percent of the sites will be occupied.

MOUNT GILEAD STATE PARK

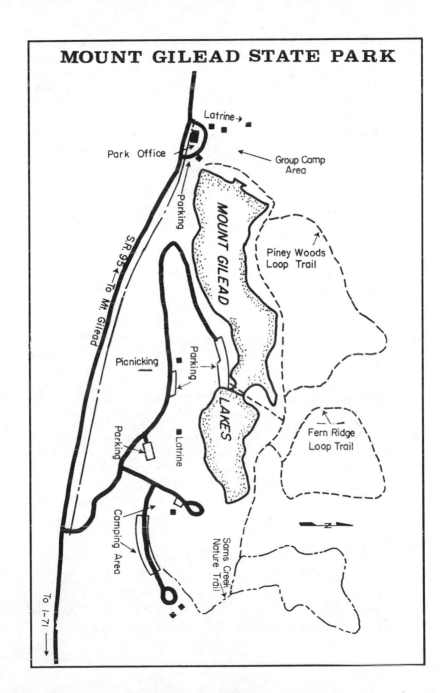

Latrine →

Park Office

Group Camp Area

S.R. 95 ←To Mt. Gilead

Parking

MOUNT GILEAD

Piney Woods Loop Trail

Picnicking

Parking

Parking

LAKES

Fern Ridge Loop Trail

Parking

Latrine

Camping Area

Sams Creek Nature Trail

N

To I-71 →

Day-use Areas: Adjacent to the campground on the ridgetop is a picnic area with three shelters, tables and grills in an open area. A road then winds steeply off the ridge and emerges from the woods on south shore of Mount Gilead Lakes, where there are additional tables, grills and benches overlooking the water.

Fishing: Mount Gilead Lakes is a 30-acre reservoir divided into two tiers by a dam in the middle. Within the picnic area on the south shore there is a ramp to launch boats on the lower half of the reservoir while canoes and other small boats can be hand-carried into the upper end. Fishing is considered fair within the park for bass, bluegill and other panfish. There is an electric-motor only regulation for boaters while shore anglers often gather at the second dam on the west end.

Hiking: The park has six miles of foot path, all located in an undeveloped area on the north side of the reservoir. A trailhead at the west end of the lakes leads to Piney Woods Trail, which begins with a bridge over Sam's Creek and quickly passes its confluence with Whetstone Creek. A posted trailhead to Sam's Creek Nature Trail is located in the campground while between the two loops is Fern Ridge Trail. All three trails are interconnected, approximately a mile long and involve some ridge climbing. An interpretive brochure available at the park office corresponds to the numbered posts found along the entire system.

Nature Notes: There is an amphitheater within the campground and the park hopes to restore its weekend naturalist programs when funds become available. Mount Gilead is impressive in October with stunning fall colors but also in the spring when the dogwood trees bloom and woodland wildflowers, ranging from bloodroot, hepatica and Virginia bluebells to the easy to spot great white trillium, bring the first splash of color to the woods.

Winter Activities: Mount Gilead has a lighted sledding hill near the park office that is open until 11 p.m. When the lake freezes an ice skating rink is also setup.

Historical locks and dams still operate at Muskingum River.

51 Muskingum River Parkway

Land: 117 acres at ten locks
Water: 93 miles of scenic waterway from Marietta to Dresden

The Muskingum River Parkway doesn't fit any traditional niche in the state's park system. It's a different breed of cat. Though not devoid of scenic and natural area qualities, those qualities are obscured by the overwhelming historic aura of the system of locks and dams that still operate the way they did when originally completed in 1841.

The great sandstone locks with their ponderous wood gates are essentially the same but the boats they serve today are a far cry from those they were built to serve. In 1836 area residents fired their muzzle-loaders to celebrate

273

passage of the act in the Ohio legislature that authorized the Muskingum Improvement which would make it possible for Ohio River steamboats to travel upriver from Marietta as far as Dresden. Steamers ruled the valley's freight industry and passenger business until river traffic dropped drastically with the coming of the railroads.

In 1886, the U.S. government took over the waterway's operation and repaired and rebuilt all the dams and locks that make up the navigation system. Discovery of new coal deposits in the region led to a brief resurgence of commercial traffic on the river until that, too, petered-out after World War II. In 1958 Ohio resumed responsibility for the system and have rehabilitated and maintained the entire system for the benefit of pleasure boats.

Today, the park caters to boaters but with the twist of emphasizing living historic value. Of particular interest is the Zanesville lock which is the only hand-operated tandem lock in the nation.

The dams, originally built of timber cribbing, spawned large flour mills including the picturesque mill at Stockport which took advantage of the tremendous source of water power. The locks, designed to accommodate boats up to 160 feet long and 35 feet wide, are most picturesque and primitive looking at Ellis and Luke Chute. On average the locks overcome an eight to ten foot elevation difference, although it is 16 feet at Lowell.

Information and Activities

Muskingum River Parkway
P.O. Box 2806
Zanesville, Ohio 43701
(614) 452-3820

Directions: Parkland is located at each lock except Philo (lock #9) which has no upland area. Roads follow the river valley and link the locks. To follow the parkway take I-70 to SR60 south (except Ellis which is located off SR60 north), at McConnelsville (lock #7) follow SR376 to SR266, back to SR60 to Marietta on the Ohio River.

Information: Park offices are located at Zanesville (lock #10) on an island in the Muskingum River which has both boat and foot access. By car, take SR60 south from I-70, turn right on Hughes St. and left at the electric substation. The offices are located in a 1904 structure that once housed the lock tender and Corps of Engineers.

Campground: Perhaps the most unusual campground in the park system is located at Ellis (lock #11). Here 20 sites are available for those who come by boat or car, all located in a primitive setting. Drinking water, picnic tables, fire rings, and vault toilets are provided in this very quiet, natural setting, which has the unusual feature of a manually operated lock. Where else could you enjoy a nice river setting, dam, and a historic lock that you can still witness in operation? The lock and dam here are the newest in the system. They were built in 1910 to replace the original dam in the area which collapsed. Unlike the other locks in the system, Ellis is constructed of cast concrete with steel instead of wood gates. This campground, reached by following SR60 north from I-70 to CR49, is little-used but is an undiscovered gem. There's a concrete public boat launch below the lock to boot with tie-ups. Pets allowed. Register with the lock operator.

A boater's-only primitive camp is located at Luke Chute (lock #5) near Stockport (lock #6). Water and vault toilets provided. Only tents are allowed and sites are unmarked. Boats must be tied up at the bank.

Boating: Unlimited horsepower boats, pontoon boats, canoes, row-boats and houseboats routinely travel the river. Public launches are provided at locks 4, 5, 6, and 11. Private ramps are located at locks 7 and 10.

Information on navigation charts is available from the park office. Although the entire river is navigable from Marietta to Dresden, the channel is unmarked and difficult to follow above Ellis (lock #11). Some of the rivers and streams which feed into the Muskingum are also navigable for short distances, especially by canoe or rowboat.

No trip on the Muskingum is complete without experiencing locking through one or more of the ten locks. When approaching the locks by boat, stay between the red and green buoys which mark the channel. Stay 300 to 400 feet clear of the lock and signal the lockmaster with one long whistle blast followed by one short blast. Slow speed to no wake in this zone. Upon entering the lock boaters must tie off to mooring posts on the lock walls, then stand by to take in or let out mooring lines as the lock water level changes. Each boater must have adequate mooring lines, at least 75 feet. The lockmaster is in complete charge of the process.

Recreational boating is most popular at Marietta and at Zanesville with the tailwaters below the Stockport dam and lock receiving the least usage. No boat rentals are available along the river.

Fishing: No fishing is allowed from the lock walls or the dam structures. Otherwise, fishing is excellent all along the waterway. Catfish is the most sought after fish in the system with all species of bass (smallmouth, largemouth, spotted, and rock) also very popular. Walleye, saugeye, and sauger are sought by some.

The most popular area for boat fishing is the pool above Luke Chute dam and lock. The tailwaters below the dams are the most popular with shore anglers.

Trails: A one-half mile, 18-station fitness trail with a sawdust surface follows the canal bank from the famous Y-bridge in Zanesville to the park office.

Day-use Areas: Three or four picnic tables and grills, along with drinking water and vault toilets are provided at each lock except Philo (lock #9). No shelters are provided.

Caves, ledges, and rugged terrain at Nelson-Kennedy Ledges.

52 Nelson-Kennedy Ledges State Park

Land: 167 acres

Nelson-Kennedy Ledges State Park may contain only 167 acres and lack a beach, boat launch and a campground but it's still an intriguing destination and one of the most interesting units in this corner of the state. Its limited trail system, a mere 2.5 miles in length, winds around, over and through ledges, cliffs and openings so tight they've been named Dwarf's Pass and Fat Man's Peril.

Those interested in the geological history of Ohio will find much of it written in the moss-covered rocks of the Nelson Ledges. The formations are carved in the Sharon conglomerate, a course bedrock comprised of small quartz pebbles eroded from an ancient mountain range and compacted into layers of sandstone and shale by the shallow sea that covered northern Ohio at one time. Then the forces of erosion — wind, water, freezing and thawing — reduced the softer rocks leaving the ledges and stump blocks, those huge boulders that seem to be tilted precariously over the trails.

Always a popular vacation spot, the state first purchased 40 acres of the Nelson Ledges and then added another 20 acres in 1940. In 1948, 101 acres of the Kennedy Ledges was acquired and the following year the state park was created to preserve the area. Most of the park's activities and all of its trails are in the Nelson Ledges. Kennedy Ledges remains undeveloped at this time and not accessible by vehicle. A permit from Punderson State Park is required to venture into the Kennedy Ledges.

Information & Activities

Nelson-Kennedy Ledges
(Mailing Address)
c/o Punderson State Park
P.O. Box 338
Newbury, Ohio 44065
(216) 564-2279

Directions: The park is located in the northeast corner of Portage County. From US-422, head south on SR770 to reach the town of Hiram in 5 miles and turn east onto SR305. Within 4 miles turn north onto SR282. The park is reached in 1.3 miles as SR282 splits the Nelson Ledges portion in half.

Information: There is no office or contact station in the park. For more information write or call Punderson at the above address.

Day-use Area: On the west side of SR282 are the ledges and hiking trails. On the east side is large picnic area, including a parking lot, vault toilets, drinking water, grills and tables, some in an open grassy area, others in a stand of pines.

Hiking: There are four short trails that wind through the Nelson Ledges and when combined they make a delightful 2.5-mile trek. Two trailheads, each with a map box, are posted along SR282 across from the parking lot. My recommendation is to hike the White Trail first followed by the Red, Blue and finally the Yellow, saving the best for last.

Nelson-Kennedy Ledges State Park

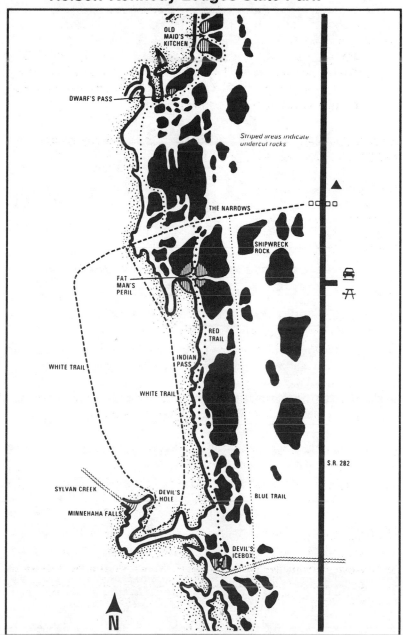

Angling at Paint Creek is among the best in the Ohio State Park system.

54   *Paint Creek State Park*

Land: 9000 acres   Water: 1200 acres

The Paint Creek region lies at the very edge of the Appalachian Plateau. This escarpment marks the boundary between the hilly eastern section of the state and the flatter western portions. This entire region of rolling hills is rich with Ohio Shale which overlays limestone of the river valleys and outcrops of ridges.

Ridges and gorges, deep valleys and wandering rivers were formed by an ice age that lasted one million years. Massive ice sheets carved much of Ohio's topography, but in areas near the park are flat places untouched from the two continental glaciers that disappeared a mere 10,000 years ago. Today, rich hillsides are covered with wildflowers in the spring, and nearby caves, still waters, rambling farmlands, and scenic vistas invite visitors from across the state.

After completion of the Army Corps of Engineers dam in 1974, which helps control flood waters of a 6510-square mile river basin, the surrounding 9000 acres of land were leased and developed into a state park . The long ridges and fertile lowlands are an ideal setting for a relaxing park visit.

Information & Activities

Paint Creek State Park
7860 Upp Road
Bainbridge, Ohio 45612
(513)365-1401
(513)981-7061 Camp Office

Directions: About ten miles east of Hillsboro, the park office is right on US-50 near Upp Road (309). The campground is north and east of the office, depart US-50 at Rapid Forge Road and follow signs.

Information: The park headquarters is located on US 50 at 7860 Upp Road on the south side of the lake. Hours are 8 a.m. - 5 p.m., daily.

Campground: Paint Creek offers 199 sites all having electricity. Located off Taylor Road about five miles north of US-50, the dump station is near the entrance. The campground is composed of two major loops, 1-69 and sites 70 - 199 is the eastern loop. The modern campground is spread around the hilly area with about 25% of the sites offering good shade. The best campsites are located in the western loop, site numbers 1-69.

There is a small camp store near site 65 that offers limited food items and camping necessities. All of the sites have asphalt pads and the perimeter camp sites usually have the best shade and privacy. Sites 29-43 are hilly and separated from other campers. Campsites 111-115 are on the water and offer a nice view.

Usually full on holidays and most weekends, the campground has self-registration near site #63. Fire rings, play equipment, showers, flush toilets, horseman's camping, and lots of picnic tables are featured.

Boating: Paint Creek Lake is designed for unlimited horsepower but there are a number of restricted areas. Near the beach, dam, and in north shallows, skiing and speed is restricted. A number of fisherman areas are also set aside as quiet areas. The Rattlesnake (off Cope Road, on west side of the lake) and Taylor Road boat ramps are nearest the fishing areas, with the dam-area ramp used by many power boats and skiiers.

There are 100 rental slips and boat rental, fuel, and other marine items are available at the marina.

Fishing:
Paint Creek, the longest creek in the U.S., feeds the structure-filled lake and offers excellent tailwater fishing, just north of US-50.

A variety of habitat makes the large reservoir an attractive destination for angler, tournaments, and even a well-known *Crappiethon* that annually offers over one-third million dollars in prizes. Crappies can be huge!

The lake is not stocked (except for saugeye, tiger muskie and pike), but has excellent natural reproduction of white and black crappie, bluegill, smallmouth and spotted bass, rockbass, suckers, darters, and channel catfish. In fact, the former world record saugeye, a seven pounder, was caught in 1988 at Paint Creek. Paint Creek has become a saugeye hot spot. Most saugeye are caught in the tailwaters from late fall until early spring. Live bait techniques are the most popular means of fishing the 1200 acre body of water. A fishing map, complete with location of underwater dikes, trees, rock piles, channels, and so on is available from the US Army Corps office (tel. 513-365-1470).

Bluegill are underfished, but once you find them they can be pulled in using wax worms, crickets, small plastic baits and poppers. Catfish love liver at Paint Creek. Paint Creek is a great place to fish.

Hiking/Bridle Trails:
Paint Creek has eight miles of hiking trails and over 25 miles of bridle paths. There are three bridle path loops, the Main Loop of 18 miles, the Middle Loop of 13 miles, and the Short Loop of seven miles. The horsemen's staging area, where riders can get a trail map, is near the Pioneer Farm on Upp Road, north of the park office. A rider's rest area, complete with hitching post is located next to a pond along the trail.

PAINT CREEK STATE PARK

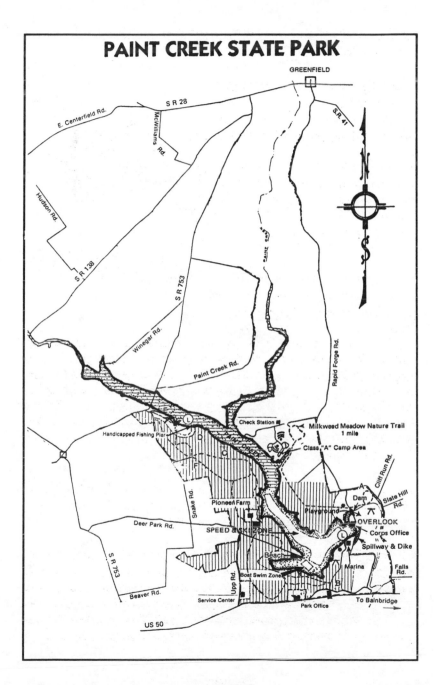

Day hikers will find six loops that traverse hillside, bottomlands, fields and meadows. The Milkweed Meadow Nature Trail, only one mile long, is adjacent to the campground and offers a pleasant upland walk. The Little Pond Trail near the dam offers overlooks, while the remaining trail on the west side of the lake usually winding in concentric circles along a variety of hills, mixed forest-areas, and fields. Well-marked, the trails have benches and twisting pathways of interest.

Day-use Area: Two miles from US-50 a small dark sandy beach is never very crowed on weekends. The beach is about 350 yards long and there are plenty of picnic tables, grills, and restrooms. In a very rural area, the beach is a favoite of those that have discovered it.

A variety of habitats makes the reservoir an attraction destination for amglers.

284

There are 26 cabins at Pike Lake State Park.

55   Pike Lake State Park

Land: 600 acres   Water: 13 acres

Pike Lake State Park makes an ordinary day, extraordinary!

That's the park staff's motto summing up the attributes of the park that they've grown to know and love. It's not just the park they love, it's the people. The thousands of people who dropped in once and have been coming back ever since. The people you might call the park staff's extended family, and there's no criteria to becoming part of the family other than to enter the park gates.

To be sure, this sort of close relationship between park visitors and staff is very common throughout the Ohio State Parks. But at Pike Lake they've raised it to a truly lofty level. It's apparent from the moment you arrive. It's in the programs, in the service, the friendly atmosphere that permeates the park. A visit to Pike Lake has the feel of a weekend trip to visit good

285

friends or close relatives.

And while the larger state parks certainly have their fine points, the smaller scale at Pike Lake adds to the friendly atmosphere.

The park itself is cozily nestled in a beautiful valley surrounded by the Pike Lake State Forest. Everything, it seems, is conveniently located within easy walking distance. The campground is close to the lake, so are the cabins, the picnic area, the park commissary, and park headquarters. All the trails begin nearby. The lake is small but beautiful, perfect for families with small children.

One of the few groups of visitors who came to the area but, for obvious reasons, chose not to return was Morgan's Raiders. Morgan's Raider's, sweeping through southern Ohio on a Confederate Raid during the Civil War, headquartered for a time in the nearby Eager Inn, built in 1797. A Union soldier, identity unknown, was killed in a skirmish with the raiders and buried in today's Pike Lake State Park. Not surprisingly, many landmarks in the area bear the name "Morgan."

The picturesque privately-owned inn still stands south of the park at Pike Lake and Morgan's Fork Roads and is reportedly being restored. The well-maintained soldier's grave is located near the park office.

Information and Activities

Pike Lake State Park
1847 Pike Lake Road
Bainbridge, Ohio 45612
(614) 493-2212

Directions: From the north take US-23 south to Chillicothe, at Chillicothe go west on US-50 to Bainbridge, then south on Potts Hill Road to Pike Lake Rd.

From east or west follow US-50 to Bainbridge, turn south on Potts Hill Road to Pike Lake Road.

From the south try US-23 to SR124, follow SR124 to Morgan's Fork Road to Pike Lake Road.

Information: Park headquarters is located on Pike Lake Rd. in the heart of the park. The office is open Monday through Friday from 8 a.m. to noon and 1-5 p.m.

Campground: If it had flush toilets and showerhouses (and they may well be built in the near future), Pike Lake Campground would be filled every weekend. Even as it is, it fills to capacity on summer holiday weekends and during the fall color season. Two fall weekends to make note of are the third weekend in October when the nearby City of Bainbridge rolls out the welcome mat for the Fall Festival of Leaves, and the last weekend in October when Pike Lake does its own Harvest Moon Campout. The Campout is a down-home weekend-long family affair with a square dance, pumpkin carving contests, games, a wood-fire cooked dinner, a costume parade, and a must-not-be-missed Saturday evening hike in the spirit of the Halloween season.

The campground features 101 sites with electric hook-ups and 11 tent sites tucked along a narrow strip south of the main camp loop. Twenty-four of the electric sites are pull-throughs. Every site in the heavily-forested campground is level, shaded and, in spite of the crew's best efforts, without grass. Most of the sites along the east edge of the camp are widely spaced and back up to Morgan's Fork Stream, check site numbers between 73 and 98 on the east side of the drive.

Campers will find a playground in the middle of the camp, and a basketball court, softball field, and horseshoe courts near the group camp at the campground entrance. It's a very easy and safe walk from campsites to the dam and lake area.

Pike Lake recently changed its no pets rule and now allows them on all sites. Designating certain sites as pet areas is under consideration.

Cabins: Pike Lake has 26 cabins, #1 is now the park office, numbers 2-14 are standard cabins built by the Depression-era CCC, and 15-26 are family cabins built in 1972. Family cabins are available year-round,

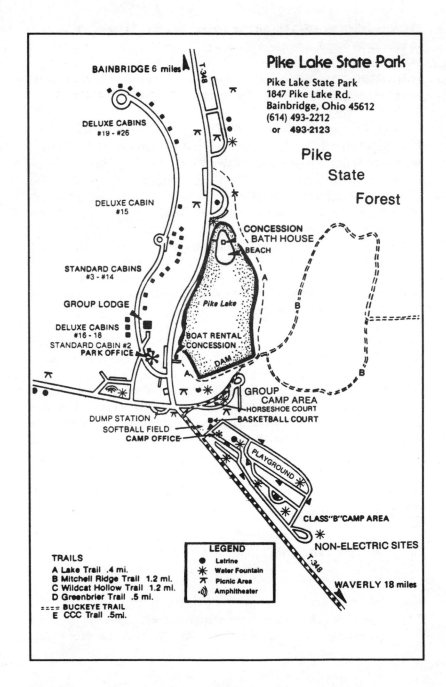

Pike Lake State Park

Pike Lake State Park
1847 Pike Lake Rd.
Bainbridge, Ohio 45612
(614) 493-2212
   or   493-2123

Pike

State

Forest

BAINBRIDGE 6 miles

T-348

DELUXE CABINS
#19 - #26

DELUXE CABIN
#15

STANDARD CABINS
#3 - #14

GROUP LODGE

DELUXE CABINS
#16 - 18
STANDARD CABIN #2
PARK OFFICE

CONCESSION
BATH HOUSE
BEACH

Pike Lake

A

B

BOAT RENTAL
CONCESSION

DAM

A

B

GROUP
CAMP AREA
HORSESHOE COURT
BASKETBALL COURT

DUMP STATION
SOFTBALL FIELD
CAMP OFFICE

PLAYGROUND

CLASS"B"CAMP AREA

NON-ELECTRIC SITES

T-348

WAVERLY 18 miles

TRAILS
A Lake Trail .4 mi.
B Mitchell Ridge Trail 1.2 mi.
C Wildcat Hollow Trail 1.2 mi.
D Greenbrier Trail .5 mi.
==== BUCKEYE TRAIL
E CCC Trail .5mi.

LEGEND
● Latrine
✳ Water Fountain
木 Picnic Area
•)) Amphitheater

standard from April 1 through October. All are on very nice sites, although cabin #2 is in the open and in the middle of activity. Cabins 4 through 12 are down a slope from parking areas, situated along a paved path. The family cabins have screened porches while the standard cabins do not. All the family cabins are nice, especially cabins 20-24. Cabin 26 is most isolated.

Lodge:
Pike Lake Group Lodge should not be confused with the resort lodges of other state parks, it is instead a facility similar to the Laurel Lodge at Lake Hope State Park. The reservable lodge sits on a small ridge above Pike Like and sleeps a group of up to 20 people in two bedrooms and a seven bunk dormitory on the second floor. The rustic lodge, which was built originally as the CCC headquarters, is wood-panelled throughout, features a large porch overlooking Pike Lake, and has complete kitchen and eating facilities along with central heat and air conditioning.

Boating:
Pike Lake hardly fits the mold of the big lakes typical of so many state parks. Yet at 13 acres it fits the close and comfortable feeling of the park. Trees crowd the east shore of the lake, the dam is on the south, an island beach on the north, and boat rental concession and commissary on the west.

Pike Lake is restricted to electric motors only. A small, primitive boat launch, which is more of a service drive that dead ends at the water off the beach parking area, can be used to put small boats in the water. Canoes, rowboats, and paddleboats -- no electric motors -- are available for rent at the Pike Lake Commissary right on Pike Lake across from the park office. The Commissary, open weekends in April, May, September and October, is open 8 a.m. until 8 p.m. from Memorial Day through Labor Day. Sandwiches, cold drinks, and basic camp supplies and groceries are available.

Fishing:
Pike Lake, originally hand-dug by the CCC as a water supply for their camp, is now a beautiful fishing and swimming hole. The lake was drained in January, 1993, so that it could be dredged and structure added. When refilled it is 16-18 feet deep at the dam and the nice weed beds will no doubt return. It will be restocked with bass, bluegill, and catfish and be an even better fishing lake than before.

Bank fishing is very popular here. A floating fishing platform is provided south of the commissary, complete with a picnic table that you don't have to be a fishing enthusiast to enjoy. Bait and fishing licenses are available at the commissary.

Hiking/Bridle Trails: Five hiking trails are featured in Pike Lake, along with a section of the Buckeye Trail and ten miles of bridle trails through the surrounding 10,586-acre Pike Lake State Forest.

Greenbriar Self-Guided Nature Trail (0.5 mi., loop) Stop in at the office for a brochure to acquaint you with the trees and geology along this easy to moderate trail. Begins at maintenance area.

CCC Trail (0.5 mi., one way). A new trail which serves to continue to the Greenbriar Trail into a larger loop. Easy.

Lake Trail (0.4 mi., one-way). Begins at the commissary, crosses the dam, follows the wooded east shore of Pike Lake past the beach to the main picnic area. Easy to moderate.

Mitchell Ridge Trail (1.2 mi., loop). Begins from the dam area, actually a loop trail that the Buckeye Trail shoots off from at the mid-point. Trail traverses difficult, rough terrain, climbs a steep ridge through heavy forest.

Wildcat Hollow Trail (1.2 mile, one way). Begins from the maintenance area or the campground. A steep trail through the hollow climbing to the ridge, moderate on the ridge-top. Some sandstone outcrops along the route.

Bridle Trails. Miles of bridle trails are available in the adjacent Pike Lake State Forest.

Day-use Areas: The lake is the focal point for day-use facilities. Picnic sites are scattered along Pike Lake Road north of the lake and along the lake itself. On a small island on the north end of the lake is a 155 foot beach and recently built handicapped-accessible beach concession with showers, flush toilets, changing areas and food concession. Offshore is a swimming platform. The concession's grill serves hamburgers, sand-

wiches, pizza slices, cold drinks and ice cream from Memorial Day through Labor Day.

Nature Notes: What the park bills as an outdoor nature center is perhaps best billed as a native animal display area. Located in two parts along Egypt Hollow Road near the park maintenance area and near the western park boundary, the center has no permanent residents so each year is something different. The summer displays often include local snakes and amphibians, raccoons, opossum, skunks and the like, and usually there is a resident or two in the park's deer enclosure. Most of the animals come to the park injured and are released back to the wild when they return to health.

A campground amphitheater, also located near the park maintenance area, is the focal point for weekend fireside programs and movies.

Hunting: Although hunting is not allowed in Pike Lake State Park, excellent hunting opportunities for deer, wild turkey, and ruffed grouse are available in the surrounding state forest.

Winter Activities: While winter's ice and snow doesn't often dip this far south into Ohio, when it does Pike Lake seems to get more than its share. Winter can be very special especially when there's snow for sledding on the dam and the lodge hill, and ice skating on the lake.

Quality habitat and regular stocking provides good fishing at Portage Lakes.

56 Portage Lakes State Park

Land: 1000 acres   Water: 2520 acres

Perhaps the most famous portage in Ohio was the eight-mile stretch between Cuyahoga and Tuscarawas Rivers, the only land crossing Indians had to make when paddling from Lake Erie to the Ohio River. The Indians quickly learned the easiest route; a series of glacially-carved lakes that lies between the two rivers.

Today the group of 13 lakes is called Portage Lakes and is the major feature of this heavily used state park in Summit County. Although the unit offers a fine campground, Portage Lakes is a haven for day visitors because of its urban surroundings. Two lakes actually lie inside the city limits of Akron while encircling the chain to the south is Canton.

That's no surprise. Portage Lakes played an important role in Ohio's Canal era, a short-lived chapter in the state's history but one that did much to bring prosperity to this region. The Ohio and Erie Canal which opened in 1833, passed between Nesmith and Long Lake to the north and the rest of the chain was used as feeder lakes to maintain the necessary four-foot depth in the "big ditches." The canal construction prompted development along the banks and led General Simon Perkins, a surveyor and land agent, to establish Akron. By 1854 the canals were already losing money due to new railroad lines and by 1913 they were abandoned.

The Ohio Department of Public Works took control of the waterways for recreational purposes and in 1939 the Nimisila Reservoir was built to raise the level of the lakes lowered by a series of droughts. Eventually Portage Lakes were transferred to the newly created Ohio DNR in 1949 to be administered as a state park.

Information & Activities

Portage Lakes State Park
5031 Manchester Road
Akron, Ohio 44319-3999
(216) 644-2220

Directions: From Akron head south on SR93 for 8 miles to reach the entrance to the park's day-use area and headquarters on Turkeyfoot Lake. From Canton head north on I-77, depart at exit 118 and continue north on SR241. Head west on SR619 to cross the lakes and reach SR93.

The headquarters is 5.6 miles from the campground on Nimisila Reservoir, the other major area of the park. To reach it head south on SR-93 for a mile and then east on Center Road for 1.5 miles to South Main Street. Turn north on South Main Street, east on Caston Road briefly and then south on Christman Road which will wind past two boat launches and the campground.

Information: The park headquarters is located in the day-use area off Turkeyfoot Lake. Hours are 8 a.m. to noon and 1-5 p.m. Monday through Friday.

Campground: Portage Lakes has 74 rustic sites on the east side of Nimisila Reservoir, an electric motor-only lake. None of the sites are within

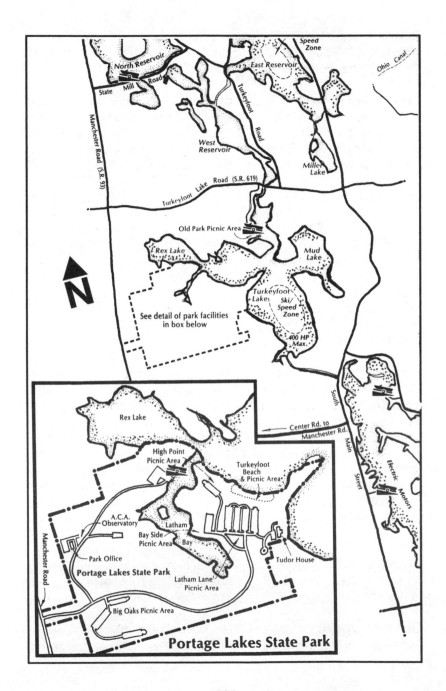

North Reservoir
State Mill Road
East Reservoir
Speed Zone
Ohio Canal
Turkeyfoot Road
West Reservoir
Miller Lake
Manchester Road (S.R. 93)
Turkeyfoot Lake Road (S.R. 619)
Old Park Picnic Area
Rex Lake
Mud Lake
N
See detail of park facilities in box below
Turkeyfoot Lake
Ski/Speed Zone
400 HP Max.
South
Center Rd. to Manchester Rd.
Rex Lake
High Point Picnic Area
Turkeyfoot Beach & Picnic Area
Main Street
Electric Motors
A.C.A. Observatory
Latham
Manchester Road
Bay Side Picnic Area
Bay
Park Office
Tudor House
Portage Lakes State Park
Latham Lane Picnic Area
Big Oaks Picnic Area

Portage Lakes State Park

view of the water but all are in a wooded area and well isolated from each other. Sites 57-70 are in a stand of pine for an interesting setting while 13 through 27 are designated for pet camping.

Facilities include paved spurs, fire rings, tables and vault toilets. There is also a unimproved boat launch within the campground and near the contact station a visitor's parking lot on the lake that attracts shore anglers. The campground generally fills up Memorial Day and 4th of July weekends but sites can usually be obtained the rest of the summer.

Day-use Areas: The park has five picnic areas with four of them located off Turkeyfoot Lake. Big Oaks, the first after entering the park, is the largest with three separate parking lots servicing a huge area of tables, grills, toilets and shelters. Turkeyfoot Beach features a 900-foot sandy shoreline and marked swimming area along with changing booths in the parking area and lifeguards. Overlooking the beach on a lightly shaded hill is an area of tables and grills. Adjoining the large parking lot for the beach are High Point and Latham Lane Picnic Areas, both on Latham Bay. Finally Old Park Picnic Area off of SR619 has tables, grills and a shelter in a lightly wooded area overlooking the water.

Boating: Within the day-use area on Turkeyfoot Lake the park maintains a four-lane launch facility with loading docks and a large parking area. From Turkeyfoot Lake you can access Rex Lake, Mud Lake, West Reservoir and East Reservoir through channels. Both Turkeyfoot and the East Reservoir have ski and speed zones where motors of up to 400 HP are permitted. These are clearly marked with buoys and speeding and water skiing are done in a counter-clockwise direction inside. The zones also have designated hours that alternate between speeding, skiing and, on Sundays and holidays, sailing. The activity and time periods are posted at the launches and the park office.

All other areas should be considered "no wake" unless posted otherwise. Nimisila Reservoir, limited to electric motors, supports the most launches; one the west side off South Main Street and three off of Christman Road. The restricted reservoir has become something of a haven for wind surfers, especially on the weekends. Other launches are in Old Park Picnic Area off SR619 for quicker access into West Reservoir and on North Reservoir and Long Lake. Summit Lake also has a boat launch but parking is limited to what is available along the street.

Fishing: The main areas for anglers is Nimisila Reservoir, the five connected lakes and reservoirs that are often referred to as Portage Lakes and Long Lake. Turkeyfoot, the deepest lake at 50 feet, has been stocked regularly with walleyes and beginning in 1988 with saugeye. Largemouth bass are found throughout the chain while crappie fishing is considered good in the spring and bluegills in the six to eight-inch range are plentiful.

Portage Lakes is one of the few places in Ohio where anglers can fish for chain pickerel and in 1961 the state record of 6-pounds, 26-inches came out of Long Lake. The North Reservoir is fished for pike and muskie while Nimisila Reservoir, a relatively shallow body of water with extensive weed beds, is stocked annually with northern pike and fished for bass, crappie and bluegill as well.

Hiking: There are five miles of trails in the day-use area on Turkeyfoot Lake, that winds from the woods and open fields to the park facilities. The best hike is Pheasant Run Trail, a 0.75-mile loop into the woods and along Latham Bay from the Big Oaks Picnic Area. Other walks include Shoreline Trail, a 3.25-mile loop from Big Oaks to the beach, and Rabbit Hill Trail, a mile loop accessed near the boat launch.

Facilities for the Handicapped: The parking lot on North Reservoir off of Portage Lakes Drive features a handicapped accessible fishing dock.

Winter Activities: Snowmobiling is permitted on the lakes during the winter while others use the frozen surfaces for ice boating and ice fishing.

The English Tudor-style lodge at Punderson offers a relaxing setting.

57   Punderson State Park
Land: 900 acres   Water: 90 acres

Yes Virginia, there are natural lakes in Ohio. Not a lot but a few, with most of them located in the northeast region of the state where 10,000 years ago the last glacier retreated north, gouging out basins and leaving behind large blocks of ice that melted into lakes. The largest of these ancient bodies of water is Punderson Lake, the centerpiece of Punderson State Park.

The lake picks up its name from Lemuel Punderson, who in 1808 was a young ambitious land agent and Newbury Township's first permanent settler. Punderson called the sparkling lake his "big pond" and built a small dam at the south end to power his grist mill with the outflowing water. With the by-products of the milling operation, Punderson also ran a distillery operation and both the mill and his powerful brew proved to be extremely profitable ventures.

It allowed the Punderson family to develop a small estate along the lake which became a popular gathering spot for Newbury Township settlers and eventually evolved into a resort area for those who wanted to escape the bustling city of Cleveland. Cottages and a small hotel were built on the hillsides overlooking the lake and in 1929 construction began on the English Tudor-style Manor House.

Today Punderson Lake, which became a state park in 1951, draws more than 500,000 visitors annually for a variety of activities that range from camping, swimming and golf to sledding and cross-country skiing in the winter. Manor House, which took almost 20 years to complete, underwent major structural renovation from 1979 to 1982 and now is one of Ohio's premier state park lodges.

Information & Activities

Punderson State Park
11755 Kinsman Road
Newbury, Ohio 44065
(216) 564-2279

Directions: From the Cleveland area and I-271 head east on US-322 for 12 miles and then south on SR44 for miles. Turn west on SR87 and the park entrance is reached in 2 miles.

Information: The park office is quickly passed after entering the state park and is open Monday through Friday from 8 a.m. until noon and 1-5 p.m. To check availability of campsites call the campground office at (216) 564-1195. For information or tee times on the golf course call (216) 564-5465.

Campground: The campground is situated on the east side of Punderson Lake on the site of a former Indian village. The facility features 201 sites on a half dozen loops equipped with electric outlets, paved spurs, tables and fire rings. The sites are close together, many are in wooded areas that provide a bit of isolation from your neighbor. Although some are situated on a bluff above the lake there is no clear view of the water through the trees. Sites 134-155, however, are located on an open hilltop above Stump Lake.

Other facilities include three laundry and showerhouses, play equipment, a pet camping area and four Rent-A-Camps. From near site number 26, a path leads to a fishing pier on the lake. On summer holidays and any nice weekend in August the campground can fill up, but otherwise campers can count on an open site. Raccoons is the one problem campers face in Punderson State Park. Don't leave your food or supplies unattended.

Day-use Areas: Just beyond the park office is the Punderson Lake beach and picnic area. The beach is not large but pleasant with a gentle sloping sandy bottom in its marked off swimming area and changing booths. On a bluff above the shoreline of the lake is a picnic area with tables and grills in both a wooded setting and open grassy area. Nearby is play equipment and a basketball court.

There is also a small picnic area near the boat concession and park marina. Punderson Camp Store and Marina (216-564-5246) is open daily from 7 a.m. to 8 p.m. during the summer and on Friday, Saturday and Sunday in May and September. Canoe, rowboat and pedal boat rentals are available along with bicycles while the store sells camp supplies, food and firewood.

Fishing: Punderson is the largest and deepest natural lake in Ohio with 90 surface acres and a depth of more than 75 feet in the middle. It's stocked several times a year with golden trout that can survive year-round in the deep, spring-fed lake. But in reality the majority are probably taken within weeks of their release. Most anglers tip jigs with wax worms and maggots to entice the trout and a 14-inch fish is not an uncommon sight during the summer.

The lake also contains largemouth bass, bluegills, crappies and perch. Only electric motors can be used on Punderson and can be rented from the camp store. A boat launch with a cement ramp is located at the marina while shore anglers will reach fishing piers with a short walk from site number 26 in the campground or by following the Iroquois Trail from the south end of the beach.

Hiking: The park has 14 miles of trails, most of it a 10-mile network on the west side of the park, north of the golf course, that is groomed in the winter for cross-country skiers. These trails can be accessed for a parking lot and trail head near the service building, from the park office, the sports chalet and from the lodge. From the campground the Erie Trail departs as a 1.5-mile loop that winds around Stump Lake and along the west side of the lake the Iroquois Trail follows the shoreline from the marina to the lodge.

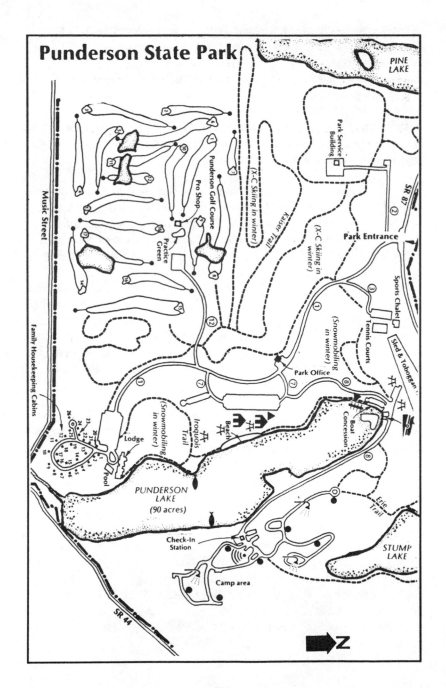

Punderson State Park

PINE LAKE

Music Street

Family Housekeeping Cabins

Punderson Golf Course

Pro Shop

Practice Green

(X-C Skiing in winter)

Kaiser Trail

(X-C Skiing in winter)

Park Service Building

Park Entrance

SR 87

Sports Chalet

(Snowmobiling in winter)

Tennis Courts

Sled & Toboggan

Park Office

(Snowmobiling in winter)

Iroquois Trail

Lodge

Pool

Beach

Boat Concession

PUNDERSON LAKE
(90 acres)

Check-In Station

Camp area

Erie Trail

STUMP LAKE

SR 44

N

300

Cabins and Park Lodge: Overnight accommodations at the park include 26 cabins, perched above the lake at its south end. The two-bedroom cabins include a living room, full kitchen and bath, television sets and a screened porch with a picnic table. Cabins two through six feature a lakeside view.

The Punderson Manor is a 31-room lodge that was completely renovated in 1982 but still retains its charming Old English decor, including some suites with fireplaces or wall to ceiling windows overlooking the lake. Other features of the Manor are an outdoor pool, basketball court and a close proximity to the park's 18-hole golf course. Advance reservations for the lodge or the cabins are strongly recommended and can be obtained by calling 1-800-282-7275.

Nature Notes: The park offers naturalist programs almost daily throughout the summer that range from wildflower hikes and birding adventures to tours of nearby Nelson-Kennedy Ledges State Park and evening slide shows. All programs meet at the amphitheater in the campground unless otherwise noted. Located near the marina is the park's Butterfly Garden, a small area landscaped with flowers that attract a variety of butterflies, while during the summer a "water nature trail" is set up on the lake. Paddlers can pick up interpretive brochures at the campstore that correspond to numbered posts on the lake.

Winter Activities: Located in Ohio's "snow belt" Punderson offers the widest variety of activities in the winter of almost any state park. The trails are some of the best in the state and the site of the annual Ohio Championship Cross-Country Ski Race. Ski rentals are available in the Sports Chalet on weekends and holidays and from there skiers follow groomed trails that pass through a mostly wooded and rolling terrain. Generally you can count on a half dozen weekends of adequate snow on the trails.

58 Pymatuning State Park

Land: 3500 acres Water: 14650 acres

After the glaciers departed Ohio 14,000 years ago, in the northeast corner of the state the melting ice resulted in kettle lakes, bogs and ponds that eventually became a vast swamp. A rich wetland, the Pymatuning Swamp supported an abundance of wildlife, including black bears and wolves, and was surrounded by an impossible impenetrable forest, much of it towering white pine. The area was a favorite hunting and gathering place for the Indians, whose name "Pymatuning" meant the crooked mouthed man's dwelling place. Early immigrants, however, went out of their way to avoid the swamp for land that was easier to settle.

But little by little the wilderness wetland lost its character. Trappers entered seeking beaver pelts and loggers took the white pine that was in high demand for the construction of sailing ships masts. By the early 1800s even settlers arrived and farmed the edges of the marsh with a cash crop of onions. In 1933, large tracts of the swamp were cleared for the construction of a dam to regulate the flow of the Shenango and Beaver rivers. The result was Pymatuning Reservoir, a 14650-acre impoundment where there once was a vast wetland.

Less than 4,000 acres of the lake lie within Ohio, but in 1935 the state already saw the recreation potential of the area and began to acquire the western side of the reservoir. By 1950, the state had acquired most of the shoreline and the Division of Parks began developing it as Pymatuning State Park. Today, the Ashtabula County park draws close to 1.2 million visitors a year who arrive to swim, boat, fish and camp.

Information & Activities

Pymatuning State Park
Route 1
Andover, Ohio 44003
(216) 293-6030

Directions: Pymatuning is 40 miles north of Youngstown and 65 miles east of Cleveland on the Pennsylvania border. From either I-90 or I-80, depart on SR11 to US-6. Head east to Andover and continue east on SR-85. Within 3 miles is the junction with Pymatuning Lake Road just before SR85 crosses the lake as a causeway. Park facilities are located both to the north and south from here. The campground, park office and cabins are south of SR85 along Pymatuning Lake Road.

Information: The office is 1.5 miles south of SR85 on the corner of Pymatuning Lake Road and NR-30, the scenic park road the loops the main section of Pymatuning. Hours are 8 a.m. to 5 p.m. Monday through Saturday. The campground check-in station is also staffed daily during the summer.

Campground: Pymatuning has a huge modern campground located near the south end, three miles from the park office. Situated along three loops are 373 campsites of which 352 are equipped with electric outlets. The first and second loops are for the most part lightly shaded grassy sites, a few of them near the water. They are divided by a tent-only camping area, as well as play equipment, a nature building and amphitheater. The third loop to the north is the most wooded by far but still features electric hook-ups. Its shoreline sites are the gems of the campground.

Pymatuning Lake State Park

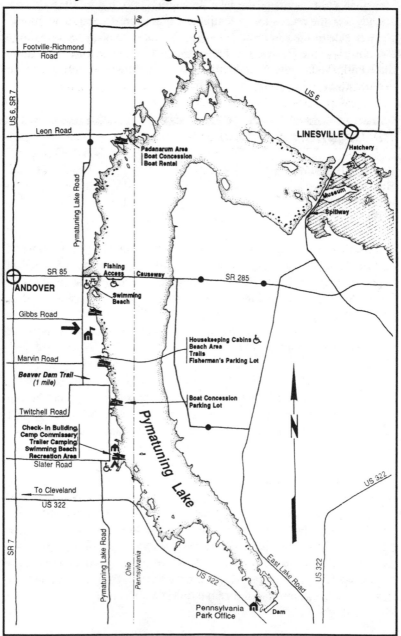

Also located in the campground are four washhouses with modern restrooms, showers and laundry facilities, a camp store, a dump station and a small beach and swimming area. Off of the first loop in the middle is a boat launch with cement ramp and limited parking for additional vehicles and trailers. The campground traditionally fills up on holiday weekends and is 80 percent filled on most summer weekends. To check on availability of sites call the camp office at (216) 293-6684.

Cabins: Located off NR-30 near the park office are 35 standard cabins and 27 family cabins. Standard cabins are single-room units that sleep four on a double bed and fold-out sofa and contain a small kitchen area and bathroom. They are available by the night and are rented out from May through October. Family cabins are heated for year-round use and sleep six in two bedrooms with twin beds and a fold-out sofa. They also have a living room, full kitchen and a screened porch.

Family cabins are available only by the week during June, July and August and none of the units, family or standard, have fireplaces, telephones, televisions or air conditioning. Grouped close together, the cabins are about a half mile north of a beach and picnic area. Like all state park cabins, these are in heavy demand throughout the summer and must be reserved in advance. Pymatuning has a special reservation telephone number (216)293-6329 and cabins can be reserved up to a year in advance.

Day-use Areas: There are five picnic areas within the park, all with tables, grills and a view of the lake. Just north of the campground is Poplar Grove Picnic Area that has a shelter in a shady area overlooking the water. Birches Landing also contains a few tables while another shelter is found at the Swimming Beach and Picnic Area near the cabins.

The largest beach is just south of the causeway and features a 1000-foot swimming beach along with bathhouse, snack bar, volleyball courts and a separate picnic area with a shelter. And finally, the Padanaram Day-use Area, 3 miles north of SR85, has a limited number of tables and grills.

Boating: The park maintains five boat launches, four south of SR85 and one north at Padanaram Day-use Area and all are posted along Pymatuning Lake Road. The launch facilities at Padanaram and Birches Landing 3 miles

south of SR85, also feature a boat livery service that sells gas, oil, bait and tackle as well as rents a variety of boats from canoes and 14-foot motorboats to 24-foot pontoons. Call Pymatuning Boat Livery (216-293-6660 or 216-293-4414) for more information about rentals and rates. The large lake lends itself to an afternoon cruise but keep in mind that it's a heavily used boating area and the maximum size of motors is 10hp.

Fishing: The lake is best known for its Pymatuning Spillway, where every year so many visitors stop to feed the ducks and carp that the waterfowl end up walking on the backs of the fish crowding in. But Pymatuning has more than just carp. The lake features 77 miles of shoreline in two states and often is regarded as one of the most productive fishing lakes in northeast Ohio. The main species is walleye and biologists estimate that anglers harvest more than 50,000 a year, averaging better than 16 inches each and some weighing up to 10 pounds. May and June are the best months for walleyes before the water has a chance to heat up.

The 14,000-acre lake supports fisheries of bluegill, white bass, perch and crappies that most anglers pick-up in the spring. There is also a strong bass population with anglers catching predominantly smallmouth. Special regulations are applied to the lake in both states and include a 15-inch minimum size on walleye, 12 inches on bass and 30 inches on muskies. The daily limits for walleye are six, eight for bass and two for muskies. As long as you stay in your boat, you can fish any section of the lake with an Ohio or Pennsylvania fishing license. Within the park, shore anglers often gather at Fishing Point near the cabins on NR30 and along the breakwall at the park's beach and picnic area just south of the causeway.

Hiking: The park has a pair of short hiking trails for a total of 2 miles. The Beaver Dam Trail is a mile-long loop located near the Swimming Beach Picnic Area and has 15 numbered posts that correspond with a interpretive brochure available at the park office. Among the things pointed out on the walk are signs of beavers and a dam they have constructed. Located near Fishing Point is a posted trailhead to the mile-long Whispering Pines Trail.

Nature Notes: During the summer a naturalist is on duty at the Nature Center in the campground and conducts a variety of programs, including hikes, fishing derbies, workshops and wildlife clinics. At night campfires, slide presentations and movies that are staged at the amphitheater.

Facilities for the Handicapped: Within the campground and the main beach south of the causeway are handicapped accessible showers while Poplar Grove Picnic Area has a barrier free vault toilet.

Winter Activities: Pymatuning lies in something of snow belt, making it a popular park for winter recreation. Ice boating and ice fishing are popular on the lake while others stay on the mainland to enjoy winter camping and cross-country skiing.

The park maintains five marinas.

Stewart Family Mansion at Quail Hollow State Park.

59   Quail Hollow State Park

Land: 698 acres Water: 2 acres

When Conrad Brumbaugh emigrated from Maryland to what is now Middlebranch in 1811, he encountered dense timberland, vast swamps and one of Ohio's few natural lakes. He marked off a homestead with his tomahawk and then embarked on the harsh life as one of the first settlers in northeast Ohio. Bears were known to kill his pigs, rattlesnakes were numerous in the swamps and the huckleberry patches south of his property so dense that "pickers occasionally became lost, a few never returned."

But Brumbaugh prevailed, raised 11 sons and four daughters and his "Brumbaugh Homestead" was such a prosperous farm in the 19th century that eventually the land was acquired by another great family. Harry Bartlett Stewart purchased the homestead in 1914 and other adjacent properties until he had totaled 720 acres. In 1929, he built a mansion featuring the Greek Revival architectural so popular in the Western

Reserve area of Ohio. The 40-room manor went on to become the residences of three generations of Stewarts, including Harry Bartlett Stewart, Jr., the chairman of the board for the Akron, Canton and Youngstown Railroad.

The family resided in the home until 1975 when it was offered as a gift to the state. In 1981, Quail Hollow State Park, named for the bobwhite quail so commonly seen in the area, opened to the public. It's now a mecca of cultural and natural history.

You can trace the lives of two great Ohio families by visiting the former Stewart Family manor, renamed the Natural History Study Center, or taking a stroll through the Brumbaugh family cemetery. Or you can enjoy miles of interpretive trails that wind through a variety of habitat, some not unlike what Brumbaugh encountered when he arrived from Maryland.

Information & Activities

Quail Hollow State Park
13340 Congress Lake Ave.
Hartville, Ohio 44632
(216) 877-6652

Directions: Quail Hollow is on the border of Stark and Portage Counties, northeast of Canton. From I-77, depart at exit 120 and head south on Arlington Road for a short ways then east on SR619. Within 7 miles you reach the town of Hartville where you turn north on Congress Lake Road. The park entrance is reached in a mile.

Information: The park office is located in the Natural History Study Center area of the park and is open from 8 a.m. to 5 p.m. Monday through Friday.

Day-use Areas: Quail Hollow has two picnic areas. Shady Lane is the first passed and features tables and grills in an open grassy area. Nearby is the park's nature study pond with an observation deck while a paved path leads to the Stewart manor which includes Spruce Grove picnic area. This facility includes tables, grills and a fire ring adjacent to the herb garden.

Historical Areas: Brumbaugh Historic Cemetery is posted along the park drive and has vault toilets, drinking water and a short path to the family plots. The small cemetery is an intriguing spot where you can study headstones that date back to the 1890s.

Much of the Natural History Study Center is used as a conference center for educational and civic groups. But also inside is a Visitor's Center which orients people to the park with 10 rooms of natural and cultural history displays. The center is staffed by the Quail Hollow Volunteer Association and open 9 a.m. to 5 p.m. year-round and 1-5 p.m. when there are volunteers available. Keep in mind that the mansion is not a museum with historic furnishings. Most of the house is empty.

The Stewart lawn and gardens have been restored, including herb gardens where various plants have been identified. What can never be replaced, however, are the 55 great elm trees that once surrounded the home and lined the driveway but eventually fell victim to Dutch Elm disease. The Quail Hollow Herbal Society holds guided tours through the gardens at 2 p.m. on the last Sunday of every month from June through September.

Hiking: The park has more than 10 miles of trails that wind through a wide variety of habitat. In fact, the trails are named for the habitat they feature and the reason most of the 100,000 annual visitors come to Quail Hollow. All the trails are less than 2 miles in length but can be linked together for longer walks. Trailheads with maps are located adjacent to the herb garden.

From the southern trailhead you can combine the Tall-Grass Prairie, Sedge Marsh, Meadowlands and Beaver Lodge trails for a 4.5-mile hike. The rest of the network lies to the north and includes paths though coniferous forest, deciduous forest, a peat bog and woodland swamp that features a bird blind.

Camping: The park maintains a primitive group campground available on a reservation basis and open to incorporated organizations. The campground can accommodate 100 people.

Bridle Trails: There are four miles of bridle trails located throughout the west half of the park. Shady Lane serves as a parking and staging area.

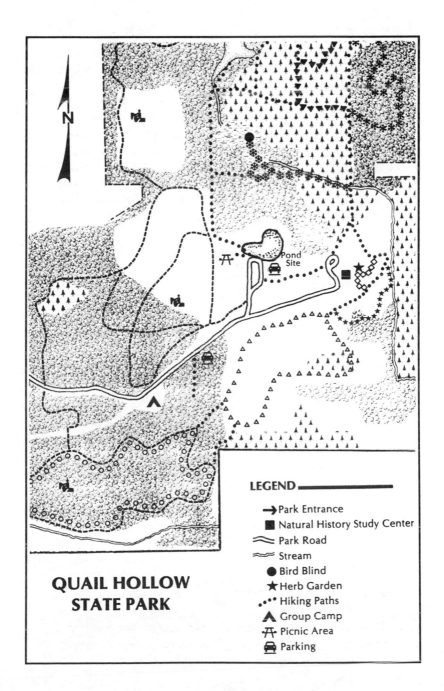

**QUAIL HOLLOW
STATE PARK**

LEGEND

➜ Park Entrance
◼ Natural History Study Center
〰 Park Road
≋ Stream
● Bird Blind
★ Herb Garden
•••• Hiking Paths
Λ Group Camp
⅄ Picnic Area
🚗 Parking

Nature Notes: Quail Hollow hosts a wide variety of natural activities as well as serving as the meeting place for a number of groups. Organizations ranging from birding clubs and historical groups to the Herbal Society meet through the year at the park and all meetings are open to the public. Call the park office for a schedule of activities and meetings.

Facilities for the Handicapped: The natural pond study area is barrier free as well as the picnic areas and Natural History Study Center. In 1994, the park will unveil its Quail Hollow All-User Trail, a half mile-long paved path through three natural habitats and equipped interpretive displays for the sight and hearing impaired.

Winter Activities: Cross-country skiing is a popular activity in the park when there is three inches or more of snow on the ground during the winter. Skiers take to the interpretive trails and a concessionaire rents out equipment from the Natural History Study Center noon to 5 p.m. Sunday through Friday and 9 a.m. to 5 p.m. Saturday.

History buffs will enjoy the old cemetery at Quail Hollow.

McCoppins Mill, 1829, near East Shore Park, Rocky Fork State Park.

60 Rocky Fork State Park

Land: 1384 acres   Water: 2080 acres

Only a couple of miles east of Hillsboro, which is the home of many stockyards, Highland House Museum, Parker House, and Christopher's Steak House is popular Rocky Fork State Park.

Nestled among a patchwork of farmlands and fertile decidious woodlots, Rocky Fork (a name that sounds like an actor on the Beverly Hillbillies TV show) is surrounded by private campgrounds, bait and tackle shops, party stores, RV storage, and marinas.

The reservoir, which shares the same history of many other water impoundments, has miles of grassy shorelines that outline the busy lake. Unlimited horsepower boats pull skiers and cruise the open zone, while small rental boats may probe the east and west no wake, or quiet zones. Rocky Fork is a comfortable park offering most amenities that enable campers a long and fun stay. The amenities are really spread out along the entire shoreline, offering shady coves and overlooks. Rocky Fork is only ten minutes from Paint Creek State Park.

Information & Activities

Rocky Fork State Park
9800 N. Shore Drive
Hillsboro, Ohio 45133
(513)393-4284

Directions: About a one hour drive east of Cincinnati on US-50. At the village of Boston take Beechwood Road south to North Shore Road (TR 274), then west two miles to the park office.

Campground: Complete with a "Chapel in the Woods," 225 camp sites are adjacent to a playground, amphitheater, six latrines, and a camp store that offers rock-hard ice cream, small pizzas, and a view of the ballfield and grassy open spaces. The swimming beach is narrow, but busy.

The campground is full most weekends by Friday afternoon. Weekday check-in is usually a breeze. A small boat marina is near the office, with the Bee Loop Hiking Trail beginning in the campground. Sites number 1-70 are a little cramped but shady, sites 179-184 have an excellent water view with the playground a short walk away. Sites 54-62 and 65-78 are spacious and shady with the latrines nearby. Sites 129-137 are near heavy traffic.

East Shore Marina - restaurant, dock, fishing.

315

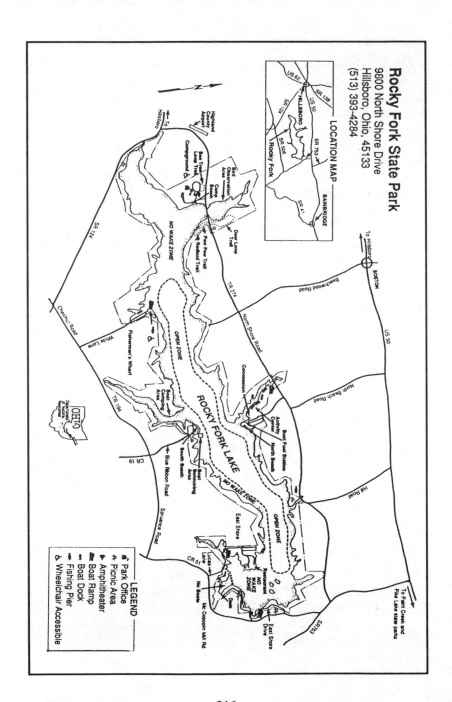

Rocky Fork State Park

9800 North Shore Drive
Hillsboro, Ohio, 45133
(513) 393-4284

LOCATION MAP

US 62
SR 138
HILLSBORO
SR 124
US 50
SR 506
Rocky Fork
SR 753
SR 41
BAINBRIDGE

N

To Hillsboro

Highland County Airport

Bird Observation Area

Camp Beach

Bear Trail Loop Trail
Campground

NO WAKE ZONE

Deer Loop Trail

Paw Paw Trail
Redbud Trail

SR 124

Chestnut Road

White Lane

Fisherman's Wharf

OPEN ZONE

TR 194

OHIO
Department of
Natural
Resources

TR 274

North Shore Road

Concession

Boat Camping Area

ROCKY FORK LAKE

Blue Ribbon Road

South Beach

CR 19

Spruance Road

Activity Center

North Beach

Boat Fuel Station

NO WAKE ZONE

OPEN ZONE

East Shore

Lucas Lane

CR 51

East Shore Drive

Restaurant

NO WAKE ZONE

No Boats

Dam

Mc Coppin Mill Rd.

East Shore Drive

SR 753

To BOSTON
To Hillsboro

Beechwood Road

US 50

North Beach Road

Hill Road

To Paint Creek and
Pike Lake state parks

LEGEND

- ■ Park Office
- ⚐ Picnic Area
- ⚑ Amphitheater
- ▦ Boat Ramp
- ▬ Boat Dock
- ▼ Fishing Pier
- ♿ Wheelchair Accessible

316

Boating: Unlimited horsepower is allowed, but all boaters must obey the 300 foot from shoreline "no wave" zone, and the east and west no wake zones. The five boat launching ramps are busy. The East Shore Marina & Restaurant offers docking for dozens of sailboats, launch ramp, and complete food service. The South Beach and Fisherman's Wharf launch, both on the south shoreline, are popular with anglers. The North Beach ramp, located south off of North Shore Road, has a fuel station, many pontoon boat rentals, and supplies. Pleasure boaters use this ramp heavily.

Fishing: Rocky Fork has excellent crappie fishing. About 100,000 walleyes are stocked annually, and about 4,000, 10 to 12-inch muskies are released each year. Musky angler should troll large plugs, or use common walleye tactics offering large lures, bait, and light wire leaders. Don't be afraid to use really big plugs, and troll at variable speeds. If you get musky fever, try Cowan Lake, the action is considered good to excellent.

Hiking: Rocky Fork has four miles of hiking trails, with much of the grassy shoreline great for easy to moderate walks. The Deer Loop, Paw Paw, and Redbud Trails are located east of the park headquarters and offer easy hiking near the lakeshore.

Day-use Areas: One of the more spread-out state parks, Rocky Fork has lots of grassy open spaces, picnic areas along the jagged edges of the lake, a playground in the camping area, shoreline fishing by the mile, and plenty of room for family gatherings. The North Beach (south of North Shore Road near North Beach Road) has dark sand and is about 200 yards long, located near the marina, concession stand, and volleyball courts. The South Beach (at the end of CR19) offers plenty of parking, changing house, buoyed-off swimming area and picnicking. The Indoor Activites Center near the North Beach features a kitchen, grills, screened-in eating area and lots of parking for group gatherings. The activity center must be booked in advance by calling the park headquarters, (513) 393-4284.

Nature Notes: Blue Bird Trail at the east end of the lake offers a short hike and grassy open spaces where the Appalachian Audubon Society conducts research. Common wildlife are often observed at the park, walk softly, you might see some great birds, a deer, or other mammals.

317

Salt Fork State Park has water side camping for RV units.

61   *Salt Fork State Park*

Land: 17,229 acres   Water: 2,952 acres

The only thing flat in Ohio's largest state park is Salt Fork Lake.

Not that Salt Fork is mountainous. Just persistently, pervasively, pleasantly hilly. Pleasant unless you're a golfer, that is, in which case you'll find the hills of Salt Fork Golf Course a diabolical challenge -- rent a cart unless you want a real workout, and keep on the lookout for the 16th hole which is renowned for its exceptional beauty and difficulty.

Even if you're not a golfer, the golf course should be a focal point. The golf course, lodge and cabin area, and nearby roadsides are perhaps the easiest places in the state to view whitetail deer, especially around dawn and sunset when they are commonly seen by the dozens. There's no need to leave your car to see deer, in fact they've grown so used to automobiles that it's better to just slowly drive the roadways and stay on the look-out without ever leaving your car.

The pro shop for the golf course sits on one of the highest knolls in the area. At the mid-point of the parking lot, looking east, is the best view of Salt Fork Lake I've ever found. It's worth the look.

Salt Fork is a great park for wildlife because of its size and its well-balanced mix of habitat. Roughly one-third of the land in the park is in second-growth oak-hickory dominated hardwoods, much of it on the steep slopes and along the lake and streams. Another third is either land still managed with crops to benefit wildlife or is former farmland or old pasture now in meadow. The final third is in mixed shrubby and grassland habitat.

Bluebirds thrive there -- odds are if you're there in spring or summer you'll see them, too, on or around the bluebird boxes that line the roadsides. So do red fox, gray fox, ruffed grouse, bobwhite quail, wild turkey, woodcock, gray and fox squirrels, muskrat, mink, beaver, hawks, owls, and a wide variety of songbirds also thrive in the park. Salt Fork also has some excellent wetlands which are home for mallards, black ducks, teal, Canada geese and other waterfowl. Wood ducks are common along the forested backwaters and feeder streams.

Fourteen miles of hiking trails await you, with miles of main and back roads to explore. Take the time to do both, and don't be shy about venturing back on the gravel roads, that's where you'll make some of the best discoveries.

It should be noted here that although the entire area is state park, much of the land other than that encompassing the resort buildings, campgrounds, and visitor activity areas is managed by the Division of Wildlife as the Salt Fork Wildlife Area.

Information and Activities

Salt Fork State Park
P.O. Box 672
Cambridge, OH 43725
(614) 439-3521

Salt Fork State Park Lodge
Box 7
Cambridge, OH 43725
(614) 439-2751, (800) 282-7275 Reservations

Directions: Take I-77 to US-22 (exit 47), follow US-22 east approximately seven miles to main park entrance.

Information: The park office is located on Park Road 1 very near the main park entrance off US-22. The office is open Monday through Friday, 8 a.m. until 5 p.m. After 5 p.m. from early spring to late fall and on weekends there's usually someone available in the camp office. The desk in the Salt Fork Lodge is staffed 24 hours a day.

Campground: A fine campground that opened in 1970 with 212 sites, all with electric hook-ups and convenient to showers and flush toilets. The campground offers a nice variety of open and wooded sites in gently rolling terrain, some with great views. Pets are permitted in Loop E. In season register at the camp office, off season registrations are accepted at the park office.

Every loop has its own showerhouse except E. The loop A showerhouse is open year-round, others are winterized the first weekend of November.

Generally speaking, loops A and C offer the best sites, with good choices to be had on loop G as well. Site A-21 is shady and isolated, with a glimpse of the lake, A-26 is nicely surrounded by trees. Also check sites C-1, E-18 to 20 and 30-32, F-19 to 25, and G-20 to 25.

Loop C consists of 18 sites designed for handicapped campers. Sites 12 and 13 are closest to the showerhouse and 13 has a special drinking fountain that accommodates those in wheelchairs.

Loops F and G have the most convenient access to the lake where a campers-only beach and marina are available.

Salt Fork Campground fills every weekend from Memorial Day to Labor Day so arrive early on summer weekends, even earlier if it's a holiday weekend. A camp store with basic groceries, treats and supplies is located in the lodge.

A primitive group camp with 150 person capacity is located off Township 587, one-half mile off US-22. A 20-site horsemen's camp is on PR1 near parking areas for Stone House and Hosak's Cave Trails.

Cabins: Fifty-four modern family cabins are beautifully situated below the lodge along the shore of Salt Fork Lake. The view from this shore is across an arm of the lake with heavily wooded hillsides rising from the shore. In the midst of the cabin area is a small sandy camper's beach and public boat launch with courtesy docks for cabin and lodge guests only.

The lakeside cabins are understandably the most popular, my choice would be cabin 20 which sits by itself on the lake at the north end of the beach. Cabin 21 is also popular, especially with boaters because it's closest to the docks. The odd-numbered cabins from 21 to 37 are all on the lake, as are the even numbers between 40 and 54. Cabins 52 and 54 are situated on a hillside with a steep drop to the lake. They have a great view over a beautiful little wooded cove and out into the lake.

Cabin 9 is outfitted with a wheelchair ramp, and cabins 5, 7, and 11 all have easy access, however none of the cabins has a bathroom properly outfitted for wheelchairs.

Every cabin has a television as well as all the basic amenities. In spite of efforts to correct problems, TV reception is sometimes poor. Bring a VCR or video games for the children, or rent them, as well as new video releases, from the lodge desk.

Cabin guests have access to lodge facilities including the pools, game room, and exercise equipment. A paved trail up a steep wooded hillside to the lodge begins near the boat launch. It's a very pretty walk and it's not uncommon to see deer along the way.

The cabins are heavily booked one week at a time through the summer, and on weekends through the rest of the year. Call for reservations as early as you can, reservations are accepted one year in advance.

Lodge: The Salt Fork Lodge and Conference Center is the largest in the state parks. Guests in its 148 rooms have numerous recreation and dining options including indoor and outdoor pools, tennis, volleyball, indoor and outdoor shuffleboard, a candy shop, gift shop, exercise room, sauna, game room, and playground equipment. In addition to the dining room there's a lounge, and a snack bar serving burgers, sandwiches and more in the pool area. Five rooms are wheelchair accessible as well as all public areas of the lodge.

The lodge atmosphere is a very comfortable mix of a modern resort complex blended with a rustic atmosphere enhanced by huge wood-beamed ceilings, stone fireplaces, and wood-panelled rooms.

When contemplating a visit, inquire in advance about special events coming up in the lodge. There are winter special rates, special theme weekends, and special packages for the holidays.

Boating: No horsepower restrictions are enforced on Salt Fork Lake although large areas of the lake are enforced as no wake zones. The upper lake areas above Sugartree Fork Marina and Salt Fork Marina as well as the lodge/cabin area are no wake zones. Two zones are marked with buoys for water skiing, one at the dam and the second in the general area between the camper's beach and the lodge/cabin area.

Five improved boat launches are available as well as several access points for car-top boats. The largest launch facility is Salt Fork Marina which offers a pair of two-lane launches. Modern two-lane launches are also located at Sugartree Fork Marina, the campground beach, in the cabin area, and behind the park office. A paved launch is also available across the lake from Sugartree Fork at the end of County Road 35 near North Salem. Several small car-top boat launches with parking are located at Hosak's Cave, off County Road 851 in the north end of the lake, at the dam, and on the east side of US22 on the lake.

There are 470 docks available for seasonal rental, 364 docks at Salt Fork marina but the docks at the newer (1981) Sugartree Fork seem to be more popular. They're bigger, closer to the water ski area, and the new marina has a more comfortable feel to it. Both marinas offer marine fuel, bait, snack bars (indoors at Sugartree), plenty of parking and rental boats from rowboats to several kinds of pontoon boats, bass boats, and ski boats. A 65-passenger cruise boat operates in season making daily excursions around the lake that last about one hour and 15 minutes. The sightseeing cruises begin from Sugartree Fork.

Fishing: Salt Fork Lake has its greatest depth, 35 feet, at the dam and

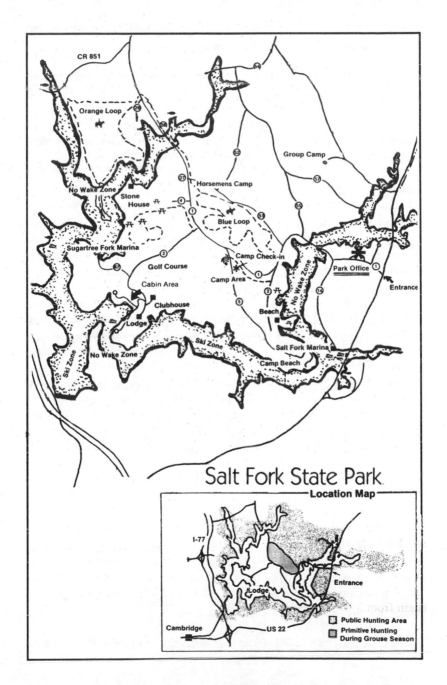

Salt Fork State Park
Location Map

Public Hunting Area

Primitive Hunting During Grouse Season

averages 12 to 14 feet deep through its pair of relatively narrow V-shaped arms that expose 74 miles of shoreline.

The lake harbors bluegill, crappie, catfish, bass, walleye and muskie. During recent netting studies the survey team was pulling up about a half dozen muskie each day in the 20 to 40 pound range. But the lake is best known for panfish and largemouth bass. Although fishing is popular year-round, April through June are the hot fishing times for most species, except muskie fishing which is best in summer.

Hiking/Bridle Trails: In spite of its large size, the walking trails at Salt Fork are relatively short and, except for the paved trails, are moderate in difficulty. The Buckeye Trail skirts Salt Fork on the northeast following a series of roads. Two bridle trail loops are available, both beginning from the Horsemen's Camp. The 10-mile blue-marked loop heads southeast from the camp and is an easy ride over dry, rolling terrain with not much water available. The northerly orange-marked loop is 20 miles long and includes rough stretches in rocky areas, a bridge crossing and some riding on abandoned blacktop roads. Lots of water on this loop. A 16-mile snowmobile trail (only) begins at the first parking lot on PR2 approaching the main beach.

Seven walking trails are connectors or scenic trails in the campground area. If you walk the Waiting Trail it's likely it will be the first one you try in the park. It's a one mile trail that's used by families waiting to register for a site in the campground. It begins from the parking area at the camp office. The Shadbush Trail (2.0 mi., one-way) connects the camp with the golf course pro shop through rolling woodland. Gunn's Glen Trail (1.0 mi., one-way) traverses a mixed hardwood forest, while both the Overlook Trail (200 yds., one-way) and the Sunshine Brook Nature Trail (0.7 mi., loop) are level, paved, and wheelchair accessible.

The Forest Crest Nature Trail (0.3 mi., one-way) connects the campground with the beach, the Valley Brook Loop Trail and Deer Run Trails are short out and back trails through the woodland off Loop G. The Hillcrest Trail is a one-mile loop within the campground and Beach Point Loop is a one-mile trail to a view over the lake.

Stone House Loop Trail (1.8 mi.) begins from a parking lot off PR1 in the northern sector of the park. The trail leads to a beautiful stone house built with locally quarried stone in 1837 by David Kennedy. Today the house is listed in the National Registry of Historic Places.

Hosak's Cave Trail (0.5 mi., round-trip) begins from a parking area off PR1 across an arm of Salt Fork Lake from the Stone House Trail. A beautiful trail, especially in spring and fall, back to one of the most impressive rock formations of the park. The cave, really a large rock overhang, is fascinating but visitors should exercise caution here and stay on the marked trail. Because of the terrain this area of the park closes at dark.

Morgan's Knob Loop Trail (0.8 mi.) and Pine Crest Loop Trail (1.0 mi.) both begin from a 20-car parking area off PR3 approaching the lodge. Both are woodland trails that have nice views of the lake at their midpoints, especially when the leaves are off the trees.

Day-use Areas: Three swimming beaches spread out the pressure for spots to splash around the lake and catch some rays. The main beach is the nicest and at 2,500 feet is the largest inland beach in Ohio. It comes complete with plenty of changing areas, restrooms and showers. A snack concession sells burgers, hot dogs, fries and more.

Picnic areas are scattered through the park but main areas are on the lake along PR14 on the way to Salt Fork marina and near the main beach. Three small picnic areas with drinking water and vault-type toilets are spaced along PR4 off PR1 north of the turn-off to the lodge and cabins. A wheelchair accessible picnic area is located on PR1 opposite the horsemen's camp. It's equipped with three shelters and flush restrooms, grills, special extended picnic tables, and paved walkways connecting the shelters.

The 18-hole, par 71 championship course is a real beauty in rolling wooded terrain. Rent a cart unless you want a real work-out. The clubhouse also has a snack bar with sandwiches and snacks. Call well in advance for weekend tee times.

Nature Notes: Salt Fork is an exemplary wildlife area and it's worth taking in some of the nature programs offered Wednesday through Sunday through virtually the entire summer (there is sometimes a period in August

Scenic shorelines are in all directions at Salt Fork Lake.

when the naturalist must be in Columbus for the State Fair). A program schedule that includes bird walks, junior naturalist programs, and weekend movies is posted each week and easily available in the park.

Hunting: Approximately 12,000 acres of Salt Fork is open to hunting but some areas are restricted. Contact the Ohio Division of Wildlife for a map detailing the restrictions, or lack of them, in the various sectors. Hunting for squirrel, ruffed grouse, rabbit, wild turkey, whitetail deer, and some woodcock is available.

Scioto Trail State Park.

62 Scioto Trail State Park

Land: 218 acres   Water: 30 acres

Eleven miles south of Chillicothe, along a busy section of US-23 where the forested hills crowd the roadway, is an intersecting road that instantaneously takes you away from the highway hustle. Watch carefully, if you blink you'll miss it.

Make the turn off US-23 and the beautiful cool green forest swallows the road immediately as it climbs and twists and climbs some more, out of the valley away from the traffic. Often, the wild mood is enhanced by a light fog hanging in the air. The park roads begin just one-quarter mile off the highway. Without a doubt, Scioto Trail is one of the most easily accessible, yet isolated, parks in Ohio.

Scioto Trail is in rugged territory, the foothills of the Appalachians. That fact coupled with its poor, thin soils delayed pioneer settlement of the park area. Although it is located in the region of the "Mound Builders," the ancient Adena and Hopewell cultures, there's no evidence of their presence in the park area. Certainly, though, this was a rich woodland wildlife area then as it is today.

The park and surrounding 9,369 acre Scioto Trail State Forest overlooks the lower Scioto River valley, the river itself abuts the state forest to the east. The park is split in two parts, each surrounding a 15 acre lake. Where these lakes now set was the target of artillery gunners training during World War I. In 1922, the state began purchasing the land, the lakes were constructed by Civilian Conservation Corps crews in the 1930s, and the land put to more appropriate use as a park and state forest.

The area has been the land of the Shawnee, the Iroquois and then the Shawnee again. Daniel Boone and Simon Kenton roamed the hills. And it was through this area that an important Indian trail and trade route, the Scioto Trail, stretched from rich southern hunting grounds across the Ohio River, through the Scioto River valley, and on to the Great Lakes.

Today, while rushing along on our modern paved trails, take that winding road that leads into Scioto Trail and enjoy a piece of Ohio preserved very much as the earliest settlers would have seen it. While you're there, be sure to drive up Lake Road (one way road from the fire tower area) to the two-way North Ridge Road for the scenic overlooks. Either follow North Ridge Road back around to the park, or backtrack onto Lake Road which will return you to the campground. You won't regret the effort.

Information and Activities

Scioto Trail State Park
144 Lake Road
Chillicothe, Ohio 45601
(614) 663-2125

Directions: Take US-23 depart at SR372, east one-quarter mile.

Information: Follow SR372 to Park Road #1 (Stoney Creek Road), past Stewart Lake to Park Office on Park Road #3.

Campground: The main campground north of the park office and Caldwell Lake has 57 sites, 20 with electric hook-ups, in a beautiful oak-hickory forest setting. Mostly gravel and grass pull-ups, no showers, no flush toilets, and no hot water. But you'll find a picnic table and fire ring at each site, and sites capable of handling up to 35 foot RV's. Pets are allowed on sites 37-57, there are no electric hook-ups in this area, a fact which is more than compensated by their location up a beautifully inviting side ravine along a feeder stream to Caldwell Lake. This is a campground to get away from the crowds. The only competition is for sites with hook-ups on the three major holiday weekends, otherwise you'll find a nice spot. The VIP can be found in season at site #13. Limited firewood is available, nearest supplies are in Chillicothe and Waverly (10 miles).

At the camp entrance is the log church, a replica of the First Presbyterian Church erected as part of the Northwest Territory Sesquicentennial celebration. The church is an interesting and stark reminder of the spartan life led by the early settlers.

There are two tent-only primitive camps here, one above the Stewart Lake parking area in a wooded setting with vault toilets and drinking water about 100 yards away. More open sites are located in a walk-in camp area on the west end of Stewart Lake. Drinking water and all other supplies must be carried in. Vault toilets are provided.

Boating: Because of the small size of the lakes, only electric motors are allowed. Caldwell Lake has a small launch ramp, Stewart Lake is strictly carry-in. Not surprisingly, it's mostly canoes and johnboats on the lakes.

Fishing: "Yeah, they catch some nice fish here," is the word from locals. Both lakes have been periodically stocked with largemouth bass, bluegill, and catfish. Caldwell Lake was drained in the mid-1970s, structure added and restocked. While there's nice fish in both lakes, Caldwell seems to be home for the bigger fish. Both are V-shaped bottom lakes, Caldwell is 20 feet deep, Stewart, 40 feet.

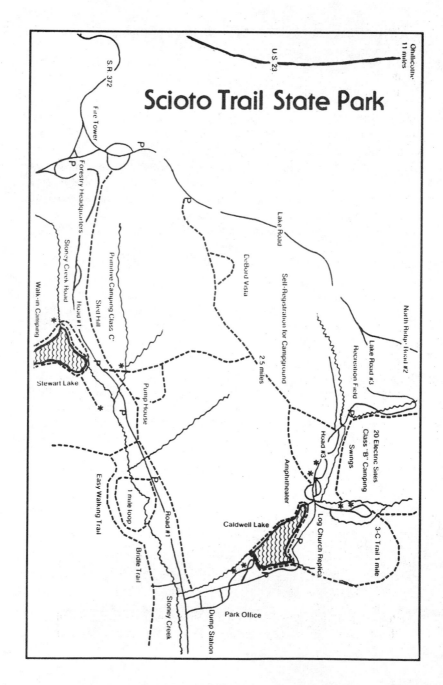

Scioto Trail State Park

Chillicothe 11 miles

U.S. 23

S.R. 372

Fire Tower

Forestry Headquarters

P

P

P

Walk-in Camping

Stony Creek Road

Road #1

Sled Hill

Primitive Camping Class "C"

Stewart Lake

Pump House

P

Lake Road

Redbud Vista

Self-Registration for Campground

2.5 miles

North Ridge Road #2

Lake Road #3

Recreation Field

20 Electric Sites Class "B" Camping

Swings

Road #3

Amphitheater

Caldwell Lake

Log Church Replica

3-C Trail 1 mile

Easy Walking Trail

1 mile loop

Road #1

Bridle Trail

Stoney Creek

Dump Station

Park Office

Hiking/Bridle Trails:

Church Hollow Trail (2.0 mi., loop), is a rugged trail out of the main campground that skirts the hillsides. Though not recommended for children or older adults, it's a very pretty trail through the oak-hickory forest.

DeBord Vista Connector (2.5 mi. to fire tower, one way), also begins at the main camp and leads through the state forest to the DeBord Vista, a nice look-out that typifies those also found along some roadsides and at the fire tower. It continues to the 60-foot high State Forest Fire Tower which can be climbed at your own risk but there's no access to the look-out. Take it slow on the first half mile of the trail, and the rest is a nice walk along a ridge line through a chestnut oak-dominated woods. The trail can be made a loop by following a mowed power line easement a distance of 1.75 miles past Stewart Lake and back to the camp.

CCC Trail (1.0 mile, loop), a newer trail cut by the modern CCC, runs from the Log Church Replica, back a hollow and around to Caldwell Lake.

Bridle trails and additional hiking trails information is available in the state forest. Contact Scioto Trail State Forest, 2731 Stoney Creek Road, Chillicothe, 45601.

Day-use Areas: Picnic areas are provided below both dams and above Caldwell Lake near the main camp. There's also picnicking out on an island in Caldwell Lake, accessible by bridge, that would be the spot I would pick. Over 150 picnic tables, grills, and vault toilets are available. Playground equipment is located near the recreation field above the campground. No swimming is allowed in the lakes.

Nature Notes: The park and forest are ideal hill country habitat with healthy populations of deer, wild turkey, ruffed grouse, squirrels, hawks, owls and more. Spring wildflowers bloom in profusion and fall colors are spectacular.

Naturalist programs are offered in the campground's natural amphitheater with movies and slide programs shown on weekends and holidays.

Shawnee State Park.

63   *Shawnee State Park*

Land: 1,100 acres   Water: 68 acres

Shawnee, located in the Appalachian foothills on the banks of the Ohio River, has the largest state forest surrounding it. For most park visitors, where the state park ends and the surrounding 60,000 acre Shawnee State Forest begins is just an imaginary line that matters only to the employees who manage the sites.

So don't think of Shawnee as merely a respectably-sized state park, think of it as a dramatically hilly, wilderness island of nearly 62,000 acres of unbroken forest. It is the largest contiguous forest in the state, a forest that when seen from any one of the breathtaking overlooks seemingly stretches to the horizon. So many trees that there is a blue haze hanging in the air as a result of the moisture generated by the millions of trees. It is this haze that hangs among the Shawnee Hills which has led to Shawnee's nickname, "the Little Smokies of Ohio."

Think of Shawnee as an enclave with modern comfortable facilities to serve park visitors. Venture out in any direction from the facilities and the scene is wild and natural. In spring the hillsides are splashed with the color of wildflowers including the Pink Lady's slipper or Moccasin flower and, to a lesser extent, the Yellow Lady's slipper. In Fall, the scene is a spectacular splay of colors.

No visit to Shawnee is complete without venturing into the Shawnee State Forest. Do it on foot, on horseback, with a backpack or from an automobile along the 170 miles of roadways that the Division of Forestry maintains. If you do nothing else, try the Panoram Scenic Loop Drive for its scenic route through the forest and stops at unforgettable overlooks.

Gaze across the Shawnee Hills, part of the hunting grounds of the Shawnee, toward what was Lower Town, a major Shawnee village at the juncture of the Scioto and Ohio Rivers. And look to the Spaylaywitheepi (Ohio River) and beyond to Kentucky which was, for them, a sacred hunting ground where no one was to make a home. These are views reminiscent of the legendary Raven Rock. Raven Rock was a sacred spot of the ancient ones, a lookout high above the Ohio River where it is said Indians lay outfitted for war waiting for pioneer flatboats to float past.

Today, the park and surrounding forest is still a land rich in wildlife and scenery, it is a land where bobcat and black bear can still be occasionally seen. It is still a wild land.

Information and Activities

Shawnee State Park
Star Route, Box 68
Portsmouth, Ohio 45663-9703

Shawnee State Park Lodge
P.O. Box 189
Friendship, Ohio 45630-0098

Telephones

Park office:	(614) 858-6652
Camp office:	(614) 858-4561
Lodge/Cabins:	(800) 282-7275 Reservations
Lodge/Cabins:	(614) 858-6621
Marina:	(614) 858-5061
Golf Course:	(614) 858-6681
Canoe Livery:	(614) 353-8333

Directions: Most visitors arrive via US-23 and pick-up US-52 west at Portsmouth. Follow US-52 west for seven miles to SR125, turn right (northwest) and follow SR125 another seven miles to the park. The first entrance will be for the campground and the second, two miles further, is for the lodge and cabin area.

From the Cincinnati area, take US-32 east to the town of Seamen. At Seaman, turn right (south) on SR247 to West Union a distance of about 10 miles. Out of West Union follow SR125 east to Shawnee State Park, about 25 miles.

The golf course and marina, although part of the park, are located on the Ohio River off US-52, two miles west of its intersection with SR125.

Information: The park office is prominently situated along the road to the lodge and cabins and is open Monday through Friday, 8 a.m. to 5 p.m.

The campground office at Roosevelt Lake is open daily from 8 a.m. until 5 p.m. during the peak camping season.

Campground: A deluxe facility with 107 sites, only three without electric hook-ups, and two showerhouses complete with laundromats and flush toilets. The three sites without hook-ups, 12-14, are tent-only sites located up some steps on a hillside above the pet camp. Pets are allowed on sites #1-33 directly above the park office, close to the amphitheater and Roosevelt Lake swimming beach.

Roosevelt, a small, but very pretty lake, with its beach, picnic areas and nice scenery is just a short walk from the campground which is situated in an oak forest between Roosevelt and Turkey Creek Lakes. Many sites sit in the shade of mature trees, others have been cleared but are adjacent to the shady woods. Most sites in the loop including 34-46 have been cleared from the road to the back of the pad. Sites 74, 76, 77, 79, and 81 back to a stream. Site 73 is across the road, rather isolated and an easy walk to a showerhouse and playground. Also check sites 92, 97 and 99.

Shawnee Campground gets its heaviest pressure on holiday weekends, for the annual trout derby held the last Saturday in April, and for the Fall Hike and Campout held the third weekend of October. At least one showerhouse is open from late April through the hunting season in mid-January. If winter camping pressure is light, the only restroom open is the vault toilet at the Roosevelt Lake picnic shelter.

The 58-site Bear Lake Horsemen's Camp with 110 stalls, vault toilets, drinking water and water for horses is located in the state forest north of SR125 with access up Forest Road 3 one-half mile west of the Shawnee Lodge entrance.

One mile east of the campground entrance is a scout camp, Camp Oyo.

Lodge: The 50-room Shawnee Lodge, opened in 1973, has tremendous personality. All the lodges are great, but Shawnee ranks as my favorite. Though modern in every way, the Lodge has an extraordinary rustic flavor perfectly accented with a Native American motif.

The small sitting area across from the lodge desk is rivalled for comfort and atmosphere only by the larger lounging area that overlooks the lodge's outdoor pool and sundeck and on to the tremendous view of Turkey Foot Lake and the ridges that stack up into the distance. Don't pass up the opportunity to walk out onto the deck off this room and savor what has to be one of the best views in Ohio. Big stone fireplaces, huge timber framing, collections of arrow and spear points, and a full size birchbark canoe all enhance the setting.

If you don't go onto the deck, the view is just as good from the window-side tables of the dining room. The food is excellent, but even if it wasn't, the cleverly designed menu loaded with Shawnee lore and legends is worth the visit all by itself.

Next to the dining room is a lounge and bar, downstairs is an indoor pool, whirlpool, sauna and exercise room.

The rooms were just nicely refurnished, those on the third floor have vaulted ceilings and walls done in pine. The walls are perfectly accentuated with Native American designs, nature posters and reproductions of carvings in rock.

Cabins: Shawnee features 25 family cabins, all on shaded sites with porches on a ridge paralleling the lodge. Cabin #16 is specially modified to accommodate the wheelchair bound. If you're looking for privacy check cabins 14 and 15, 16 through 25 are just over the edge of the ridge looking into the woods and are a little nicer than the others.

Boating: Shawnee State Park has a split personality when it comes to boating, put in at Turkey Creek or Roosevelt Lakes and enjoy a quiet leisurely paddle, maybe floating a bit and casting for bass in some placid coves. Or put in a powerboat at the big marina on the mighty Ohio River and set out on a whole different kind of adventure.

Shawnee State Park Marina offers three two-lane launch ramps into the Ohio River, a large car/trailer parking area, gasoline and diesel fuel dock, and 150 docks for boats and sailboats up to 60 feet. Water and electric hookups are available at the docks which are located in a boat basin protected from the main channel of the Ohio River. Overnight and weekly docking is welcome. No boats are available for rent. The marina and launch serves a 70 mile section of the Ohio River between the Greenup Locks and Dam above Portsmouth and the Capt. Anthony Meldahl Lock and Dam toward Cincinnati. It is a beautiful section of the river, largely natural area on both sides, with some bottomland farms and a few homes.

Turkey Creek Lake below the lodge and cabins, Roosevelt Lake below the campground, and Shawnee Lake (aka Pond Lick Lake) near the CCC headquarters in the State Forest are all restricted to electric motors only. A two lane launch ramp is available on the southeast end of 55-acre Turkey Creek Lake and a smaller ramp is located on the south end of 13 acre Roosevelt Lake, off Mackletree Run Road. A small boat rental is also available on Turkey Creek Lake at the beach off the lodge road. Canoes, johnboats, and paddleboats are available for rent as well as some electric

Shawnee State Park

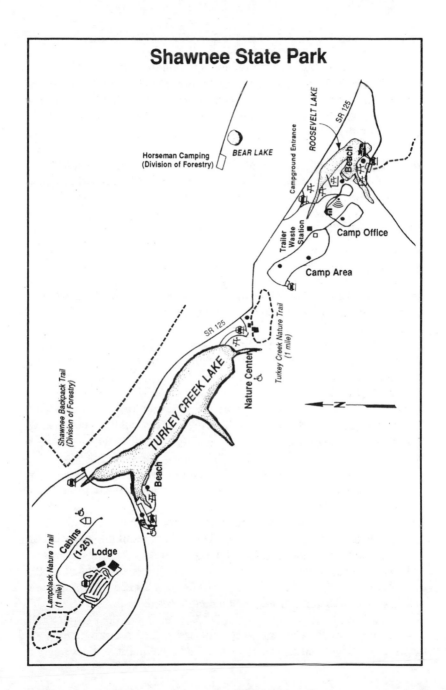

motors.

Fishing: In addition to the fishing opportunities on the Ohio River, Roosevelt Lake and the deeper, larger Turkey Creek Lake are both decent fishing lakes. Largemouth bass, panfish, and catfish are there for the catching in both lakes. Bass fishing is especially popular. In early spring try white or chartreuse jigs for the biggest bass. In the dead of summer try the lake just after dark with a top water bait. Turkey Creek Lake is also stocked annually with trout just before derby held the last Saturday in April. Turkey Creek Lake is deepest along SR125 where the old Turkey Creek once flowed.

Hiking/Bridle Trails: Three walking trails are available in the park as well as the Shawnee Backpack Trail and 75 miles of bridle trails in the state forest.

Lampblack Nature Trail (1 mi. loop). A moderate trail through hardwood forest that begins from the northwest end of the lodge parking area.

Turkey Creek Nature Trail (1 mi. loop). An easy trail along Turkey Creek that's especially nice in fall. Begins from the Turkey Creek Lake boat launch area.

Look-Out Trail (1 mi. round-trip). A more difficult trail that begins from the parking area on the south side of Roosevelt Lake, but the effort is well-rewarded with a nice view of the hills and trees of the valley.

The Shawnee Backpack Trail (43 mi. loop) affords perhaps the best opportunity for a true wilderness experience in Ohio. By incorporating a 10.5 mile side trail into the Shawnee Wilderness Area it's possible to spend nine days on the trail without spending more than one night in any of the eight backpack camps. It's also possible to split the trail into a north loop (23 miles long) and south loop (29 miles) and also cut your time on the trail. No matter what your route, the place to start is the trailhead at the intersection of the road to the Shawnee Lodge and SR125 where adequate parking and a self-registration station are provided.

The terrain along the trail is rugged and challenging, requiring moderate levels of skill and endurance. This is a wild area and it's important that backpackers use sturdy footwear, proper clothing and good equipment. For a trail map contact the Shawnee State Forest, Rte. 5, Box 151C, Portsmouth, OH 45662. Or call that office at (614)858-4201.

Auto Trails

Among the 170 miles of roadway maintained in the park and forest is a route designated the Panoram Scenic Loop Drive, a 25 mile or so route over well-maintained gravel roads that provides excellent looks into the forests and spectacular overlooks. The drive begins and ends on Forest Road 1, about four miles east of the campground off SR125. Allow at least half-day to truly appreciate the scenery. The road is two-way, so a shorter drive is possible.

Another fine overlook is north of SR125 near the Shawnee Lodge and is reached by following Forest Road 3 to Road 6 to reach the Copperhead Fire Tower site.

Day-use Areas: Add picnicking, swimming, and golfing to the preceding list of activities at Shawnee.

Secluded and scenic picnic sites are scattered throughout the park. Some of the best sites are at the beach on Turkey Creek Lake near the canoe rental concession, which also serves up sandwiches, snacks and cold drinks. Two picnic shelters and a number of very nice sites are located on the shores of Roosevelt Lake.

Public beaches with change booths are located on Turkey Creek and Roosevelt Lakes. The Turkey Creek beach has a lifeguard on weekends and holidays.

The Shawnee Golf Course is an 18-hole, par 72 championship course that opened in 1980. The pro shop for the 6,400 yard course is located next to the marina. Because it's in the bottomlands the course is flatter than you might expect but the trees are maturing nicely and there are a number of water hazards to add a challenge. The fifth hole affords a great view down the Ohio River. In the pro shop is a grill serving up sandwiches and burgers. Across the parking lot from the pro shop is the Marina Cafe, open May 1 to October 31 (weekends before Memorial Day and after Labor Day), with its view of the marina and river complimenting the house specialty, smoked ribs.

Nature Notes: A word of caution is appropriate. Shawnee is

wilderness, rugged country where careless hikers can get lost or hurt. If you get lost, follow a hollow down until you come to a stream or road. Stay on the trails, but if you insist on straying step on---not over---logs because this is copperhead and timber rattlesnake country. Be careful where you sit, especially in rocky areas. Park Manager Jan Saffer has never heard of anyone being bitten by a poisonous snake in 18 years and it is extremely unlikely a visitor will even encounter one, but they are present and reasonable caution is advised.

Nearly 8,000 acres in the southwest section of the state forest has been specially designated as wilderness to minimize human impact and protect the area in as natural a condition as possible. The area can be viewed from either the Lower or Upper Twin Creek Roads and from a section of the Shawnee Backpack Trail.

The entire park and forest area is dominated by an oak-hickory forest. Some virgin timber still exists in some of the deep hollows with some fine examples of oak, beech and tulip-tree in the Vastine and Cabbage Patch Hollows in the designated wilderness.

The nature center at the head of the Turkey Creek Nature Trail which traditionally has been a focal point for programs and live animal displays was closed in 1992 and its future is uncertain. However, throughout the summer, nature walks, program and fireside presentations are offered Wednesday through Sunday.

Bikers in Put-in-Bay on South Bass Island.

64 South Bass Island State Park*
Land: 36 acres Water: Lake Erie

South Bass Island is best known for Put-in-Bay and Perry's Victory and International Peace Memorial. The national monument, the third highest in the country at 352 feet (following the St. Louis Arch and Washington's Monument), honors Oliver Hazard Perry's navy victory over the British in the War of 1812.

The battle, which took place just west of South Bass Island, was one of the few American successes in the unpopular war and the first time in history an entire British fleet was captured. The moment was immortalized by Perry's famous note to General William Harrison "We have met the enemy and they are ours: two ships, two brigs, one schooner, and one sloop."

*53-Oak Point State Park, a one-acre access to Lake Erie is on So. Bass Island

Eventually at the turn of the century South Bass Island became a mecca of tourism with steamboats from Detroit, Toledo and Cleveland making Put-in-Bay a regular stop. Presidents Grover Cleveland and William H. Taft made annual summer visits to the island and when the Hotel Victory was built it was not only billed as the largest summer hotel in the world but also boasted a revolutionary idea; the first co-ed swimming pool.

The hotel burnt down in 1919 and tourism suffered a devastating set-back with the institution of Prohibition in the 1920s and the Great Depression the following decade. But South Bass Island has long since rebounded with tourists, especially boaters. More than 413,000 visit South Bass Island State Park annually where they can pitch a tent, rent a cabin, launch their boat or take in the remains of Hotel Victoria and that historical pool in the park's campground.

Information & Activities

South Bass Island State Park
Put-in-Bay, Ohio 43456
(419) 285-2112

Directions: South Bass Island is located three miles from the mainland just north Catawba Island Peninsula. Miller Boat Line runs a ferry from Catawba Point at the north end of SR53 from late March to mid-November with runs every half hour during the summer. Call the boat company at (419)285-2421 for a schedule and fares. Put-in-Bay Boat Line Company (800-245-1538) maintains jet express service from the Jefferson Street Dock in Port Clinton from May through mid-October. The Jet Express lands in Put-in-Bay but cannot take vehicles. You can also take Island Airlines out of Port Clinton.

The state park is located at the southwest corner of the island and reached heading out on Catawba Avenue from the downtown area of Put-in-Bay. Catawba Avenue ends at the park's entrance.

Information: A park office is located on the island and doubles up as the campground check-in station. It's open daily during the summer. During the off-season call Catawba Island State Park at (419)797-4530. For more information on renting bicycles, golf carts or lodging on the island call the Put-in-Bay Chamber of Commerce at (419)285-2832.

Campground: South Bass Island has a spectacular campground located on a bluff above Lake Erie. The facility has 134 sites with 32 of them considered cliffside sites and restricted to tent campers with no more than one vehicle. Most of these sites hug the edge of the bluff and from your table you enjoy a stunning view of Lake Erie and the island's rugged western shoreline.

The campground can be divided into the lower level that is heavily wooded with spread out sites and the upper loop which is more open and campers are closer together. Facilities include showers, vault toilets and a group camping area that can handle up to 50 people. There are also eight pet sites. The campground is filled every weekend from Memorial Day to Labor Day, usually by noon on Friday. When all sites are filled, no vacancy signs are posted at all ferry docks.

Cabins: The park has four hexagonal cabins for rent called "cabents." The single room, wooded structures feature high fabric roofs and are located on a wooded hillside away from Lake Erie. They contain an efficiency kitchen with a small refrigerator, picnic table, shower and bunks for six people. The cabins are rented on a weekly basis only from Memorial Day to the last weekend in September. Rental is done on a lottery basis from the Catawba Island State Park, which can be contacted for an application. All applications must be submitted before Jan. 31 and the drawing is held the second week of February.

Boating: The park maintains Oak Point Docks located west of the boat harbor in Put-in-Bay. The facility can accommodate 22 boats and is used on a first-come-first-served basis.

Day-use Areas: A lightly shaded picnic area with tables, grills, limited play equipment and a large shelter is located within the park overlooking Lake Erie. Nearby is a stone beach that attracts swimmers. A picnic area is also maintained at Oak Point Docks.

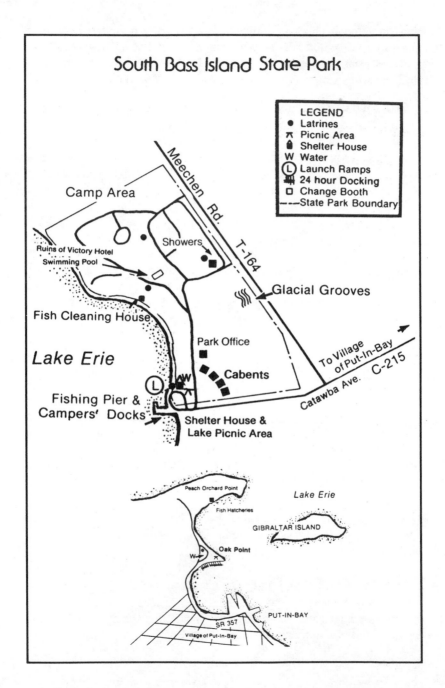

South Bass Island State Park

LEGEND
- • Latrines
- ⤬ Picnic Area
- 🏠 Shelter House
- W Water
- ⓛ Launch Ramps
- 📶 24 hour Docking
- ☐ Change Booth
- --- State Park Boundary

Camp Area

Meechen Rd.

T-164

Showers

Ruins of Victory Hotel

Swimming Pool

Fish Cleaning House

Glacial Grooves

Lake Erie

Park Office

Cabents

To Village of Put-In-Bay

Catawba Ave. C-215

Fishing Pier &
Campers' Docks

Shelter House &
Lake Picnic Area

Peach Orchard Point

Fish Hatcheries

Lake Erie

GIBRALTAR ISLAND

Oak Point

PUT-IN-BAY

SR 357

Village of Put-In-Bay

344

Fishing: Near the campground is a single-ramp boat launch with a loading dock and a L-shaped fishing pier that makes for a scenic spot to cast a line with the park's shoreline cliffs in the background. The Western Basin of Lake Erie is a renown fishery, especially around the islands. Peaking in April and May several species, including perch and crappies, move into the shallow waters around South Bass Island to spawn and can be caught off the pier with minnows and jigs and curly tails.

Smallmouth bass fishing picks up in May with anglers bouncing eighth and quarter-ounce jigs and tails across off-island reefs 10 to 15 feet deep while walleye peaks from late May through June. The most popular technique for walleyes is drifting weight-forward spinners with a gob of nightcrawlers. The lure is cast and counted down to the fish zone at a drop of one foot per second after a school of walleye is found with electronic locators.

Biking: Although South Bass Island has only 17 miles of road, bicycle touring is extremely popular during the summer. Bikes can be taken across on the ferries for an additional fee or rented from a number of bicycle stables on the island.

Nature Notes: Although not nearly as impressive as Kelleys Island, South Bass Island has a small set of glacial grooves posted near the group campsites in the state park.

Winter Activities: Ice fishing for walleye takes place from January through mid-February during normal winters and many anglers consider South Bass Island as the best place to consistently catch large walleyes, many exceeding 10 pounds. You can reach the island via Island Airlines (419-734-3149) and then hire a fishing guide in Put-in-Bay who will provide transportation to a heated shanty as well as bait and equipment. Most anglers return to the mainland that same day. Call the Put-in-Bay Chamber of Commerce for a list of fishing guides.

Small boats enjoy Stonelick's quiet lake.

65   *Stonelick State Park*
Land: 1058 acres   Water: 181 acres

Where prairie meets forest, the Stonelick State Park reflects a time when warmer climates and tall grasses flowed like oceans across the Midwest. Only a half-hour from eastern Cincinnati, Stonelick is one of the older and most innovative, but least used state parks.

Truly a quiet retreat-type of park, the long lake is smooth and the campground is rarely filled. Small boats, shoreline anglers, and many families compose much of the repeat business that keeps the park popular among those that are seeking a quiet place to camp, fish, or hike.

Park tours, guest speakers, and a rollicking canoe race are part of the activities scheduled by the lake association. An old cemetery, the William Sloan Civil War area, and a landmark of the first settlement of Wayne Township and also within the park boundary.

Information & Activities

Stonelick State Park
2895 Lake Drive
Pleasant Plain, Ohio 45162
(513)625-7544

Directions: In southwestern Ohio, 15 minutes east of Milford. Depart I-275 at Route 131 east, take 727 north at junction to park entrance and follow signs. The park is about 25 miles east of Cincinnati.

Information: The park office is on SR727 and open mostly by chance. The rangers are usually nearby patrolling in the park and campground. Maps are available outside the office and at the small campground contact office. Hours are by chance.

Campground: The Stonelick campground was the first Ohio State Park to offer the now popular Rent-A-Camp program. Four sites, 80-83 have a tent, a dining canopy, table and fire pit. Also included in the renting program are two foam sleeping pads, two cots, a cooler, light and stove, fire extinguisher, broom, and so on. The program is terrific for those fledgling campers that would like to try camping before buying expensive equipment. The camps can accommodate four adults, or two adults and three children. Cost is $15-$22, and reservations should be made in advance.

A Primitive Group Camping area, with vault toilets, can be reserved and permits are required. A clean washhouse is centrally located near sites #8 and #9, with five other restrooms scattered around the campground. One of the least crowded state parks, the shady sites are located around the perimeter of most loops. Pets can accompany you on sites #20-36, and the following sites do not have electricity: 26-28, 37-42, 49 and 50. Sites 37-50 are on the water and sometimes flooded during spring. Sites number 140 - 150 are good for large RV rigs.

Bring your canoe and camp next to the water on sites 37-50, 58 and 59. A small amphitheater is the site of limited naturalist programs during the summer. It is located northeast of the campground check-in station and auxillary parking area.

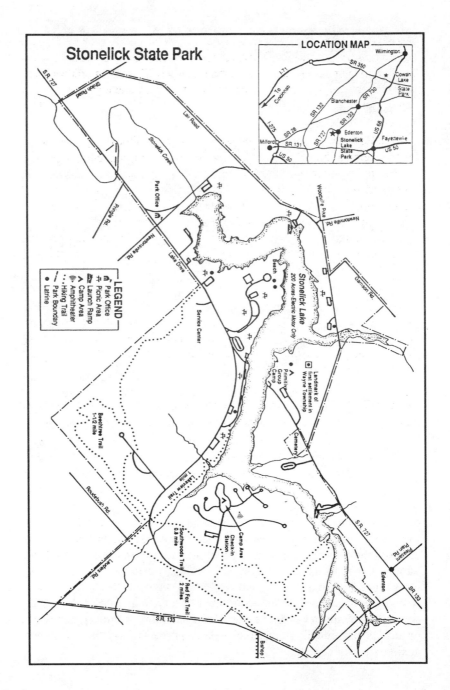

Stonelick State Park

LOCATION MAP

348

Boating: The small 181 acre lake was impounded in 1950 and gas motorboats are prohibited. Small sailboats and electric motors are allowed. Two small launch ramps are both located off SR727, one is at the west end near Newtonsville Road, the other is just past the cemetery near the east end of the lake.

Fishing: Fairly shallow with plenty of stumps and bass-type cover, the lake once held the state record for spotted bass. The scattered weedbeds hold crappies and members of the bass family, all susceptable to correctly presented live baits, rubber crawlers, and surface lures for small and largemouth bass. Channel cats are taken with crayfish and soft crawls on the bottom. Planting of threadfin shad to increase the forage base is repeated annually due to the winter die-off. As biologists improve the forage base, the lake fishing will improve. Kids will have a ball catching small bluegills from the shore.

Hiking: Prairie-like, the seven miles of trails are flat, but teaming with flora. The Red Fox Trail, a short two mile hike begins near the campground check station and has a leisurely stretch that takes you to the lake shoreline. Southwoods Trail, a short .8 mile route, links the Red Fox to the westerly 1.5 mile Beechwood Trail.

Day-use Areas: The south side of the lake has the most picnic sites with dozens of tables and grills dotting the open spaces and shady spots within sight of the smooth lake. The small beach is clean and a lifeguard is on duty during busy times. Changing rooms, open spaces, and picnic tables are near. The narrow but sandy beach is a good one for small children.

Nature Notes: Seasonal naturalist programs are offered to campers on many evenings. Activites include hikes, films, and nature talks. Because of the light public use at Stonelick, amateur naturalists have an excellent opportunity to engage in birding on both land and on the lake. Small canoes can silently cruise the coves and shoreline seeking birds and other wildlife. Migratory songbirds, like spring and fall warblers, have been regular visitors to the flats and lake corridor at Stonelick. Late spring and mid-summer wildflowers are also of interest, featuring many tall prairie species found in this southwestern portion of the state.

Strouds Run State Park.

66   Strouds Run State Park

Land: 2,606 acres   Water: 161 acres

I've seen the sign to Strouds Run more times than I can count, zipping by on US-33 on the way to business in Athens or to one of those beautiful "big name" parks like Burr Oak, Hocking Hills or Lake Hope. For years I resisted, never taking the bait, never taking the quick detour to this place that was known to me only as a name on a highway sign.

Strouds Run is perhaps the most outstanding of all the wonderful discoveries that I was privileged to experience in the course of researching this book. I expected big things -- and got them --out of the well-known state parks. But Strouds Run was different, it was totally unknown to me until the moment I drove in and realized it is one of those places that had to be destined to be a park.

There is a distinct feeling here of a comfortable marriage between nature and park visitor. The man-made lake, beach, picnic areas, campground -- they all seem to fit the wilderness flavor of this park. Maybe it's because the visitor facilities are all concentrated at the north end of Dow Lake, preserving the long pristine look down the length of the lake crowded to its shore with hillsides and ridges covered with tall timber.

Strouds Run is an old forest of oak, hickory, sugar maple and beech. Here and there are pieces of the original woodland, remnants of the nearly unbroken hardwood forest that those first settlers from the east found. On the ridges, in the heavy woods above the lake, are some white oaks five feet in diameter and easily over 200 years old.

In the upper end of the lake, along Strouds Run, the work of beaver and muskrat is readily apparent. Screech and barred owls rule the night, wood ducks nest in the privacy of the coves, bluebirds pluck grasshoppers and other insects to feed their young in the numerous nesting boxes along the lake and roadside. A pair of ospreys visits like clockwork in spring and fall to work the lake for trout, while sharp-shinned and red-tailed hawks patrol the day-time skies for their meals.

Springtime brings a tremendous display of spring wildflowers along with a colorful array of migrating warblers that intermix with the native flowering dogwood and redbud trees lining the lakeshore.

The Linscott Spring, located near the park office, is like the heart of the park, pumping 200,000 gallons of water a day into Strouds Run to feed the lake. The spring, one of the largest in Ohio's hill country, has been an area landmark since the early 1800s. Today it flows from under an old stone springhouse where early farmers once kept their milk cool.

If you drive past the Strouds Run sign and don't stop, you've missed a lot.

Information and Activities

Strouds Run State Park
11661 State Park Rd.
Athens, Ohio 47501
(614) 592-2302

Directions: For most park facilities follow US-33 into Athens to the Columbus Road exit, turn left on North Lancaster Road which becomes

Columbia Avenue then Strouds Run Road (CR20). The route crosses over US-33, turn right when the road deadends on the far side of the bridge. Follow Strouds Run Road into the park. Total distance is about five miles and the route is not nearly as difficult as the directions might suggest.

To reach picnic and trail facilities below the dam on the south end of the lake, take the US-50 bypass east of Athens and watch for the well-marked entrance just after the roadway goes down to two lanes.

Information: Park headquarters is located left off of CR20 on T212, past the campground.

Campground: The proximity of Ohio University and Hocking Tech gives the Strouds Run campground a different usage season than those in other parks. Among the heaviest use days are those first nice days of spring when students are hungry to cure cabin fever, and again in the fall when classes are back in session. But even on the heaviest use days Strouds Run will have a few spots left. Don't be put off by the college crowd, the word from the park rangers is that the college campers are well-behaved and not a problem.

There are 80 campsites to choose from at Strouds Run, including 10 pet sites (29-38) on a cul-de-sac, three Rent-A-Camps (sites 57-59), and a cabent (56) which has the same amenities as the Rent-A-Camps with the additional luxury of wood walls. No showerhouse, flush toilets, or sites with electricity are available although studies are underway to upgrade the campground facility.

The wooded campground runs parallel to and between Township Road 212 and Strouds Run. There are some partially open sites but many are shaded by big hardwoods, especially sycamores. The most popular sites are 5 through 11 and 59 through 75. The latter grouping is under tall trees and features long pull-up pads capable of handling 35 foot rigs. Sites 30 to 80 back up to the stream which is very pretty with a mostly gravel bottom. Sites 37 and 40 are especially popular in spring because they are near a hillside that invariably has a tremendous display of great white trilliums in bloom.

On busy weekends the park staff shows movies on Saturday nights in the amphitheater at the campground entrance.

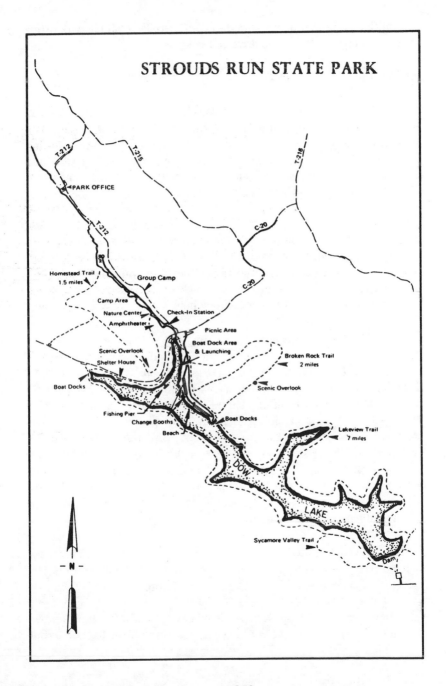

STROUDS RUN STATE PARK

T-212

T-215

T-218

PARK OFFICE

T-212

C-20

Run

Homestead Trail
1.5 miles

Group Camp

C-20

Camp Area

Nature Center

Check-In Station

Amphitheater

Picnic Area

Boat Dock Area
& Launching

Scenic Overlook

Broken Rock Trail
2 miles

Shelter House

Scenic Overlook

Boat Docks

Fishing Pier

Change Booths

Boat Docks

Lakeview Trail
7 miles

Beach

DOW

LAKE

Sycamore Valley Trail

Dam

— N —

A primitive group camp accommodates 150 people. Call the park office at least 14 days in advance to arrange for its use.

Camp supplies are readily available in nearby Athens.

Boating: Dow Lake, named for Ohio University Professor Clarence Dow who was instrumental in designating the area as a state park, is a beautiful boating lake. It's long narrow configuration, the many small and not so small coves to explore, and the pristine appearance of the steep and heavily wooded shorelines give it the feel of a wilderness lake, even though it's only a stone's throw from a city.

There is a 10hp limit on Dow Lake and boats are prohibited from venturing inside the buoyed area at the swimming beach. A very wide, easy to use boat ramp is provided on the north end of the lake off Strouds Run Road. Fifty-three tie-ups located near the launch ramp are available for rental by the season through park headquarters. Rowboats and canoes -- no motors -- are available for rent at a concession where snacks are also available.

Fishing: Dow Lake is a decent fishing lake with a V-shaped bottom that's 45 feet deep at the dam tapering back to shallow weed beds up some of the coves and in the northern part of the lake. There's pretty good fishing there for largemouth bass, channel catfish and bluegill. Use spinner baits for the bass and simple banklines baited with cheeseballs or chicken livers for catfish. Each year, in mid-April, 3,000 or so rainbow and golden trout are released just before the annual trout derby. Structure was added to the lake in the 1980s. It's an even split here between those who like to bank fish and those who prefer it from a boat. The Lakeview Trail runs the entire perimeter of the lake so virtually any portion of the lake can be reached by foot. Either way, the challenge is to get the lake to yield another 12-pound, 24 inch largemouth, like it did in 1989.

Hiking/Bridle Trails: Sixteen miles of hiking trails are in the park, and the park crew reopened an old eight-mile bridle trail in 1993. A horsemen's camp is being considered for the future.

Lakeview Trail (7 mi. loop) A prominent heavily-used trail which follows the naturally-wooded perimeter of Dow Lake. There are no big climbs but the trail is up and down due to ravines and the contours of the coves. Access is via any of the lake-side parking areas.

Vista Point is a beautiful scenic spot high an a ridge that looks down the length of the lakeshore from north to south. Vista Point can be reached via either of two trails, the Homestead Trail (1.5 mi. round-trip) or Vista Point Trail (1.0 mi. round-trip). The Vista Point Trail is more difficult because it takes a shorter route up the ridge face.

Pioneer Cemetery (0.7 mi. round-trip) is an easy, almost level walk up a valley, along a feeder creek, to the Gillett Family Cemetery, one of the area's earliest families.

Broken Rock (2 mi. loop) A rough climb up to a ridge, easy walking once on top. Some maps show a scenic overlook on this trail but the site is overgrown.

Both the **Sycamore Valley** (0.5 mi., loop) and **Indian Mound Trails** (1 mi., loop) are on the south end of the lake and can be accessed either from the Lakeview Trail or from the picnic area below the dam off the US-50 bypass.

Day-use Areas: Strouds Run is a heavy day-use park, with picnic area and beach users more numerous than overnighters. Picnic areas and individual picnic sites are scattered along park roadways. Three shelterhouses are available, one at the launch ramp, the largest is on the lakeshore near the park entrance, and the third is in WPA Hollow at the end of Lake Road at the beach. WPA Hollow is a very nice picnic area. Vault-type restrooms are easily accessible from all sites.

A very inviting 900-foot sand beach at the end of Lake Road is favored by sunbathers and swimmers. Restrooms and two change booths are available. Scuba diving with proper equipment is permitted, but it is prohibited to dive alone or in the beach area.

Nature Notes: The forests of Strouds Run are among the finest to be found in Athens County, no small accomplishment in this part of the hill country.

Sycamore State Park Office, 4675 N. Diamond Mill Rd., Trotwood, Ohio.

67 Sycamore State Park

Land: 2295 acres   Water: 5 acres

In the mid-1970s they almost built a housing development on the current Sycamore State Park property. Fortunately the Federal Land and Water Conservation Fund and state monies were mustered to purchase the property and develop it in 1979. The terrain is flat, much of it now second growth farm fields, but the eastern trails do enter some excellent woodlands crowded with giant sycamore trees.

Hunting and fishing is a popular activity at this park, which is located only minutes west of Dayton. Virtually all of the state parks have a hunting season, but regulations differ by park. The master plan at Sycamore includes interesting provision for hunting as well as land acquisition, development of a campground and continued improvements for horsemen.

The P.A.L.S. (Police Activities League Service) has recently leased nearby property to develop youth programs, horseback riding, and other activities funded through the efforts of area police officers.

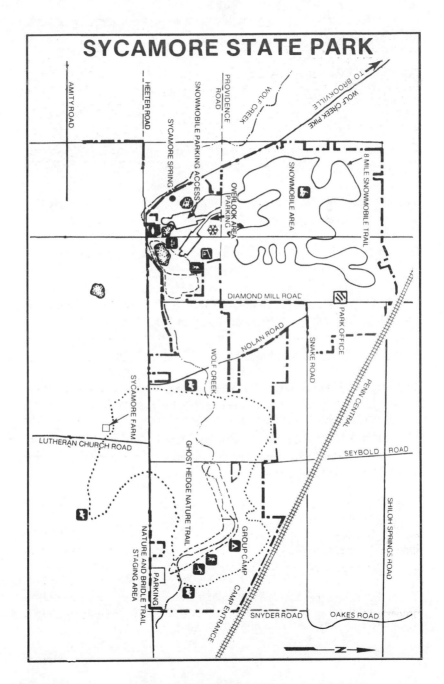

SYCAMORE STATE PARK

Information & Activities

Sycamore State Park
4675 N. Diamond Mill Road
Trotwood, Ohio 45426
(513)854-4452

Directions: Only minutes west of Dayton, depart US-35 at Diamond Mill Road and go north to the park office.

Information: The small office is open by chance, but staff is usually nearby on the park property seven days a week.

Campground: Primitive group camping by advanced reservation.

Fishing: The three small ponds, with the largest being 3.5 acres, offers fair panfishing, some bass and catfish are also taken. The ponds were stocked in 1980, but are not now managed or stocked.

Hiking: 4.5 miles of trails await day-use visitors to this small, but very clean and neat state park. The Ghost Ridge Nature Trail, which is accessed near the parking lot on Heeter and Snyder Road, is the main trail offering flat, but interesting hiking or cross-country skiing.

Day-use Area: The cleanest picnic facilities in the state! A year-round pavilion, tables and grills are located near the small ponds on Providence Road just south of the park office.

Bridle Trails: Sycamore State Park is popular for trail riders. About seven miles of bridle trails are maintained and heavily used and constantly improved by the Ohio Horse Council.

Winter Activites: Eight miles of snowmobile trails are located east of the park office, with parking and a staging area off Providence Road just west of Diamond Mill Road. Ice skating, ice fishing, and cross-country skiing are also popular during the winter season.

Shady campsites attract families to scenic Tar Hollow State Park.

68   Tar Hollow State Park

Land: 520 acres   Water: 15 acres

Tar Hollow is tucked into one of the most scenic sections of Ohio, an area that was once home to moonshiners and squatters, and before that was a hunting ground for the Shawnee and Mingo Indians.

Its unusual name comes from the pine tar that was once taken from the heartwood and, especially, the knots of the park's native pitch pines which grow on the poor, thin soils of the ridges. Pitch pine was an extremely important tree for Ohio's early settlers. Its resins were used to produce what was said to be the best axle grease for wagons, as well as turpentine, pitch, and animal liniments.

Most of Ross County is fertile and wide bottomland, ideal for agriculture, overlooked by hillsides and ridges of poor, thin soils. Approaching Tar Hollow, the ridges and hills take over, gradually creeping in on the wide fertile farms fields, crowding them, encroaching on them, until finally there is only a narrow crop-filled avenue leading to the park entrance.

Soils in the bottoms are fertile at Tar Hollow, too, but there aren't that many bottoms. It is a land of long, steep hillsides rising in V-shapes from the hollows to relatively flat ridges. The forest has been cut over, but is still a beautifully maturing mix of pine and oak.

In the 1930s, Federal revenue agents removed the area's inhabitants, relocated them to areas where jobs were available, and the land was purchased for conservation purposes. The land was passed from the Federal government to Ohio's Division of Forestry and finally, in 1949, a prime section of the state forest was turned over to the newly created Division of Parks so that it could be developed for outdoor recreation. Today, the park sits in the middle of the 16,126 acre Tar Hollow State Forest.

Information and Activities

Tar Hollow State Park
16396 Tar Hollow Road
Laurelville, Ohio 43135
(614) 887-4818

Directions: From US-23 take US-50 east out of Chillicothe to Londonderry, then ten miles north on SR327 to Tar Hollow Road, turn left.

From US-33 take SR180 west to Adelphi, then eight miles south on SR327 to Tar Hollow Road, turn right.

Information: Park headquarters are located on Tar Hollow Road near the park entrance.

Campground: Big, small, shaded, open, secluded -- whatever your preference, there will be something among Tar Hollow's 95 campsites to please you. The 95 sites are split between two hollows, sites near the bottom of the hollows tend to be long and open, becoming narrower and more shaded as you drive in. All sites are self-registering, none has electricity although it is being considered for installation in the lower sites of Ross Hollow. A showerhouse open during the warm season (look for the pop machine there, as well) is located at the beginning of the drive into Ross Hollow, all restrooms in the camp -- throughout the park, for that matter -- are vault-type.

Approaching the campground, Ross Hollow is on the left and Logan Hollow is on the right. On the Ross loop the most popular sites are 1-5, they are big, open, level sites with easy access to the showerhouse and playground. A nice gravel bottom stream flows behind sites 24-34 then crosses under the roadway and borders sites 1-15. On either side of the hollow hillsides and forest crowd to the edges of the sites. Site 14 is a very pretty and popular site on the stream. Site 45, also near the showerhouse, is modified to better accommodate those in wheelchairs. Sites 20-27 are nicely wooded at the end of the hollow.

Pets are allowed in Logan Hollow where a shallow stream, even nicer than the one in Ross Hollow, flows behind sites 52-71. Sites 52-60 are very deep and easily able to accommodate trailers up to 35 feet long. Generally, Logan Hollow sites have more trees on the sites than in Ross Hollow, especially deeper into the hollow. Site 62 is very nice, as are 66-75, but my favorite when conditions are dry would be site 71 which sits right on the stream but low enough that a deluge of rain could cause problems. Also be sure to check sites 91-95 which are located up a short ravine. They're open sites but very secluded, nestled into the hillsides and woods.

Tar Hollow Campground seldom fills to capacity and usually has a few spots available even on holiday weekends.

If those sites don't fit your needs, there's a primitive group camp at the head of Logan Hollow, an open and semi-open grassy area capable of accommodating up to 75 people. Reservations for this area are through the park office, 14 days in advance.

High on a ridge top up Tar Hollow Road are 16 walk-in tent sites with fire rings, vault toilets and drinking water, excellent spots for getting away from

Tar Hollow State Park

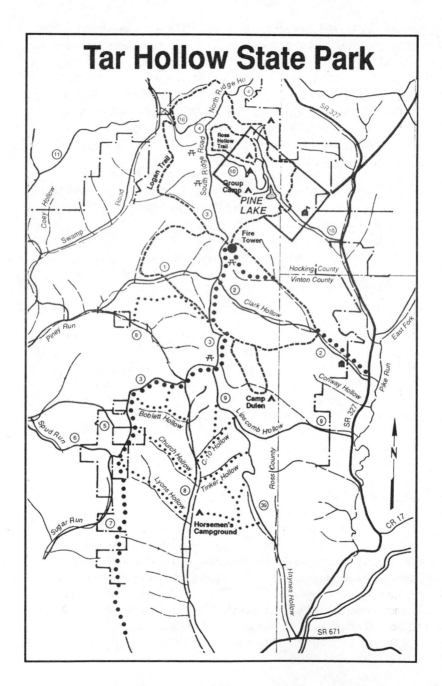

the crowds. It's a short walk up from parking to the sites, be sure to walk all the way up the hillside and check out the furthest site before pitching your tent.

A primitive backpack camp for scout troops is located in the surrounding Tar Hollow State Forest serving hikers on the 16-mile Chief Logan Trail. Vault toilets are provided, but water must be brought in to these sites. Also in the state forest is a horsemen's campground with vault toilets, water for horses, and some stalls.

Resident Camp:
The Tar Hollow Resident Camp, also known as the Four Hills Resident Camp, is a facility unique to the system. The camp is ideal for youth groups, institutions, environmental groups, and the like numbering 175 people or more for workshops, retreats, camp programs, whatever. The secluded complex consists of 28 sleeping cabins, each able to accommodate eight people, three staff cabins, and a recreation/dining hall equipped with a modern kitchen. Included, too, is a private beach on Pine Lake and access to canoes and rowboats. It is advised to call well in advance to reserve use of the camp which is very reasonably priced.

Boating:
Pine Lake is a small, relatively shallow recreation lake built during the Depression by the Civilian Conservation Corps. Canoes, rowboat and boats equipped with electric motors of less than four horsepower are permitted on the lake. A gravel launch ramp is located just off Tar Hollow Road past the park office. It is also possible to launch a small boat into the creek at the swimming beach.

Fishing:
Fishing is only fair in Pine Lake but don't leave the rod at home. There's little structure in the lake but bluegill, bass and catfish are still there. Most of the locals fish the lake for catfish and crappie, nightcrawlers are a favored bait.

Hiking/Bridle Trails:
Ross Hollow Trail (2 mi. loop). Begins at the Ross Hollow camp area and climbs to the top of a ridge looking back down into the deep woods of the hollow. The trail starts with a steep climb but is otherwise nice with fairly easy grades. Park crews plan to rework the start of the trail.

Chief Logan Trail (16 mi. loop). A hiking trail that traverses both park and state forest lands. The trail, which is sometimes strenuous, is set up in north and south loops that meet at the state forest fire tower on South Ridge Road. Tar Hollow Road deadends into Ridge Road west of the park, turn south (left) to the firetower. The north loop of the trail can be picked up at the Pine Lake dam.

Tar Hollow is a midpoint on the blue-blazed Buckeye Trail between Scioto Trail and Hocking Hills State Parks.

A network of bridle trails and a horsemen's campground are available in the Tar Hollow State Forest. For information write them at Route 1, Londonderry, Ohio 45647 or call (614)887-3879.

Day-use Areas:
Tar Hollow is an excellent picnickers park, no wonder when the combination of forests, topography and availability of facilities is considered. Eight picnic shelterhouses in hollows and on ridgetops are available, four with lights and electricity. All sit in the middle of picnic areas and are very popular for family reunions and other gatherings. Seven are first-come, first-served, the large shelter located on the drive into Logan Hollow is reservable one year in advance through the park office. Many have vault toilets and drinking water nearby, the shelters on the ridgetop along Tar Hollow Road will have water in the near future.

A 200 foot long sand beach is open for swimming, protected seasonally by life guards. The section of the lake where swimming is permitted is only six feet at the deepest, overall the deepest spot in the lake is only 15 feet. No changing booths are provided, but there are vault toilets and a picnic area with grills provided nearby.

Nature Notes:
Tar Hollow is mushroom heaven. Rangers say the ridges are covered in spring with as many mushroom hunters as wildflowers. Three of those wildflowers -- green adder's-mouth, Great Indian-plantain, and stiff-leaf aster -- are rarities in Ohio, and the largest smooth sumac recorded in Ohio can also be found here.

Weekends between Memorial Day and Labor Day are great times to learn more about Tar Hollow when nature programs, walks, and evening movies are offered in the amphitheater between the beach and the campground.

Hunting: Tar Hollow State Park and State Forest provide a real challenge for hunters. The huge acreage and rough terrain are home for large populations of wild turkey and whitetail deer, and good populations of other game. Hunting is permitted in season except within 400 feet of roadways, trails, buildings, and other recreation areas.

Tar Hollow is located in one of the most scenic regions of Ohio.

Take a nap, soak up the rays, go for a swim at Tinkers Creek.

69 Tinkers Creek State Park

Land: 740 acres   Water: 10 acres

Tinkers Creek State Park is a small day-use park southwest of Aurora just inside Portage County. The park lacks both camping and boating facilities but when combined with adjacent Tinkers Creek State Nature Preserve offers a handful of trails that wind through an interesting marshland habitat. Approximately 75 percent of the state park is wetlands while the nature preserve has even more extensive marshes.

Originally, the area was a private park known as Colonial Spring Gardens for which a 10-acre man-made lake was dug. With the assistance of Federal Open Space Program, the state acquired the land in 1966 and initially administered it as a wildlife area. The park was developed in the early 1970s and dedicated in 1973. A year later a portion of the state park was re-designated Tinkers Creek State Nature Preserve to be maintained by the Division of Natural Areas as a nature sanctuary.

The park receives a moderate number of visitors on the weekend and is lightly used in mid-week, a time when you can have the trails to yourself.

Information & Activities

**Tinkers Creek State Park
(Mailing Address)
5708 Esworthy Road, Route #5
Ravenna, Ohio 44266-9659
(216) 562-5515**

Directions: From the Ohio Turnpike depart at Gate 13 and head north on SR14/I-480. Depart at the first exit, head east on Frost Road (T197) but immediately turn left at the first road which parallels the interstate briefly. At the T-intersection of Wellman and Aurora-Hudson Roads turn right and the park entrance will be reached a mile north on Aurora-Hudson Road.

Information: A small park office is located near the beach but not maintained on a regular basis. For information contact West Branch State Park at (216) 296-3239.

Day-use Area: The heart of the park is the 10-acre man-made lake which features a small beach and a marked swimming area. The lake has been stocked with grass carp in an effort to control the aquatic vegetation but it's still quite weedy. Changing booths and restrooms are connected to the park office.

Nearby is a shelter equipped with electricity and a picnic area shaded by white oaks and featuring tables, grills and limited play equipment. A second picnic area with tables and grills is located further into the park and away from the lake.

Hiking: The park has a limited network of three trails that can be combined for a 2-mile trek. None of the trailheads are posted but departing from the second picnic area along a pipeline clearing is Gentian Trail. The 0.5-mile path quickly swings into the woods and ends at Pond Run Trail which begins at a gravel parking area nearby. The 1.2-mile Pond Run Trail is the most interesting by far as it skirts a large pond, a good place to sight

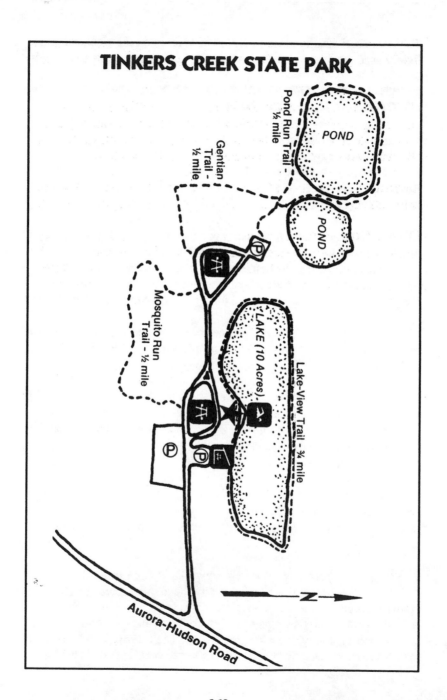

TINKERS CREEK STATE PARK

POND

Pond Run Trail - ½ mile

Gentian Trail - ½ mile

POND

Mosquito Run Trail - ½ mile

LAKE (10 Acres)

Lake-View Trail - ¾ mile

N

Aurora-Hudson Road

wildlife, before swinging into a lowlying woods and then ending at Lake View Trail. Lake View is a 0.7-mile walk along the shore of the man-made lake.

Within Tinkers Creek Nature Preserve is Seven Ponds Trail, a 1.5-mile path that features a boardwalk through the wetlands and an observation deck for viewing waterfowl. The trail begins from a parking area off of Old Mill Road reached by continuing north along Aurora-Hudson Road.

Fishing: There is limited fishing activity in the 10-acre lake, by shore anglers off the Lake View Trail, for largemouth bass, bluegill and catfish.

Nature Notes: Wildlife in the area includes beavers, muskrats and whitetail deer. During the spring and fall migrations thousands of ducks use the marsh area for shelter and food while mallards, wood ducks and Canada geese and songbirds nest here annually.

70 Van Buren State Park

Land: 236 acres   Water: 60 acres

One mile east off I-75 on SR 613, Van Buren State Park is one of the smallest parks in the system with a mailing address of Box 117, Van Buren, Ohio 45889, call (419)299-3461. The modest park has no beach, but day-use amenities include three picnic shelter houses, a small playground, limited fishing in the shallow lake, and a 2.5 mile hiking trail around the lake.

The wooded southside of the lake offers a good hike that is easy to moderate in difficulty. The three-foot deep lake attracts great blue herons and other wading birds. Occasionally nature programs and films are shown in the small 40 site rustic campground. Although there is no electricity (or showers or flush toilets), the campground offers 15 waterside sites, and a group camping area that can accommodate 200 people.

Rowboats and canoes are allowed on the tiny lake using a small one-hole launch ramp, electric motors may be used. Two miles of bridle trails are maintained by the staff, and used irregularly by area equestrians.

A large commercial campground is located next door, with both facilities only 8 miles north of Findlay in north central Ohio.

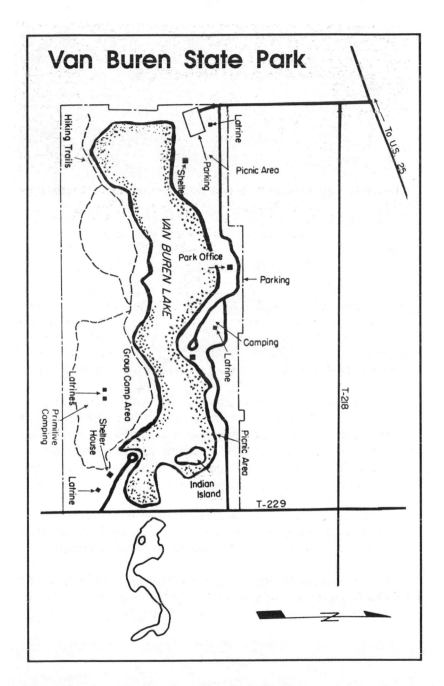

Van Buren State Park

VAN BUREN LAKE

Hiking Trails

Latrine

Parking

Picnic Area

Shelter

Park Office

Parking

Camping

Latrine

Group Camp Area

Latrines

Primitive Camping

Shelter House

Latrine

Indian Island

Picnic Area

To U.S. 25

T-218

T-229

N

Fishing, boating, skiing, pleasure crusing, all on Kirwan Lake.

71   *West Branch State Park*

Land: 5352 acres   Water: 2650 acres

To ease problems of flood control and water supply, the U.S. Army Corps of Engineers constructed a dam in 1965 that turned the West Branch of the Mahoning River in Portage County into Michael J. Kirwan Lake. In the process, they also created a recreational haven for anglers, boaters and swimmers that became West Branch State Park the following year.

West Branch includes 5,352 acres of gentle rolling terrain forested in mixed hardwoods. The north half of the park is a glaciated plateau, a lobe of the Kent terminal moraine, while in the middle is the 2,650-acre reservoir. Michael J. Kirwan Lake stretches seven miles and has a shoreline of coves, inlets and numerous forks. The park's campground itself is located on a peninsula with many sites overlooking small coves.

Indians and early settlers, mostly from Connecticut, passed through the area to harvest a salt lick that was located along the Mahoning River, southeast of Warren and in 1799 Benjamin Tappan founded nearby Ravenna. At the west end of the park is a crossroads known as Campbellsport, named for Captain John Campbell, who gathered a militia for the War of 1812 at the site and then marched them off to Cleveland. The surveyor and land agent also constructed what is said to be the oldest brick land-office building in Ohio around 1810, Prior to the flooding of the reservoir, the building was moved by the Portage County Historical Society and restored.

Today, the park is considered "heavily used" on weekends in attracting thousands of visitors, from anglers and campers to horseback riders and even an occasional backpacker as a portion of the Buckeye Trail passes through its western half.

Information & Activities

West Branch State Park
5708 Esworthy Road, Route #5
Ravenna, Ohio 44266-9659
(216) 296-3239

Directions: From I-76, depart at exit 38 and then head north on SR44/5 for 3 miles towards Ravenna. Continue west on SR5 for six miles to the posted entrance of the park at Rock Spring Road.

Information: The park headquarters is located right before the campground at 5708 Esworthy Road and is reached from Rock Springs Road by turning east on Copeland Road which becomes Esworthy. Hours are 8 a.m. to noon and 1-5 p.m. Monday through Friday.

Campground: West Branch has 103 rustic sites on four loops at the east end of Esworthy Road. Loops B, C, and D are on small peninsulas of their own, featuring well separated sites in a wooded setting. Ten sites on Loop B overlook the water from the shady edge of the lakeshore bluff, the rest are only a short descent from the shoreline. Loop A is an open grassy area in the middle of the campground which also features five Rent-A-Camps and a group camping area for up to 100 people.

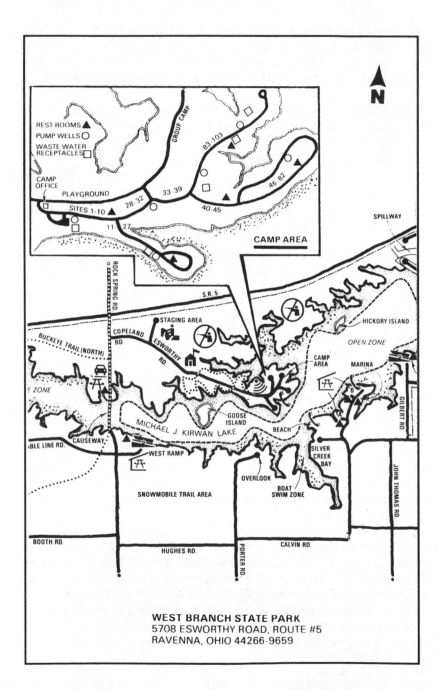

WEST BRANCH STATE PARK
5708 ESWORTHY ROAD, ROUTE #5
RAVENNA, OHIO 44266-9659

Facilities include tables, fire rings, vault toilets and play equipment within the campground while a dump station is located at the park headquarters. The campground is filled almost every weekend from Memorial Day through Labor Day and often reaches capacity by late Friday afternoon.

Boating: Michael J. Kirwan Lake is designated for unlimited horse-power but there is a no-wake zone 300 feet out from the shoreline while the reservoir west of the Causeway is also no wake. The West Ramp Boat Launch is located right off Rock Spring Road on the south side of the lake and has cement lanes with a loading dock, large parking area for vehicles and trailers and bathrooms.

The East Ramp Boat Launch is at the end of Gilbert Road at the southeast corner of the lake and has a four-lane cement ramp and two loading docks. The ramp is across a small cove from the park marina which features slip rentals as well as gas, marine supplies, food service, bait and boat rentals. The West Branch Marina (tel. 216-296-9209) is located at the end of Alliance Road on the south side of the lake.

Fishing: The variety of habitat makes the large reservoir an attractive destination for anglers. The lake is best known for a hybrid striped bass and muskie which are both stocked annually. In fact, the state record tiger muskie, 45-inch long, 26-pound, 8-ounce fish, was caught in the West Branch Reservoir on Aug. 25, 1984. The lake is also considered fair to good for largemouth bass and catfish and fair for bluegills and saugeye.

Along with the ramps mentioned above, the park also has a Fisherman's Parking Lot on the north side of the Causeway, where there is parking, picnic tables, vault toilets and a place to launch hand-carried boats. This is a popular area for shore fishermen while others head to the east end of the reservoir to fish off the dam.

Hiking: West Branch has 12 miles of foot trails with most of it in a portion of the Buckeye Trail, the 1,200-mile statewide route. The portion in West Branch is an 8.2-mile loop with trailhead in the Fisherman's Parking Lot at the north end of the Causeway. The four-hour hike circles the western half of the reservoir on a trail that passes through fields and stands of oak/hickory forest while also following a portion of Knapp Road and crossing the lake along the Causeway. The northern half is the most scenic stretch that winds through a mature beech forest and fields.

Other trails in the park are posted near the park headquarters. Club Moss Trail is a 0.8-mile walk towards the campground and merges into the mile-long Deer Run Trail that follows the shoreline back to the office. Wild Black Cherry Trail is a mile loop with much of it along the lake. At the east end of the reservoir is Little Jewel Run Nature Trail, a mile-long loop that is maintained by the U.S. Army Corps of Engineers and includes benches and an observation platform. Its posted trailhead is reached just after crossing Little Jewel Run on Wayland Road.

Day-use Areas: Picnic areas with tables, grills and shelters are located at West Ramp and East Ramp boat launches. There are also a few tables and grills at the marina and the Fisherman's Parking Lot. The two most scenic picnic areas are opposite the marina on Alliance Road and feature shelters and tables in an open grassy area with a pleasant view of the lake.

The park beach is also located nearby on Alliance Road. The 1,100-foot sandy beach is at the entrance of Silver Creek Bay and has a showerhouse, changing booths, food service and lifeguards. Its extensive parking lot is a good indication of its popularity on the weekends.

Nature Notes: The park presents a variety of naturalist programs during the summer from Tuesday through Friday. Programs range from short hikes and wildlife walks to evening slide programs at the amphitheater near the campground. A weekly list describing the activities and location of them is available at the park headquarters or the campground contact station.

Bridle Trails: West Branch has a 20-mile network of bridle trails on the north side of the lake that traverses the woods and open meadows. A staging area with a large gravel parking area is reached from Rock Spring Road by turning east on Copeland Road. To the east of the staging area is Beaver Lodge Trail, a six-hour ride that connects to several short spurs and a horse camp. To the west is Winter Hawk Trail, a mile-long loop, and Woodcock Rumble a three-mile ride.

The horse camp is designated for one riding group at a time and there is no fee for the use of it. Riders interested in the camp need to reserve the facility two weeks in advance by calling the park office.

Winter Activities: When weather and snow conditions permit, snowmobilers gather at the park, staging at the West Boat Ramp for posted trails that follow the south side of the reservoir. Other winter activities include ice fishing and ice boating on the reservoir and cross-country skiing on the trail system. There is no ski rental in the park.

Unlimited horsepower boats operate on Kirwan Lake.

Wolf Run State Park.

72 Wolf Run State Park

Land: 1,143 acres   Water: 220 acres

If someone says to you, "Why don't we fly on over to Wolf Run State Park?," the inquirer may mean it quite literally. Noble County Airport is right on the west shore of Wolf Run Lake. You can fly in, tie-down the plane, and be camping or fishing in a matter of minutes.

It's not exactly inconvenient if you're planning to arrive by car, either. The park is just a few minutes off a major interstate.

Wolf Run lies in the shadow of nearby Salt Fork State Park, one of the state's truly outstanding parks, a fact which has added to its relative obscurity. The park, however, is not unknown to local fishing and camping enthusiasts. Trout, huge catfish, and trophy bass lurk in the clear, clean, deep waters of

Wolf Run Lake which has served as a water supply, flood control and recreation lake since it was created in 1966.

The lake is fed by Wolf Run Creek and its watershed is only about five and one-half square miles. Virtually all of it is in forest or grassland cover so there is very little agricultural or urban run-off. In the park itself, the crew has reduced the amount of mowing they do, a move that has led to a tremendous recovery of wildlife in the park.

"Park visitors used to ask where the wildlife was," Park Manager Phil Stanley said. "Now they're asking what kind of wildlife it was they saw."

There's no one way to get the best view of Wolf Run. Do it from the air, from one of the prominent look-outs, at water level with a fishing rod in hand, from a trail ---a 2.5 mile section of the Buckeye Trail slices a north-south route on the west side of the lake and a two mile trail connecting the boat launch with the campground is under construction -- or from your car. One of the best views is from an obscure narrow gravel road that scales a ridge high above the lake and surrounding oak-dominated forest. The road, Noble Township Road 126, cuts off SR215 just east of Bond Ridge Road.

It's a view that shouldn't be missed. And be sure to pack a fishing rod and enjoy some of the eight-plus miles of Wolf Run Lake shoreline.

Not far from the park, in what is now the town of Caldwell, is the oldest oil well in the country, discovered in 1814 when two pioneers drilling a well for brine, struck oil instead. That well at the junction of SR78 and SR564 is open for public viewing.

Information and Activities

Wolf Run State Park
Route 6
Caldwell, Ohio 43724
(614) 732-5035

Directions: Follow I-77 to the Belle Valley interchange south of Cambridge, exit on SR821 eastbound, follow a short distance to SR215, turn left and follow SR215 to the main park entrance at Bond Ridge Road, a distance of less than one mile. The swimming beach and boat launch area is located two miles further east off SR215.

Information: The park office is located on Bond Ridge Road inside the main park entrance at the entrance to the campground.

Campground: If you want a site by Wolf Run Lake go to the campground office and say you want "one of those sites down over the hill." There are ten sites that would be considered over the hill, but really only sites 22 to 26 are on the water. Boaters, especially, like these sites because they can bring their craft right up to camp.

Most of the campground's 140 sites are high above the lake on four roadways that are extensions of the main drive. Among the best are the overlook sites, 128-132, on a cul-de-sac that affords a beautiful view down and across Wolf Run Lake. To reach them turn left after passing the campground office and follow the roadway to the end. Park regulars like sites 138-140 because they are up near the entrance and across from the showerhouse. That way they can watch for their friends coming and going and have easy access to the showers and laundry facilities. Tent campers would do well to check out the six tent only sites, 51-56, which sit on a nicely wooded peninsula high above the lake. They, too, have great views. Those with big rigs prefer site 67, a pull-through site with extremely easy access.

Showerhouse and laundry facilities are available, as is a dump station, but electricity is not available, nor are flush toilets.

Directly across the lake is the only fly-in camp in the park system. No, not a float plane fly-in area like you might expect, but a great camping area. On the ridge across the lake is the Noble County Airport where pilots can land, tie-down their planes and walk down to the lakeshore where they'll find a beautiful primitive camp on a fairly steep hillside overlooking the lake. Level sites in this camp are precious, but the view and the remote qualities of the area make it worth it. There are no roads leading to this camp, get there either via the airport or by canoe from the other side of the lake. One of the best scenics in the park is the ravine just west of this camp.

Camp supplies are available at two stores in Belle Valley.

A primitive Youth Group Camp is available at no charge at the tip of the north fork of the lake. The walk-in area must be reserved through the park office at least 14 days in advance.

Boating: Boats up to 10hp are allowed on Wolf Run Lake. A boat launch and tie-ups are available on the southeast side of the lake, check with the park office for information on the tie-ups.

Fishing: Wolf Run is an excellent fishing lake, one of the few lakes in the state, for example, that is managed for a rainbow trout fishery. Some 4,000 rainbow, golden and/or brown trout are stocked each March. It's also noted for shovelhead catfish. A 65 pound shovelhead catfish was taken in a recent Division of Wildlife net survey and two 45-pounders were taken by fishermen in 1991. Among other recent catches was a 10-pound plus largemouth bass. Fishing for crappie is also good at Wolf Run.

The Ohio Division of Wildlife recommends fishing Wolf Run look for trout in shallow waters early in March, especially after several warm days have raised the water temperature into the high 50s. They recommend light spinning or casting outfits, 4- to 6-pound test line and small (10-14) hooks. Work the rock shelves and sharp drop-offs with spinners, cheese, worms, or salmon eggs. As temperatures warm, move to progressively deeper water, as deep as 15 to 20 feet in summer.

The best largemouth fishing is also in those warm days of early spring, back in the shallow coves close to deep water. As temperatures warm, move to the shallow bays and, after spawning, to the long sloping points fished with deep diving plugs. Early in the spring live nightcrawlers work well, later live or artificial nightcrawlers and spinners are effective. In summer, early morning and late evening fishing is best, using topwater plugs. There's a slot limit in effect, bass 12 to 15 inches in length must be returned to the lake unharmed.

Fly fishing for bluegill using poppers and rubber spiders is popular. Worms work well on all rigs May through June. Crappie fishing is best in late spring using minnows or small jigs on light tackle, casting the shoreline around fallen trees. Catfish are caught on shrimp, nightcrawlers, liver, redworms, and crayfish when fishing just off the bottom in shallower areas, especially when fishing on mid-summer nights.

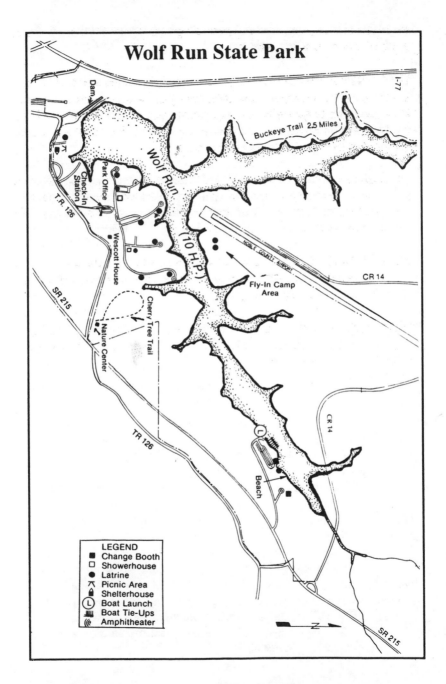

Wolf Run State Park

Buckeye Trail 2.5 Miles

Wolf Run

(10 H.P.)

Dam

I-77

T.R. 126

Park Office

Check-In Station

Wescott House

SR 215

Nature Center

Cherry Tree Trail

TR 126

Fly-In Camp Area

CR 14

CR 14

Beach

LEGEND
- ■ Change Booth
- □ Showerhouse
- ● Latrine
- ⋏ Picnic Area
- ⬣ Shelterhouse
- Ⓛ Boat Launch
- ⯏ Boat Tie-Ups
- ⦅ Amphitheater

N

SR 215

Be aware that in places the shoreline drops quickly to 30 feet of water, especially near rock outcroppings.

Day-use Areas: A very nice, well-shaded picnic area and shelterhouse is located on Bond Ridge Road near the dam, past the campground entrance. It's a good family spot with play equipment, nice areas for volleyball and the like, and a fireplace at one end of the shelter. Picnic sites are also provided in the beach/boat launch area.

The public swimming area features a 150 foot beach next to the boat launch and tie-ups. Changing booths and vault-type restrooms are provided, and there are lifeguards on duty for at least a portion of each summer day. No concessions are available.

Nature Notes: The camp amphitheater, located near sites 83-85, comes alive when volunteer naturalists lead fireside programs and movies on Friday and Saturday evenings.

Hunting: Over 700 acres of Wolf Run State Park is open to hunting in season, with shotgun or bow and arrow only. Hunting is good for grouse, turkey, deer and small game.

About the authors:

Art Weber

The camera and notepad are just excuses to keep Art Weber in his natural habitat, the outdoors. Author of a monthly nature column, his award-winning articles and photos have appeared in numerous publications including **Birder's World, Outdoor Life, The Nature Conservancy Magazine, Boy's Life, Ohio Magazine, Wildlife Conservation,** and in various publications of the National Wildlife Federation. He has served as president of the Outdoor Writers of Ohio and is an active member of the Outdoor Writers of America.

He has also served as public information manager for the Metroparks of the Toledo Area for over twenty years, a position which affords him a professional insight into parks and leisure services. He lives with his wife, Ann, and sons, Andy and Brian, in Toledo.

Bill Bailey & Jim DuFresne have written over 20 books and are publishers of Glovebox Guidebooks.